Bertrand Russell and the
Origins of Analytical Philosophy

D1293084

THOEMMES

Printed in England by Antony Rowe

BERTRAND RUSSELL
AND THE ORIGINS OF
ANALYTICAL PHILOSOPHY

Edited and introduced by
Ray Monk
and
Anthony Palmer

University of Southampton

THOEMMES PRESS

Published in 1996 by

Thoemmes Press
11 Great George Street
Bristol BS1 5RR
United Kingdom

ISBN 1 85506 475 8 – Hardback
ISBN 1 85506 476 6 – Paperback

Editor's Introduction and arrangement
© Ray Monk and Anthony Palmer, 1996

Individual essays © respective authors, 1996

Front cover illustration
'Lucidity' mosaic depicting Russell drawing truth from a well.
Reproduced with kind permission from
The National Gallery, London

British Library Cataloguing-in-Publication Data

A catalogue record of this title is available
from the British Library

CONTENTS

v

INTRODUCTION

Analytic philosophers in the mid twentieth century, asked to characterize their intellectual origins, would very soon have found themselves talking about Russell and Moore. In the last quarter of the century things have changed. Now there are even some, like Michael Dummett, who would claim that neither Russell nor Moore was even *a* source of analytic philosophy let alone singly or jointly *the* source. This revisionist thesis can find little to support it in the way of historical evidence and must rely upon what Dummett enigmatically refers to as 'causal influences which appear to operate in the realm of ideas independently of who reads what or hears what'. Russell seems to be in danger of becoming relegated to the sidelines of the twentieth century's major philosophical development not by the unearthing of hitherto undiscovered evidence but by the invocation of that most unreliable of witnesses, a *zeitgeist*. This volume of papers by Russell scholars from around the world, given at a conference at Southampton University in July 1995 should go some way towards restoring Russell's role in the development of analytical philosophy.

One reason, perhaps the main one, for the attempt to place Russell at the periphery of the development of analytic philosophy is a revaluation of the role Frege played in its development. Ray Monk in his contribution points out that Dummett precisely dates the beginning of analytic philosophy to a specific moment

vii

in Frege's *Foundations of Arithmetic*; the moment at which Frege begins by asking about the nature of number and ends by asking instead about the meanings of sentences containing number words; the moment, that is, when Frege made the linguistic turn. Now, as Monk points out, if, like Dummett, we make this linguistic move definitional of analytic philosophy then Russell would not count as an analytic philosopher. Nor would he have wanted to be counted as such. Monk is only one of several contributors to this volume to remind us that that in *The Principles of Mathematics* Russell insists that 'meaning in the sense that words have meaning, is irrelevant to logic'. Moreover, Monk argues, when, under Wittgenstein's influence, Russell did come to see logic as linguistic, this engendered in him not elation but despair. It also, in an attempt to explain the basis of language itself, threw him in the direction of a psychologism which was the exact antithesis of Frege. Constant to Russell's various changes of opinion was the conviction that 'merely' linguistic considerations were trivial and not the chief interest of the philosopher, whose real task is to understand, not language, but the world.

Several of the contributors are concerned to show that it was precisely the anti-linguistic nature of Russell's early conception of propositions and therefore his early conception of analysis which generated the successive distinctions and theories in Russell's work between 1900 and 1919. One of these, the theory of descriptions, was famously described by Ramsey as a paradigm of philosophy. It would be difficult to argue that it has not remained a paradigm for analytic philosophy throughout the twentieth century.

Nicholas Griffin argues that what has become the orthodox interpretation of Russell's celebrated 1905 paper 'On Denoting', in which the theory of definite descriptions is advanced, suffers from its failure to appreciate the *Principles of Mathematics* theory of denoting and denoting concepts which it was designed to replace. He shows that the theory of denoting and denoting concepts in *The Principles of Mathematics* arises directly out of Russell's insistence that propositions are not essentially linguistic. Propositions, Russell argues, are made up of terms, a word which he takes to be synonymous with the words 'individual' or 'entity'. This generates the problem that the analysis of a proposition destroys its essential unity. The terms, individuals or entities of which it is composed, placed side by side, do not reconstitute the proposition. Russell's early conception of propositions generated a paradox of analysis.

Russell's first effort to get round this problem was to distinguish between kinds of terms. Holding on to the idea that the consituents of a proposition are terms he proceeded to distinguish between terms which occur in propositions *as terms* and those, which while remaining terms, occur in propositions other than as terms. He called the former 'things' and the latter 'concepts'. It was this capacity of terms to occur in propositions other than as terms which prevented analyis from destroying the unity of the proposition. Now, however, a question arises about concepts when they do appear as terms. For it soon becomes clear that when they do so the proposition is not about those terms themselves, ie. not about concept terms, but something else. That something else Russell argued is what is denoted by the concept. A concept term, when it appears as a term in a proposition is what he called a denoting concept, and the proposition in which such a term occurs is not about the concept, but about what the concept denotes.

Denoting, in the *Principles*, is a relation between a concept and a term, not a relation between a word or phrase and a term. While, of course, there are denoting phrases, it is not the phrases that do the denoting, but the concepts expressed by these denoting phrases. Griffin shows to what extent the interpretation of the theory of denoting in *The Principles of Mathematics* and its rejection in 'On Denoting' has suffered from the failure to appreciate this. He argues that it lies behind the almost universal interpretation of *The Principles of Mathematics* as being essentially Meinongian or quasi-Meinongian in its ontology, hence turning Russell's rejection of the theory of denoting concepts in his 1905 paper 'On Denoting' into no more than an excercise in ontological pruning.

Harold Noonan, whose views about the theory of denoting concepts in the *Principles of Mathematics* almost entirely coincide with Griffin's, argues that when 'On Denoting' is seen in the background of a properly non-Meinongian reading of the earlier work, it becomes clear that its central argument is one which is often taken to be both peripheral and confused. The argument is generally refered to as the 'Gray's Elegy' argument. While the theory of denoting in the *Principles* had already provided Russell with a means of handling the problems in ontology which 'On Denoting' is usually thought to address, one problem remained, Noonan argues, which threatened Russell's *Principles* theory of propositions. If, as Russell insisted, terms, the constituents of propositions, were to be thought of as essentially language independent then denoting concepts themselves have to be thought of as essentially independent of language. Russell, however, realised that there did not seem to be any way of specifying a denoting concept *except* via its linguistic expression.

Noonan argues that the real aim of 'On Denoting' was to safeguard the non-linguistic nature of the analysis of propositions by the elimination of denoting concepts. 'On Denoting' should really have been called 'On not Denoting'.

The theory of terms not appearing as terms in the *Principles* was, as we have seen, Russell's reaction to the problem of the unity of the proposition. It is sometimes referred to as Bradley's problem. The extraordinary influence that this problem exerted on Russell's thinking is testified to by the contributions of Stewart Candlish, and Francisco Rodríguez-Consuegra.

Candlish traces Russell's contorted efforts to solve it from his first attempt in the *Principles* through the multiple relation theory of judgement, which lies at the heart of *Principia Mathematica*, and the theory of propositional forms in the 1913 *Theory of Knowledge* manuscript, whch Russell abandoned because of Wittgenstein's criticism of it, to his virtual surrender in face of the problem in 'On Propositions: what they are and how they mean' published in 1919. In his reply to Candlish, Mark Sainsbury argues that the problem of the unity of the proposition (or judgement), which had so exercised Russell, is solvable using the techniques of modern (Davidsonian) truth-conditional semantics, and outlines a sketch of such a solution. In an appendix to his paper, Candlish gives reasons for denying that the problem is thus solved.

Russell's virtual surrender to the problem of the unity of the proposition in the abandonment of his multiple relation theory of judgement was at least partly occasioned by Wittgenstein's criticism of it. One strand running through many of the contributions is the relation between Russell's ideas and Wittgenstein's in their discussions, which led ultimately to Russell's lectures on logical atomism and Wittgenstein's *Tractatus Logico-Philosophicus.*

Anthony Palmer argues that Wittgenstein's 'Notes on Logic' and 'Notes Dictated to Moore in Norway' show that Russell and Wittgenstein were at cross-purposes in their thinking from the very beginning. He argues that reflection on a correct symbolism for negation led Wittgenstein to the doctrine of the bipolarity of the proposition which, he argues, needs to be distinguished from Russell's insistence that a proposition is essentially either true or false. The doctrine of the bipolarity of the proposition is Wittgenstein's doctrine of the sense of a proposition, and one of its consequences was that propositions cannot have predicates or relations. He argues that many of the themes of the *Tractatus* follow from this, and that when they are seen so to follow it becomes apparent just how anti-Russellian and indeed anti-analytic the *Tractatus* is.

This idea of the failure of analysis, at least in Russell's hands, is the theme of Peter Hylton's paper. As early as 1900 Russell thought it obvious that all good philosophy should begin with the analysis of propositions. We have seen how he begins by insisting that propositions are not essentially linguistic items. Hylton argues that for Russell declarative sentences were thought of as 'more or less defective expressions of propositions'. In so far as they are less defective expressions then the structure of a sentence expressing a proposition will approximate to the structure of the proposition it expresses. If the sentence is not defective at all with regard to the proposition it expresses then of course it will have the same structure. Hylton charts the various ways in which Russell came to see more and more sentences as being defective in this respect until it became questionable whether there was such thing as a non-defective expression of a proposition. At the root of his difficulties is, once more, his non-linguistic conception of propositions. Russell thought of a proposition as being constituted by the entities which it is said to be about. Strictly speaking, on this conception, the constituents of a proposition cannot be about anything other than themselves. The idea of one thing designating another has no place within a theory which insists that the items a proposition is about are constituents of the proposition itself. Russell's doctrine of acquaintance is a direct result of this. Our acquaintance with the constituents of propositions was designed to do the job that designation would do if it only could. All of Russell's difficulties with denoting concepts, false propositions, and true negative propositions stem from this. Hylton tries to show how Russell's idea of analysis as the attempt to produce sentences which reflect the structure of the propositions they express in the end was doomed to failure.

Consuegra takes up the story of Russell's struggle with the problem of the unity of the proposition after 1919, after, that is, Russell's abandonment of the multiple relation theory of judgement, a theory which sought to solve the problem by denying the existence of propositions. This theory was in turn abandoned, Consuegra argues, because Russell came to deny the existence of judgements, at least as he had previously conceived them. In the multiple relation theory, a judgement needed a mind, a subject, to be in a series of relations with the elements of the complex judged. In Russell's theory of 'neutral monism', however, there were no such minds, and Russell was led, therefore, in a radically new direction. This new path Consuegra describes as Russell's 'perilous journey' from the atomism of his early philosophy to the 'holism' (as Consuegra calls it) of Russell's post-1919 works – *The Analysis of Mind*, *The Analysis of Matter*, *An Inquiry into Meaning and Truth* and *Human Knowledge* – all of which, on Consuegra's account, are less concerned with analysing knowledge into its atoms than in identifying its (irreducible) *structures*.

For A. C. Grayling, the development of Russell's later philosophy runs along a course that is not so much perilous as disastrous, ending in what he describes as a 'crash-landing' in the 'crude biologism' of *Human Knowledge*. The flight was unnecessary, Grayling argues. Russell was on firmer ground than he had thought in his very earliest philosophical book, *An Essay on the Foundations of Geometry*, the Kantian transcendentalism of which can be defended against the criticism it received from G. E. Moore if restricted to an *Antirealist* epistemology rather than extended to the untenable *Idealist* metaphysics to which Moore and Russell considered it to be committed.

An Essay on the Foundations of Geometry receives a rather different, though no less sympathetic, interpretation from the mathematician C. W. Kilmister, who sees in it an early manifestation of Russell's conviction that technical advances (in this case, the advance of projective over metrical geometry) can help to solve philosophical problems. This conviction, Kilmister argues, is one of the central tenets of analytical philosophy, as Russell conceived it, and, Kilmister says, one that has left behind a legacy of doubtful value. Of more certain and lasting value, in Kilmister's view, are Russell's emphasis on the importance of definitions and his demonstration that numbers could be defined as classes.

But if, as Kilmister insists, Russell's achievements in formal logic are his 'main contribution to the analytic tradition', there has been, as Gregory Landini points out, little agreement on what those achievements are. The formal logic of *Principia Mathematica*, especially, has defied numerous attempts to render it consistent, intelligible and philosophically plausible. Especially difficult is to show how the book's Introduction – with its theory of types, its theory of descriptions and the multiple relation theory of judgement – squares with the technical apparatus used in the proofs that follow. Is the formal logic of the book even consistent with the philosophical theories that supposedly provide its foundations? Many commentators have concluded that it is not, but Landini, insisting (as Russell and Whitehead famously did not) on a clear distinction between the metalanguage and the object-language of the theory, shows how the heirarchies of orders and types in *Principia* can be understood in such a way that they are not only consistent with, but the natural outcome of, the philosophical ideas of the Introduction. Thus understood, the formal logic of *Principia* can be seen as the expression of a coherent, and philosophically tenable, view of the nature of logical form.

Russell's early works on logic, mathematics and epistemology have been a continuous source of discussion throughout the century, and will no doubt continue to be so well into the next. They are a permanent contribution to the history of philosophy. The two final papers in this volume, however, stress the importance of his work in other areas of the subject.

Charles Pigden argues that Russell's work on ethics, even though denigrated in later years by Russell himself, nevertheless repays study. It turns out that Russell has interesting things to say about most of the problems which have engrossed moral philosophers throughout the twentieth century. In particular his very early 'apostolic' altercations with G. E. Moore, despite his ultimate capitulation to Moore's *Principia Ethica*, retain their value. One in particular, published in 1897, entitled 'Is Ethics a Branch of Empirical Psychology', in which Russell advances the view, as against Moore, that the good should be defined in terms of what we desire to desire, anticipated by a hundred years a view which now has currency through the work of David Lewis.

Finally, Louis Greenspan maintains that Russell's work on the history of philosophy itself still has lessons to teach us. He argues that the continuing popularity with the general reading public of Russell's *History of Western Thought*, while not reflected in the attention paid to it by philosophers, nevertheless deserves their attention. *The History of Western Thought*, he argues, is not the obituary to a tradition which died at the hands of twentieth-century analytic techniques, nor is it remarkable merely for the the identification of the sources of totalitarianism in that tradition. It should rather be seen as an important contribution to the debate which has come to assume an increasing importance as the century has progressed – namely the place and role of ideas in history, or the relation of ideas to social structures. *The History of Western Thought* is a study of the political impact of ideas. It presents us, Greenspan argues, with a drama of ideas which like all good dramas is really a warning. In particular it is a warning against the political fallout of the sceptical trend in European thought which leads to the madness of romanticism via a relativism which deems madness to be no more than a minority view. We do not have to look far around us at the end of the twentieth century to discover the monuments to such an outlook.

Ray Monk and Anthony Palmer, 1996

WHAT IS ANALYTICAL PHILOSOPHY?

Ray Monk

University of Southampton

The widespread habit of thinking of the English Channel as the border between two mutually hostile philosophical cultures has in recent years come under much fire. The division between analytical and continental philosophers, Bernard Williams has recently remarked, is a cross-categorization, like dividing cars between four-wheel drive models and those built in Japan. Among analytical philosophers, there are, of course, many who live and work in France, Germany, Spain, Italy and other continental countries. In an effort to undermine the nevertheless persistent use of this cross-categorization, Michael Dummett, in his book, *Origins of Analytical Philosophy*, has sought to remind us that there is nothing especially 'Anglo-American' about the analytical tradition; that, indeed, its roots lie precisely on the other side of the Channel. 'The sources of the analytical tradition', he writes, 'were the writings of philosophers who wrote, principally or exclusively, in the German language; and this would have remained obvious to everyone had it not been for the plague of Nazism which drove so many German-speaking philosophers across the Atlantic' (Dummett, 1993, p. ix).

For Dummett, the opposite of 'analytical' is not 'continental' but 'phenomenological', and the thesis of his book is that: 'the roots of analytical philosophy ... are

the *same* roots as those of the phenomenological school'
(*ibid*.). The two traditions, he writes, 'may be compared
with the Rhine and the Danube, which rise quite close
to one another and for a time pursue roughly parallel
courses, only to diverge in utterly different directions
and flow into different seas' (*ibid*., p. 26).

Thus he describes the courses charted by the careers
of, respectively, Frege and Husserl, which, beginning in
a common milieu that included also the work of, among
others, Brentano, Meinong and Bolzano, turned sharply
in opposing directions to form, on the one hand the
analytical school and on the other the tradition of
phenomenology. At the centre of Dummett's philosophical cartography in mapping the divergent courses
of these two streams of thought is the importance he
gives to the so-called 'linguistic turn' taken by the
Fregean analytical school. Both Frege and Husserl, on
Dummett's view, conceive philosophy to be fundamentally concerned with the analysis of thought, but Frege
took the decisive step of insisting upon what Dummett
calls 'the extrusion of thoughts from the mind'. To
pave the way for Wittgenstein's early work, Dummett
writes, 'it was first necessary that the fundamental place
should be accorded to the philosophy of thought. That
could not happen until the philosophy of thought had
been disentangled from philosophical psychology; and
that in turn depended upon the step that so perplexed
Brentano, the extrusion of thoughts from the mind and
the consequent rejection of psychologism' (*ibid*., p. 127).

So, while Husserl became enmired in the search for an
essentially non-linguistic mental act of perception that
lies at the root of our thought and that enables us to
make sense of the world – and was thus driven, via his
notion of a phenomenological or eidetic reduction, to
attempt to isolate a special kind of perception that has

as its object a form rather than an ordinary everyday particular – Frege hit upon a far more fruitful method of analysing thought through the analysis of sentences. Thus, for Dummett, 'analytical philosophy was born when the linguistic turn was taken' (*ibid.*, p. 5), and, in *Frege: Philosophy of Mathematics*, he points us to the precise moment of this decisive step. In paragraph 62 of *Die Grundlagen der Arithmetik*, Frege begins by asking about the nature of number and ends by asking instead about the meanings of sentences containing number words. '*There* is the linguistic turn', Dummett exclaims in his commentary upon this passage: 'The context principle is stated as an explicitly linguistic one, a principle concerning the meanings of words and their occurrence in sentences; and so an epistemological problem, with ontological overtones, is by its means converted into one about the meanings of sentences' (Dummett, 1991, p. 111). If it were on the strength of this, 'the most pregnant philosophical paragraph ever written' alone, Dummett claims, Frege 'would still deserve to be rated as the grandfather of analytical philosophy' (*ibid.*, pp. 111–12).

On the basis of this characterization of Frege's achievement, Dummett has provided the clearest answer yet given to the deceptively simple question: what is analytical philosophy. It is, he can claim unequivocally, 'post-Fregean philosophy'. 'We may characterise analytical philosophy', he remarks, 'as that which follows Frege in accepting that the philosophy of language is the foundation for the rest of the subject':

> For Frege, as for all subsequent analytical philosophers, the philosophy of language is the foundation of all other philosophy. (Dummett, 1978, p. 441)

This last claim, it turns out, is a grammatical remark:

analytical philosophers simply *are* those for whom the philosophy of language is the foundation of all other philosophy. Thus, when he finds in the work of Gareth Evans, for example, an attempt to, in Dummett's words, 'give an account, independent of language, of what it is to think about an object in each of various ways', he has no hesitation in declaring Evans to be 'no longer an analytical philosopher' (Dummett, 1993, p. 4).

In a previous paper (Monk, 1996), I have argued that Dummett's adherence to this rigid criterion compels him to accept that Bertrand Russell never *was* an analytical philosopher. For Russell never thought that the philosophy of language was the foundation of all other philosophy. Throughout all the various transformations of Russell's philosophical doctrines, one thing remained quite constant, and that was the conviction that, whatever it is the philosopher is concerned with, it is precisely *not* language. The 'linguistic turn' in twentieth-century philosophy indeed was something which Russell looked upon with despair. 'We are now told', he wrote in the 1950s, aghast at the state in which he found philosophy, 'that it is not the world that we are trying to understand but only sentences' (Russell, 1959, p. 217), a conception of the subject which he regarded as the abandonment of its claim to be a serious discipline.

In these later laments about the state of philosophy, Russell is sometimes regarded as having forgotten – or perhaps misunderstood – the nature of his own philosophical achievements. For isn't his theory of descriptions, for example, a 'paradigm of philosophy' precisely because it demonstrates the value of linguistic analysis in philosophy, of demonstrating that philosophical clarity can be achieved through the analysis of sentences? It is true, of course, that this is how this theory – and much else in Russell's work – has been absorbed in 'the literature', but we should, I think, not lose sight of the fact that this is not, and never was, how Russell himself understood the matter. At the very centre of his argument in 'On Denoting' is a rejection of the notion that language is the subject of the philosopher's inquiry. The pivotal step in his notorious 'Gray's Elegy' argument, for example, is his discounting of the notion that the meaning of definite descriptions might be 'linguistic through the phrase'. His assumption, here, is that, as logicians, we are simply not interested in linguistic meaning, but rather in the purely logical relation that he calls 'denotation'. As he had put it in *Principles of Mathematics*: 'meaning, in the sense in which words have meaning, is irrelevant to logic' (Russell, 1903, p. 47).

True, Russell later, under the influence of Wittgenstein, came to take precisely the opposite view of the relation between logic and language, but he did so with an attitude, not of having finally understood the proper method of philosophy, but rather of deep disillusionment. Just days after his famous meeting in Holland with Wittgenstein at the end of 1919, for example, Russell wrote a review of Harold Joachim's Inaugural Lecture, 'Immediate Experience and Mediation', in which he declared roundly: 'As for logic and the so-called "Laws of Thought", they are concerned with symbols, they give different ways of saying the same thing... only an understanding of language is necessary in order to know a proposition of logic' (Russell, 1988, p. 405). But the lesson he took from this is not that philosophers should now seek to analyse sentences, but rather that logic did not have, after all, the philosophical significance he had earlier attached to it. A similar note of disillusionment is evident in his essay 'Is Mathematics purely linguistic?' in which he writes: 'it turns out that numbers are nothing but a verbal convenience, and disappear when the propositions that seem to contain them are fully written out. To look for numbers in heaven is therefore as futile as to look for (say) "etc."' (Russell, 1973, p. 301). This conclusion, he adds, 'may be regarded as an epitaph on Pythagoras' (*ibid.*, p. 306).

The assumption here is that, in so far as something has been shown to be linguistic, it has been shown to be trivial and beneath consideration. In *My Philosophical Development*, he describes his disillusionment with logic and mathematics as 'the retreat from Pythagoras', a fall from grace so to speak from the mystical satisfaction in the contemplation of mathematical truth to the sad acceptance of the essentially linguistic nature of mathematics. 'I have come to believe', he writes, 'though very reluctantly, that it [mathematics] consists in tautologies. I fear that, to a mind of sufficient intellectual power, the whole of mathematics would appear trivial, as trivial as the statement that a four-footed animal is an animal' (Russell, 1959, pp. 211–12).

In his old age, Russell dramatized the road he had travelled in his love affair with mathematics in a short story called 'The Mathematician's Nightmare' (Russell, 1954, pp. 48–53), in which the central figure, Professor Squarepunt, falls asleep one day in his chair after a long day's study of the theories of Pythagoras and dreams of living, breathing numbers that are dancing around him in concentric circles: the first circle containing the numbers 1 to 10, the second from 11 to 100, the third from 101 to 1,000 and so on to infinity. Beside him stands the masked figure of Pi. As he looks more closely at the numbers, Professor Squarepunt notices that each has its name marked on its uniform and that different kinds of numbers have different uniforms and different shapes: the squares were tiles, the cubes were dice, etc. He then has to sit and listen as each number in turn introduces itself and explains its particular merits, while the others carry on dancing. Throughout the show Professor Squarepunt notices that one of the primes, number 137, seems unruly and unwilling to accept its place in the series. He asks it why it is rebelling. At this 137 delivers an impassioned speech against the metaphysics of Plato. 'We all found Plato's heaven dull', the number exclaims, 'and decided that it would be more fun to govern the sensible world ... Our empire now is of this world and when the world goes pop, we shall pop too.' The Professor, to his own surprise, finds himself agreeing with the views of 137, but all the others, including Pi, consider this blasphemous and turn against him, the whole infinite host descending on him in an angry buzz. For a moment Professor Squarepunt is terrified, but then, pulling himself together, he calls out: 'Away with you! You are only Symbolic Conveniences!' At which, with a banshee wail, the whole vast array dissolves in mist. As he wakes up, the Professor hears himself saying: 'So much for Plato!'

Tragically, then, Russell came to think that Plato had been wrong, and that the Pythagorean reverence for numerical relations was founded on a misconception. But, this realization, far from compelling him to accept what Dummett calls the 'priority of language over thought' sent him in exactly the other direction. In his early work, Russell had joined with Frege, in insisting on the 'de-psychologizing of logic', but behind his rejection of psychologism, and underpinning it, was his Platonism. With his Platonism destroyed by his acceptance of Wittgenstein's view of the linguistic nature of logic, Russell reverted to a psychologism that would make Dummett blush. In *The Analysis of Mind* and, later in *An Inquiry into Meaning and Truth*, Russell turned his attention to language, with precisely the opposite view about the 'relative priority of language and thought' to that which Dummett regards as definitive of the analytical tradition. He sought, that is, to understand language *through an understanding of psychology*.

The problem of meaning, in so far as it was an interesting philosophical question, was for Russell essentially a psychological problem. 'I think that the notion of meaning', he writes in *The Philosophy of Logical Atomism*, 'is always more or less psychological ... the theory of symbolism and the use of symbolism is not a thing that can be explained in pure logic without taking account of the various cognitive relations that you may have to things' (Russell, 1985, p. 45). Logic had been shown to be essentially symbolic, and therefore fairly trivial: what remained was to theorize – psychologistically – about symbolism itself. Thus, 'a proposition is just a symbol' (*ibid.*, p. 44), but as the theory of symbolism is fundamentally psychological, it follows that the nature of logic cannot be fully understood outside a study of psychology. After his rejection of Platonism, then, Russell's work took the form of *re-psychologizing* logic, the re-intrusion, so to speak, of thoughts back into the mind.

Accordingly, from 1919 onwards, therefore, Russell began to formulate a psychological, or, as he sometimes said, in the light of his conversion to neutral monism, a *physiological* theory of the proposition. In 'On Propositions' and *The Analysis of Mind*, this took the form of understanding the nature of a proposition in terms of the mind's ability to form *images*. Central to this theory was the notion of an 'image-proposition', a notion uncomfortably close, from Dummett's point of view, to that of a 'presentation' that lies at the centre of the Husserlian tradition of phenomenology. On Russell's new theory of meaning, an 'image-proposition' was a kind of proto-proposition made up, not of words but of mental images. Thus the basis of meaning is shown to be non-linguistic and to lie in a series of mental acts that are *prior* to, and the foundation of the meanings we give to words. The story goes like this: we see somebody called John, then sometime in the future we recall John by calling up an image of him. This image then 'means' John. The origin of the meaning of words, Russell maintains, is the replacement of such images by words, so that, instead of using the image of John to mean John, we use the word 'John'.

An 'image-proposition' is an image that is complex rather than particular. An image of John without any hair, for example, might be the 'image-proposition' which in words would be expressed as 'John is bald'. In general, according to Russell, 'the image-proposition is the meaning of the word-proposition. But the image-proposition itself refers to something else, namely, the objective fact which makes the proposition true or false' (Russell, 1988, p. 8). Of course it is possible to entertain in our minds any number of images, only some of which will be 'image-propositions' that we actually believe. I can *imagine* John to be bald even when I know him to have hair. So what distinguishes those 'image-propositions' that constitute my beliefs? Russell's answer to this is enough to have him drummed out of Dummett's club of analytical philosophers for life. '*Belief*', he writes, 'is a specific sensation, which ... has a certain relation to a present image or complex of images' (Russell, *ibid.*, p. 14).

If ever a philosophical doctrine deserved the name 'descriptive psychology', it is this. Russell's views at this period, indeed, recall strikingly those he had discussed in 1903 in his paper 'Meinong's Theory of Complexes and Assumptions'. For Meinong, a complex was a mental presentation which might be the content, either of an assumption if merely entertained (in the sense that we might assume, for the sake of playing with our children, for example, that a sofa is a boat, even when we know that it is not), or a judgement, if actually believed. But, not even Meinong went so far as to characterize a belief as a sensation, which is about as rampant a piece of psychologism as it is possible to imagine. In 1903, Russell had contrasted his own approach to that of Meinong by saying that, the doctrine of complexes that Meinong had arrived at psychologistically, he had reached from the other direction of logic. Now, it seems, he had jumped ship and was being carried off down-stream at an alarming rate along the same river as Meinong: the one, that is, that leads to the sea of phenomenology.

In his 1940 book, *An Inquiry into Meaning and Truth*, Russell reaffirms his commitment to the psychological and epistemological approach to language. Several times throughout the book, he castigates his opponents (he is thinking chiefly of the logical positivists) for their 'linguistic bias'. As he makes clear, the interest in language has its interest and its justification in the light it can shed on epistemological questions. The book begins, indeed, with a declaration that: 'The present work is intended as an investigation of certain problems concerning empirical knowledge' (Russell, 1940, p. 11), and when he comes to define the nature of a proposition, he does so in unashamedly psychological terms:

> ... it is necessary to distinguish propositions from sentences, but ... propositions need not be indefinable.

They are to be defined as psychological occurrences of certain sorts – complex images, expectations, etc. Such occurrences are 'expressed' by sentences ... . When two sentences have the same meaning, that is because they express the same proposition. Words are not essential to propositions. The exact psychological definition of propositions is irrelevant to logic and the theory of knowledge; the only thing essential to our inquiries is that sentences signify something other than themselves, which can be the same when the sentences differ. That this something is psychological (or physiological) is made evident by the fact that propositions can be false. (*ibid.*, p. 189)

It is clear, then, that Russell emphatically fails – at any stage in his career – to count as an analytical philosopher as defined by Michael Dummett. And as Russell is, I take it, the very epitome of an analytical philosopher, this is enough to show that Dummett's conception of the tradition needs some revision. In my earlier paper, I suggested that Dummett's view might be replaced by one which gives more emphasis to what, in his various attempts to characterize analytical philosophy, he rather curiously ignores: namely, analysis. I want now to expand upon that suggestion, and to propose an alternative cartography of twentieth-century philosophy, one in which the crucial boundary is defined neither by the English Channel nor by the 'linguistic turn', but by the commitment to analysis. On my map, Frege, Russell, Husserl and Meinong are all on the same side of the border, while Wittgenstein lies outside. And thus the opposite of 'analytical' is neither 'continental' nor 'phenomenological' but rather 'Wittgensteinian'.

I begin by noting the title of Dummett's paper in which

he first outlined his view of analytical philosophy as 'post-Fregean philosophy'. It is called 'Can Analytical Philosophy be Systematic and Ought it to Be?' His answer to both questions is: yes. And, though he recognizes that this is not an answer with which Wittgenstein would have concurred, he seems convinced that this is but a small matter compared to the commitment which he and Wittgenstein have in common to the 'Linguistic Turn' in philosophy. I want to suggest that Dummett's conviction as to both the possibility and the desirability of philosophy as a systematic discipline puts him, on the contrary – on the question that counts – closer to Russell than to Wittgenstein, and come to that, closer to Husserl.

The question at stake, I believe, in providing broad characterizations of philosophical points of view, is what one thinks philosophy is and what it can achieve. In the light of this, Wittgenstein's resolute rejection of the idea that it is the task of philosophy to provide theories and doctrines is of far more fundamental importance than the relatively superficial fact that he, like Frege, adopted a more or less linguistic method. Wittgenstein was not an analytical philosopher in the simple and straightforward sense that he did not believe in analysis. The idea, he once said, that one had to wait upon a Moorean analysis of one's words before one understood what one meant was both absurd and grotesque. At the centre of the notion of analysis that Russell inherited from Moore's famous paper, 'The Nature of Judgment' was the idea of a complex that invited us to identify its component parts. It is this notion of a complex – and the concomitant notion that to understand a complex is to analyse it, to break it down into the simples that compose it – that lies at the heart of analytical philosophy.

In a famous passage in *Philosophical Investigations*, Wittgenstein subjects just this notion to a withering piece of scorn:

We see *component parts* of something composite (of a chair for instance). We say that the back is part of the chair, but is in turn itself composed of several bits of wood; while a leg is a simple component part. We also see a whole which changes (is destroyed) while its component parts remain unchanged. These are the material from which we construct that picture of reality.

When I say: 'My broom is in the corner', – is this really a statement about the broomstick and the brush? Well, it could be any rate be replaced by a statement giving the position of the stick and the position of the brush. And this statement is surely a further analysed form of the first one. – But why do I call it 'further analysed'? – Well, if the broom is there, that surely means that the stick and brush must be there, and in a particular relation to one another; and this was as it were hidden in the sense of the first sentence, and is *expressed* in the analysed sentence. Then does someone who says that the broom is in the corner really mean: the broomstick is there, and so is the brush, and the broomstick is fixed in the brush? – If we were to ask anyone if he meant this he would probably say that he had not thought specially of the broomstick or specially of the brush at all. And that would be the *right* answer, for he meant to speak neither of the stick nor of the brush in particular. Suppose that, instead of saying 'Bring me the broom', you said 'Bring me the broomstick and the brush which is fitted on to it'! – Isn't the answer: 'Do you want the broom? Why do you put it so oddly?' (Wittgenstein, 1953, vol. 1, pp. 59–60)

Analogously, having worked through the introduction of *Principia Mathematica*, with its theory of descriptions and its theory of judgement, and then having mastered the theory of types, and proceeded from the primitive propositions through the various definitions and theorems based upon them to the famous result produced half way through the second volume, one might say: 'Do you mean that two plus two equals four? Why do you put it so oddly?'

It matters comparatively little, I think, whether a philosopher takes himself to be analysing language or the world, whether he conceives the analysis of thought to proceed through the analysis of sentences, or whether he thinks the analysis of sentences proceeds through the analysis of psychology. What matters, what distinguishes Frege, Russell, Meinong and Husserl from Wittgenstein is that they believe in analysis at all. And hand in hand with this belief in analysis goes the faith that philosophy has a hope of being a systematic discipline. Husserl once wrote a paper called 'Philosophy as Rigorous Science' in which he hoped to show, *à la* Descartes, that philosophy can provide a foundation for certain knowledge by reflection upon, analysis of, the certainty of various features of self-conscious experience. That he was not proceeding linguistically in this attempt is less important than that he thought he had some chance of success. One might say, indeed, in the face of Husserl's phenomenological reduction, of his bracketing of all 'inessential' features of experience: 'Do you mean you see a tree in front you? Why do you put it so oddly?'

Husserl's title, if nothing else, would have appealed to Russell. Throughout his philosophical career, Russell endeavoured to show how one might aspire to pursue philosophy as, if not a rigorous science, then at least a discipline imbued with what he called 'the scientific spirit'. In an article called 'On Scientific Method in Philosophy', he argued that progress in philosophy depends upon its adopting an ethically neutral 'scientific' attitude towards its enquiries, together with what he called the 'analytic method', examples of which include the use of mathematical logic in defining both numbers and points in space. 'The failure of philosophy hitherto', he writes, 'has been due in the main to haste and ambition: patience and modesty, here as in other sciences, will open the road to solid and durable progress' (Russell, 1986, p. 73). The message, then, is this: slow down, learn the techniques of mathematical logic, apply them wherever possible, and pin your faith in logical analysis rather than speculative metaphysics. Then, philosophy might hope to become a systematic discipline.

In the same spirit, Dummett writes:

> For those who value it at all, it has always been something of a scandal that philosophy has, through most of its history, failed to be systematic ... to such an extent that the question 'Can there be progress in philosophy?' is a perennial one. If philosophy is regarded, as most of its practitioners have regarded it, as one – perhaps the most important – sector in the quest for truth, it is then amazing that, in all its long history, it should not yet have established a generally accepted methodology, generally accepted criteria of success and, therefore, a body of definitely achieved results. (Dummett, 1978, p. 455)

Philosophy, Dummett feels, should *build*, piecemeal, a systematic body of doctrine, one founded upon the 'linguistic turn' taken by Frege. Thus, he writes, 'the most urgent task that philosophers are now called upon to carry out is to devise what I have called a 'systematic theory of meaning' (*ibid.*, p. 454).

Now, it would be a blind reader indeed who saw in Wittgenstein's work a consciousness of the same 'urgent task', and Dummett is not so blind. But he is at least blinkered. 'I do not feel certain', he writes, 'that Wittgenstein thought a systematic account of the functioning of language to be impossible':

> If he did, then he would, of course, repudiate the claim that any of his ideas provided guidelines for the construction of such a systematic account, but would, on the contrary, hold that they ought to deter anyone from any such enterprise. But, even if he did not, it remains that, while we can extract from his work conditions that any successful theory of meaning must satisfy, and warnings against trying to construct such a theory along certain lines, he does not provide us with any outline of what a correct theory of meaning will look like, any strategy or sketch of a strategy for constructing one. This is why I say that, fundamentally important as it is, Wittgenstein's work does not supply us with a *foundation* for future work in the philosophy of language or in philosophy in general. (*ibid.*, p. 453)

Wittgenstein, then, on Dummett's strange reading of him, is pulling in the opposite direction, but, somehow, mysteriously, on the same side.

In fact, of course, Wittgenstein's conception of philosophy is fundamentally opposed to Dummett's ambitions of building a secure foundation for the theory of meaning, or the theory of anything. There are many places in his work in which one can find repudiations of Dummett's ambitions in this respect, but perhaps the most striking is the preface to *Philosophical Remarks*.

'This book', Wittgenstein writes there, 'is written for such men as are in sympathy with its spirit':

> This spirit is different from the one which informs the vast stream of European and American civilization in which all of us stand. That spirit expresses itself in an onwards movement, in building ever larger and more complicated structures: the other in striving after clarity and perspicuity in no matter what structure. The first tries to grasp the world by way of its periphery – in its variety: the second at its centre – in its essence. And so the first adds one construction to another, moving on and up, as it were, from one stage to the next, while the other remains where it is and what it tries to grasp is always the same.
>
> I would like to say 'this book is written to the glory of God', but nowadays that would be chicanery, that is, it would be rightly understood. It means the book is written in good will, and in so far as it is not so written, but out of vanity, etc., the author would wish to see it condemned.

In Dummett's failure to grasp – or, at least, to realize the significance of – such statements of the spirit in which Wittgenstein pursued philosophy, one is reminded of Russell's surprisingly enduring delusion that he and Wittgenstein were partners-in-arms in the struggle for 'scientific method in philosophy'. As late as 1914, Russell regarded this as a cause to which he and Wittgenstein were jointly committed, against various forms of philosophical wrong-headedness, of which, for Russell at that time, the three most prevalent and pernicious were Bradley's Idealism, William James's pragmatism and Bergson's evolutionism. In this fight, as Russell understood it, the forces under his command were small in number but highly trained and well-armed with mathematical logic. And in Wittgenstein, so he thought, he had a charismatic and able second-in-command.

This combative spirit is evident in a review Russell wrote in February 1914 of A. J. Balfour's Gifford lectures, *Theism and Humanism*, which, as the lectures were not actually published until the following year and Russell was dependent upon newspaper reports of them, was something in the nature of a pre-emptive strike. In all sorts of ways, Balfour was the very personification of the views with which Russell felt himself to be at war. First of all, he was a Tory, the Prime Minister of the despised Tory administration of 1902–1905. Secondly, as the author of 'Creative Evolution and Philosophic Doubt', an article published in *The Hibbert Journal* in 1911, he had done much to foster and encourage the enthusiasm for Bergson's philosophy among British intellectuals. Finally, the tenor of his philosophical thinking, and of these Gifford lectures in particular, was anti-scientific and pro-religion. The point of the lectures was to argue for the existence of God on the basis of the accepted fact of aesthetic and ethical value, which, Balfour argues, would be unintelligible if God did not exist. Along the way, Balfour casts doubt on the certainty of the fundamental beliefs which underlie science. All in all, it was, Russell wrote to Ottoline Morrell, 'rhetorical dishonest sentimental twaddle'. The quality of Balfour's mind, he told her, 'is more disgusting to me than anybody else's in the world'. A few days later, he told her: 'It is incredible balderdash. There is something in every word of his writing that fills me with loathing' (Russell, 1986, p. 99).

In print he was slightly less scathing. Running throughout the review, however, is the opposition between Balfour's arguments and proper scientific procedure, and it concludes: 'The fundamental defect of Balfour's lectures, it seems to me, is that, in spite of their allusions to science, they are designed to discourage the scientific habit in philosophy' (*ibid.*, p. 104).

It is one of the great ironies of twentieth-century philosophy that in the very month that Russell was writing in this way, the man he thought of as the very ideal of scientific method in philosophy was doing his best to repudiate any such allegiance. On 30 January, Russell had written to F. H. Bradley, saying that he hoped to find solutions to the vexed question of the unity of the proposition through the work of 'an Austrian pupil of mine'. That Wittgenstein was no such pupil was about to be made abundantly clear.

In the same month, Wittgenstein wrote to Russell with reflections about the existential *Angst* that tormented him. 'Perhaps you think this thinking about myself as a waste of time', he added, 'but how can I be a logician before I'm a human being! *Far* the most important thing is to settle accounts with myself!' (Wittgenstein, 1974, p. 58).

This hardly sounds like the sentiments of a storm-trooper for the struggle to establish the scientific habit in philosophy, but worse was to come. In his next letter, Wittgenstein lectured Russell on the value of *thought* rather than that of a cut and dried result. How Russell responded to this we do not know, since Russell's side of this correspondence has not survived. But Wittgenstein's reply to his letter was evidently so distasteful that Russell destroyed it. This itself is, I am inclined to think, of great significance. Russell kept all his letters from Wittgenstein, *except* this one, and the next letter from Wittgenstein that survives refers to a great quarrel in the past tense, one that was sufficient to persuade him that it was fruitless for them to remain friends. 'We've often had uncomfortable conversations with one another when certain subjects came up', Wittgenstein wrote, 'And the uncomfortableness was not a consequence of ill humour on one side or the other but of enormous difference in our natures ... Our latest quarrel, too, was certainly not simply a result of your sensitiveness or my inconsiderateness. It came from deeper – from the fact that my letter must have shown to you how totally different our ideas are, E. G., of the value of a scientific work. It was, of course, stupid of me to have written to you at length about this matter: I ought to have told myself that such fundamental differences cannot be resolved by a letter. And this is just one instance out of *many*' (*ibid.*, p. 50).

From these hints, it is possible to venture a guess as to what happened: in response to Wittgenstein's remarks about the value of thought over cut and dried results, Russell – imagining perhaps that he was in agreement with Wittgenstein – replied that, as far as he was concerned the value of the lectures he was then preparing (the ones later published as *Our Knowledge of the External World*, subtitled 'As a field for Scientific Method in Philosophy') was primarily that of illustrating the value of the scientific method. He was – to continue my speculations – shocked to discover in the letter that has not survived that, far from being his closest and most powerful ally in the struggle to establish philosophy on a scientific basis, Wittgenstein did not even believe in such a thing. The disappointment of this, alone, I believe, would have been sufficient reason for Russell to destroy the letter.

Whether my speculations are right or not, it became abundantly clear to Russell in time that Wittgenstein was *not* his second-in-command in the campaign for a scientific philosophy. 'The correct method in philosophy', Wittgenstein was to write in *Tractatus Logico-Philosophicus*, 'would be this: to say nothing except what can be said, ie. the propositions of natural science, ie. something that has nothing to do with philosophy: and then always, when someone else wished to say something metaphysical, to demonstrate to him that he had given no meaning to certain signs in his propositions. This method would be unsatisfying to the other – he would not have the feeling that we were teaching him philosophy – but it would be the only strictly correct method.'

This method in philosophy – what A. J. Ayer once facetiously described as the vision of the philosopher as park-keeper, picking up the mess dropped by others – offers little hope to those who wish to see philosophy as a systematic, theory-building activity. It is the very repudiation of the scientific spirit in philosophy, and, as such, as I understand it, the antithesis of the spirit of analytical philosophy, a spirit which informs both the rivers of Dummett's apt analogy. If there is a method by which we can analyse complexes – whether these are propositions, sentences or elements of psychological experience – there is a hope for a systematic philosophy. Wittgenstein offers no such hope. 'The chief thesis I have to maintain', Russell once wrote, 'is the legitimacy of analysis' (Russell, 1985, p. 49). Whether we are for him or against him on this determines whether we are or are not analytical philosophers. On one side of this boundary lie Husserl, Frege, Russell and Dummett, and, on the other, Wittgenstein.

BIBLIOGRAPHY OF WORKS CITED

Dummett, M., 1978. *Truth and Other Enigmas* (London, Duckworth).

—— 1991. *Frege: Philosophy of Mathematics* (London, Duckworth).

—— 1993. *Origins of Analytical Philosophy* (London, Duckworth).

Monk, R., 1996. 'Was Russell an Analytical Philosopher?', to appear in *Ratio*, vol. 9, no. 3, December.

Russell, B., 1903. *The Principles of Mathematics*, (Cambridge).

—— 1940. *An Inquiry into Meaning and Truth* (London, Unwin).

—— 1954. *Nightmares of Eminent Persons* (London, Penguin).

—— 1959. *My Philosophical Development* (London, Unwin).

—— 1973. *Essays in Analysis* (London, Unwin).

—— 1985. *The Philosophy of Logical Atomism* (La Salle, Open Court).

—— 1986. *Collected Papers*, vol. 8 (London, Unwin).

—— 1988. *Collected Papers*, vol. 9 (London, Unwin).

Wittgenstein, L., 1953. *Philosophical Investigations* (Oxford, Blackwell).

—— 1974. *Letters to Russell, Keynes and Moore* (Oxford, Blackwell).

DENOTING CONCEPTS IN
THE PRINCIPLES OF MATHEMATICS

Nicholas Griffin
McMaster University

1. *'The Standard View'*

In 'On Denoting' Russell puts forward his theory of definite descriptions as the preferred alternative to two other theories. One was Meinong's theory of objects, according to which every definite description denotes an object (though not necessarily one which exists). Any sentence in which a definite description occurs in subject position is a sentence which is about this object. The other was Frege's theory of sense and reference, according to which some descriptions have both a Fregean sense (which Russell sometimes called a meaning) and a reference (ie. in Russell's terminology, the object denoted), while others (so-called empty descriptions) have sense but lack reference.[1] In 'On Denoting' Russell deploys against Meinong, a battery of relatively clear arguments which for many years were generally (though erroneously)[2] assumed to have demolished the theory. Against Frege's theory, by contrast, he develops a single lengthy argument of appalling

---

[1] Frege, 1892, p. 58. I ignore here Frege's willingness, in some other writings, to assign a conventional reference, the null class, to empty descriptions. See Frege, 1891, pp. 32–3.

[2] See, eg. Routley, 1980, pp. 86–90, 255–6, 272–3; Bourgeois, 1981; Griffin, 1985.

23

obscurity which commentators until recently have tended to ignore. The neglect of this argument can no doubt be attributed partly to its obscurity, but perhaps even more important was the widespread assumption – what I shall call 'the standard view' – that the theory of descriptions was intended primarily as a contribution to ontology, a device (as Quine, 1967, p. 305 put it) for 'dispensing with unwelcome objects'.[3] If this was the purpose of the theory, then clearly the attack on Meinong was central to the theory's success, while that on Frege might seem of less importance.

Contributing, both to this evaluation of the relative importance for Russell of the arguments against Meinong and Frege and to the assumption that the theory of descriptions was intended as an ontological device, was the view that Russell's own earlier theory of denoting in *The Principles of Mathematics* was (despite some important differences) a sibling of Meinong's theory of objects. If this were the case, then it would be natural for him to assign greatest weight in 'On Denoting' to attacking those theories which had hitherto seemed to him most plausible, ie. Meinongian ones. Thus the standard view is associated not only with a ranking of the arguments in 'On Denoting', but with an interpretation of Russell's earlier theory in the *Principles*. In both respects, however, the standard view is quite clearly mistaken. It was the argument against Frege in 'On Denoting' that Russell regarded as crucial for his new theory of descriptions,[4] and his own earlier theory

---

[3]   Although one would hardly gather as much from the literature, Russell's theory of descriptions does not mandate the elimination of non-existent objects. Montague, for example, kept Russell's analysis of definite descriptions along with a commitment to non-existent but possible objects (Montague, 1973).

[4]   cf. *Papers*, vol. 4, p. 359.

of denoting was much closer to Frege's than to Meinong's. In this paper I shall be concerned only with this second claim, that is with the interpretation of Russell's theory of denoting in the *Principles* in particular with rebutting what I shall call the 'quasi-Meinongian' interpretation of that theory.

The quasi-Meinongian interpretation of the *Principles* has been extraordinarily widespread. Consider, eg. the following characterization by Quine:

> In *Principles of Mathematics*, 1903, Russell's ontology was unrestrained. Every word referred to something. If the word was a proper name ... its object was a *thing*; otherwise a *concept*. He limited the term 'existence' to things ... And then, beyond existence, there were the rest of the entities: 'numbers, the Homeric gods, relations, chimaeras, and four-dimensional spaces' [*POM*, pp. 44, 449]. The word 'concept', which Russell applied to these nonexistents, connotes mereness; but let us not be put off. The point to notice, epithets aside, is that gods and chimaeras are as real for Russell as numbers. Now this is an intolerably indiscriminate ontology. (Quine, 1967, p. 305)

D. F. Pears' preliminary account is cruder but along the same lines. Describing the important changes brought in with the theory of descriptions, Pears writes:

> Russell had believed [in *POM*] that every phrase, long or short, must denote something, or else be meaningless. Now that theory does not imply that a word like 'dragon' denotes an actual species of animal, or that the phrase 'the daughter of Hitler' denotes an actual woman. But, when a phrase lacks an actual denotation, the theory would credit it with a

denotation not belonging to the actual world. Dragons and Hitler's children are supposed to exist in another world .... The change in Russell's theory of meaning came when he decided not to postulate that other world. The reason for his decision was what he sometimes calls 'a vivid sense of reality' [*PLA*, p. 196]. Its consequence was that he had to find some other way of explaining how phrases that lack an actual denotation acquire a meaning .... Russell offered his explanation in his Theory of Definite Descriptions, which was the first product of his new theory of meaning. (Pears, 1967, pp. 13–14)

Ayer took the same line, though he stuck closer to the text:

Anything that could be mentioned was said to be a term; and any term could be the logical subject of a proposition; and anything that could be the logical subject of a proposition could be named. It followed that one could in principle use names to refer not only to any particular thing that existed at any place or time, but to abstract entities of all sorts, to nonexistent things like the present Tsar of Russia, to mythological entities like the Cyclops, even to logically impossible entities like the greatest prime number .... Very soon afterwards, however, Russell came to think that this picture of the world was intolerably overcrowded. (Ayer, 1971, p. 28)

Many other authors could be cited in the same vein.[5] For example, Urmson has it that 'Russell ... went more or less the whole way with Meinong in the acceptance of a shadowy world of being, including essentially numbers, classes, and propositions, but containing, as

---

[5]   eg. Jager, 1972, pp. 55–6; Griffin, 1980, pp. 119–21.

an inevitable corollary, much more besides' (1956, p. 2) – a claim that gets both Russell and Meinong wrong.[6]

This quasi-Meinongian reading of the *Principles* receives *prima facie* support from a number of passages (variously alluded to by Quine, Ayer, and others). For example, Russell first introduces the notion of a term in the *Principles* as follows:

> Whatever may be an object of thought, or may occur in any true or false proposition, or may be counted as *one*, I call a *term*. This, then, is the widest word in the philosophical vocabulary.[7] I shall use as synonymous with it the words unit, individual, and entity. The first two emphasize the fact that every term is *one*, while the third is derived from the fact that every term has being, *ie. is* in some sense. A man, a moment, a number, a class, a relation, a chimaera, or anything else that can be mentioned, is sure to be a term; and to deny that such and such a thing is a term must always be false. (*POM*, p. 43)

Russell also provides a large number of other examples: Socrates, points, instants, bits of matter, particular states of mind, the points in a non-Euclidean space, the pseudo-existents of a novel, classes, numbers, men, spaces (p. 45); a teaspoon, the number 3, a four-dimensional space (p. 71); propositions and Homeric gods (p. 499) even nothing 'in some sense ... is something' (p. 73). There is enough in all this, one might think, to justify Quine's complaint about an 'intolerably indiscriminate ontology'.

---

[6] William and Martha Kneale, 1962, p. 262 repeat both mistakes.

[7] As we shall see, he subsequently introduces a wider one, 'object' – albeit reluctantly.

Although I have called the interpretation these passages have engendered 'quasi-Meinongian', Russell's theory so interpreted certainly differs in important respects from Meinong's theory of objects. Most importantly, Meinong's own realm of being was much more selective in what it would admit, though this was not generally recognized at the time the quasi-Meinongian interpretation was developed.[8] It was also recognized that Russell's theory lacked a good deal of the labyrinthine complexity that marks Meinong's theory and also that Meinong's psychological and epistemic interests were entirely absent in the *Principles*. On the other side, it was admitted that Meinong's theory lacked Russell's notion of denotation. None the less, it was thought that Russell's terms were very much like Meinong's objects, except that Russell endowed all terms with 'being', an ontic status that most of Meinong's objects lacked. The differences between Meinong's characterization of objects and Russell's characterization of terms were thought to derive mainly from a difference of approach. Meinong, a psychologist turned philosopher, was concerned primarily with objects as objects of thought, the object of a mental state; Russell, the philosopher of mathematics, was concerned primarily with terms as constituents of propositions. When these differences of approach were allowed for, it was thought both men had arrived at rather similar positions.

---

[8] It was generally assumed that Meinong thought that all non-existent objects subsisted. When this was recognized as a mistake it became common to think that it was one Russell had originated. That also is a mistake: see Griffin, 1977. Though Meinong did maintain that some abstract objects subsist, most of his objects, abstract and concrete, neither exist nor subsist.

2. Contents in 'An Analysis of Mathematical Reasoning'

Russell's theory of terms, on which the theory of denoting in the *Principles* is based, made its appearance in unpublished manuscripts five years before the *Principles* was published. The earliest and most important among these is a most remarkable document, 'An Analysis of Mathematical Reasoning' (*AMR*), which Russell wrote and abandoned in 1898. The flaws in what survives of 'An Analysis of Mathematical Reasoning' are evident enough, but, ironically, it is the flaws that constitute the historic importance of the manuscript. For it was written at exactly that juncture in which Russell abandoned neo-Hegelianism and embarked upon what has become known as analytic philosophy. And the manuscript's flaws arise largely from its having still a foot in both camps.[9]

Although the theory of terms in the *Principles* originates in Moore's 'Nature of Judgment' and Russell's 'Analysis of Mathematical Reasoning', the theory as presented in these two early pieces is not in all respects the same theory as that which appeared in the *Principles* five years later. The most important development of the theory of terms in the *Principles* is the addition there of the theory of denoting, part of which will be my main concern in this paper. It is not clear when Russell first seriously investigated the notion of denotation. He *uses* the words 'denotation' and 'denotes' in earlier works but without discussing them and without supplying the special technical sense they have in the *Principles*. So far

---

[9]   As is well-known, G. E. Moore broke with idealism at around the same time – and in a similar direction. Moore's theory of concepts (Moore, 1899) originated in his Fellowship dissertation of 1898 and has many similarities to Russell's theory of terms – though the latter was developed a good deal more fully even in the unpublished manuscripts. Russell's early theory of terms is discussed in detail in Griffin, 1991, chap. 7; for Moore's theory, see Baldwin, 1990, chap. 2.

as I know, Russell did not discuss the concept of denotation until he wrote an early draft of Part 1 of the *Principles*, in May 1901.[10]   One of the innovations of the *Principles* is the idea of a *denoting concept* which appears explicitly there for the first time.   In this case, however, the idea is pre-figured in the 'Analysis' by the notion of *contents*.

In the 'Analysis', as in the *Principles*, Russell uses the word 'term' for '[w]hatever can be a logical subject' (*AMR*, p. 167).   'Every possible idea, everything that can be thought of, or represented by a word, may be a logical subject' (*AMR*, p. 168; cf. *POM*, p. 43).   In the absence of any device, like the later theory of descriptions, which would reveal 'real' logical subjects behind apparent ones, it follows, since we can plainly think of what does not exist, that not all terms exist.   But all of them, Russell asserts, have being: 'Being ... belongs to whatever may be the subject in true judgements; and every possible idea, ie. every idea which does not involve a contradiction, may be a logical subject.' (*AMR*, p. 168).[11]   Terms which don't exist Russell calls '*contents*'.   All predicates and relations are contents,[12] so, more importantly, are such terms as *any point, any moment* and *thing*.   These last – contents which are not

---

[10] cf. *Papers*, vol. 3, pp. 196–201.   Most of this material appears in chapter 5 of *POM* on denoting.   In the early draft, however, Russell offers no discussion of the concept of denoting itself.   The 1899–1900 draft of the Principles does not contain any material corresponding in subject matter to that in Part 1 of the published version (cf. *Papers*,vol. 3, paper 1).

[11] The consistency constraint imposed here is not explicit in *POM*, leaving Quine (for one) to wonder whether Russell countenanced impossible terms in *POM* (Quine, 1967, p. 305).   Russell excluded them in *AMR* because he hoped to mirror the domain of terms with a domain of predicates and he imposed consistency constraints on predicate combination (*AMR*, p. 169).   These reasons were not operative in *POM* and it seems plausible to suppose that some terms would be impossibilia.   Russell does not make much of them, but on p. 73 he mentions 'the even prime other than 2'.

[12] In the 'Analysis' Russell includes relations among predicates.

predicates or relations – I shall call 'pure contents', though not for any good reason. Russell provides no name for them and says too little about them to suggest anything more evocative.

Despite the sketchy account he provides, pure contents had an important role to play in Russell's philosophy of mathematics as presented in the 'Analysis':

> All the terms used in Geometry, or in any branch of Mathematics not applied to actual particular existents, are contents. For, even when the term means *any* existent, it does not mean one actual existent. Thus, in the general theory of gravitating bodies, the terms are contents; but when this theory is applied to calculate eclipses, or the motion of the moon, our terms become existents. The distinction of *content* both from existent and from predicate is of great importance. Thus a particular actual thing is an existent, *thing* is a content, but not a predicate; *thinghood* is both a content and a predicate ... . Contents such as *thing* are names [*sic*.] for any term of a class; when the class is defined by a common predicate, the contents in question imply this predicate, but are nevertheless distinct from it. (*AMR*, pp. 176–7)

There is one characteristic terminological confusion in this passage. Russell's talk of *thing* as a '*name* for any member of a class' is a slip, even though he repeats it a few lines later when he refers to pure contents as 'names for unspecified terms of specified classes' (*AMR*, pp. 176–7). Such contents *cannot* be names since they are terms and terms in general are not linguistic.[13]

---

[13] On the other hand, his use of 'predicate' for non-pure contents is *not* a mistake, despite appearances. For Russell expressly introduces 'predicate' to refer, not to the word, but to what the word refers to, that is to a term

None the less, one can sympathize with Russell's difficulty.[14] It is all too natural to talk about pure contents in grammatical terms, as consisting either of a class name on its own or of a class name preceded by the quantifier expression 'any'. What we need is some terminology which will pick out the non-linguistic items that are expressed by class names and class names preceded by the word 'any'. For the former, I shall use Russell's phrase 'class concept' (*POM*, p. 56), despite the fact that it belongs to a later period and Russell does not put the word 'concept' to serious use in the 'Analysis'. In the second case, I shall distinguish between a 'quantifier expression', which is a word or phrase, and a 'quantifier' which is what the word or phrase expresses. At this point we need some systematic notation for the mention of such non-linguistic items. Russell does not provide any, though he often (but not invariably) uses italics. In what follows I shall enclose mentioned propositions and mentioned constituents of propositions within slashes (as in Griffin, 1980). Thus 'human' and 'Socrates' are words and 'Socrates is human' is a sentence; by contrast, /human/ and /Socrates/ are terms and /Socrates is human/ is a proposition. In practice, the slashes in '/Socrates/' are superfluous and will be omitted. With this notation the word 'dog' is a class name which expresses the class concept /dog/; and the quantifier expression 'any' expresses the quantifier /any/. I do not wish to imply there is (or that

which, in addition to be able to function as the subject of a proposition, can also occur, to use Russell's phrase, as 'meaning', ie. as the element which binds together the other constituents of the proposition into a unity. (Similar remarks apply to Russell's use of 'adjective' in the *Principles*, for which he is often unjustly criticized. Following F.H. Bradley, he intentionally uses the word for what we would now call 'properties'.)

[14] As we shall see, his problem arises precisely because, in *AMR*, he lacks the concept of denotation.

Russell thought that there was) a term which was expressed by the quantifier expression 'any'.[15] On the other hand Russell seems committed to the view that there must be something that it expresses. 'Words', he says 'all have meaning, in the simple sense that they are symbols which stand for something other than themselves' (*POM*, p. 47). In that idiom (not faithfully adhered to by Russell), /any/ is what 'any' means.

The need to express this in some neutral language results from the fact that Russell had no viable theory of quantification throughout the period covered by this paper. Even in the *Principles*, he had no adequate account of variables (he laments its lack at *POM*, pp. 5–6), and his account of quantification there is, as a result, notoriously idiosyncratic.[16] In the 'Analysis' things were worse, because there he had not even fixed upon the variable as a crucial ingredient in his account of pure contents.

This lack in the 'Analysis' shows up in the uncertainty one feels about the intended extension of 'pure contents'. Russell gives just two kinds of example: /thing/ and /any point/,/any moment/. It is tempting here to think of /thing/ as a class concept. But to do so would be a mistake, because a class concept is a predicate and not a pure content. It seems, rather, that what Russell has in mind would be more naturally expressed by the phrase 'a thing'. He says, for example, that pure contents are used in judgements of class-inclusion such as /Socrates is a man/ or /3 is a number/ (*AMR*, pp. 174, 177). Taking this suggestion to heart,

---

[15] In *AMR* he doesn't treat quantifiers at all. In *POM* he takes the whole phrase 'any dog' to indicate, not a term, but a certain kind of object.

[16] See Dau, 1986 and Geach, 1962, chap. 3. It was not until he studied Frege, just after completing the *Principles*, that he came upon anything approaching the modern treatment of quantification.

I shall suppose that Russell thought there were two kinds of pure content, which I shall call /a/-form and /any/-form pure contents.

Now it is hard to suppose that the theory toward which Russell is here struggling is likely to prove successful. On the other hand, it would be a mistake to suppose that Russell's approach was an obvious dead end. It seems not implausible to suggest that the idea that Russell sought to capture by means of /a/-form pure content was the one that Hilbert subsequently did capture by means of his ϵ-operator (cf. Hilbert and Bernays, 1934, vol. 2, sec. 1). Russell's /a/-form pure contents are very much like Hilbert's ϵ-terms. Indeed, ϵ-terms are often explained in a way reminiscent of Russell's account of /a/-form pure contents. Thus Kneebone (1963, p. 101) explains that if any item has the property F then the ϵ-term $(\epsilon x)F(x)$ 'designates some entity, not further specified, with the property'.[17]

Similarly, Russell's /any/-form pure contents bear some affinity to the arbitrary objects Kit Fine uses to formulate natural deduction systems. It is not quite accurate to think of Russell's /any/-form pure contents as analogous to Fine's arbitrary objects, they are rather terms which should be thought of as denoting such objects.[18] In both cases, it seems, the idea led nowhere in Russell's hands, not because it was inherently flawed, but because Russell discovered Fregean quantification

[17] Compare Russell (*AMR*, p. 177): 'Contents such as *thing* are names for any term of a class; when the class is defined by a common predicate, the contents in question imply this predicate.' What's missing in Russell's account, apart from the variable, is Kneebone's notion of designation (equivalently Russell's later notion of denotation) which permits the ϵ-term to be neither a linguistic expression nor the item the expression refers to. The absence of this notion makes it difficult for Russell to state his theory.

[18] Except, of course, that Russell does not yet have the concept of denoting. The important point here is how close he is to that notion: he has a theory which cannot be coherently stated without it.

theory. Although, even by the time he wrote the *Principles* (ie. before he read Frege), he was already arguing against arbitrary objects (*POM*, pp. 53, 90–91).

Making an elaborate distinction between words and the items which they express does not solve our difficulty in saying what exactly pure contents are. For, while it is clear that they can't be what Russell called them, 'the names of unspecified terms of specified classes' (*AMR*, p. 177), it is also clear that they cannot be the unspecified terms themselves. For, in the case where the specified class is a class of existents, then the unspecified member of the class would be an existent. But contents are, by definition, terms which do not exist. The pure content, therefore, must be some term with a status intermediate between the word and the term to which the word refers, a term which designates (to use Kneebone's word) an unspecified member of the given class.

There is, though Russell doesn't mention it in what survives of the 'Analysis', another feature that pure contents have. When an ordinary term occurs in a proposition as its logical subject, the proposition is about that term.[19] But when a pure content occurs in a proposition as its logical subject, the proposition cannot be about the pure content itself. Consider, for example, the proposition /any integer has a definite number of prime factors/. This proposition cannot be about the pure content /any integer/, for it is about integers and the pure content, as we have just seen, is not an integer. Thus a pure content is a term which is neither a word nor what the word refers to, but is an intermediary between the word and what it refers to, in the sense that,

---

[19] This doctrine only appears explicitly in *Principles* (p. 45), though it fits equally well with the views put forward in the first two chapters of the 'Analysis'.

when the pure content occurs as the logical subject of a proposition, the proposition is not about the pure content but about a term or terms which are referred to by the word which expresses the content. This relationship between pure contents and terms is what Russell calls 'denoting' in the *Principles*.

We have here the essentials of Russell's account of denoting in the *Principles*. The main differences are: first, that the account is generalized in the *Principles* from terms formed with the quantifier /any/ and /a/ to terms formed with other quantificational devices (viz. /all/, /every/, /some/, /the/); and, second, that, in the eccentric quantification theory of the *Principles*, pure contents are treated (along with other terms expressed by quantifier expressions) as denoting concepts which denote what Russell calls 'objects'. He uses 'object' in a broader sense than 'term' to include, in addition to terms (all of which can be counted as one), items which, are not one but many (*POM*, p. 55&n.) and also items which, he says, are 'absolutely peculiar' in being 'neither one nor many' (*ibid.*, p. 58). Objects which are many Russell later called 'plurals' (*MTCA*, p. 27). But it is the objects which are neither one nor many which are denoted by most of the denoting concepts considered in the *Principles*. He calls them 'combinations' since they combine terms without the aid of relations (*POM*, p. 58). Denoting concepts of all types denote combination except for those formed with /the/ which always denotes a single term.[20] By introducing the word 'object'

---

[20] The introduction of object is a retrograde move as regards the original pure contents /a *u*/ and /any *u*/. There is no need to invoke objects to deal with /a *u*/ (nor, for that matter, to deal with /any *u*/, if arbitrary terms are admissible – cf. Fine, 1985). In the theory of pure contents of 1898, one could interpret the content /a *u*/ as denoting the particular *u* chosen – rather than the elaborate disjunctive object (u_1 or u_2 or ... u_n) Russell supposed in *POM* (p. 59). It seems that Russell introduced objects to ensure uniformity

to include terms as well as combinations Russell is able to give a uniform statement of the main principle of his theory of denoting: denoting concepts of all types denote objects. The uniformity of statement, however, does not yield a uniformity of treatment. Denoting concepts expressed by definite descriptions are accorded separate treatment in the *Principles*.

Knowing how things developed, it is easy to see that Russell's account of pure contents in the 'Analysis' is the precursor of his theory of denoting concepts in *The Principles of Mathematics*. However, in the 'Analysis', the arguments just considered about the aboutness of pure contents are not invoked, even as problems, though they lurk close to the surface. In their absence, the concept of denoting itself did not emerge explicitly until later.

3. *Denoting in 'The Principles of Mathematics'*

Russell starts his discussion of denoting with the remark that 'like most of the notions of logic, [it] has been obscured... by an undue mixture of psychology' (*POM*, p. 53). 'There is a sense', he goes on, 'in which *we* denote, when we point or describe, or employ words as symbols for concepts.' But this is not the sense Russell is concerned with. What concerns him, rather is 'the fact that description is possible – that we are able, by the employment of *concepts*, to designate a thing which is not a concept' This, he says, 'is due to a logical relation between some *concepts* and some terms, in virtue of

of treatment for the various denoting concepts (except, of course, /the *u*/). Even so, there seems clear evidence of inconsistency in Russell's treatment in *POM*. Compare what he says about /a man/ on p. 53 with what he says on pp. 54, 59. See below.

There is in fact a seventh type of denoting concept in the *Principles* which has been little noticed, namely that expressed by the plural of a class-name (eg. 'men'). The denoting concept /men/ denotes the class as many (a plural in Russell's later terminology), cf. *POM*, p. 54.

which such concepts inherently and logically *denote* such terms' (*ibid.*; 1st and 2nd italics added). Denotation, then, in the sense in which Russell uses the word, is a relation between concepts and terms – not between words and terms.

Russell has no settled usage for the relation between words and terms. On pp. 44, 47 he uses 'indicate', which seems to have stuck in the secondary literature (no doubt because it is one of the few words in the area that he didn't use in some other sense). But elsewhere he uses 'stand for' (p. 47), 'mean' (p. 47),[21] 'express' (p. 49), and even 'denotes' (pp. 55–6) – though this last is clearly a mistake. This terminological chaos might be extenuated (though not entirely excused) on the grounds that it is this relation between words and terms which is what Russell is *not* concerned with. None the less, it confused so astute a reader as Victoria Welby, to whom we are indebted for preserving Russell's long and extremely helpful letter of clarification (see appendix).

In the *Principles* Russell treated denotation as an indefinable notion (*POM*, p. 106). In introducing it he says merely this:

> A concept *denotes* when, if it occurs in a proposition, the proposition is not *about* the concept, but about a term connected in a certain peculiar way with the concept. (*POM*, p. 53)

The 'peculiar way' in which a denoting concept is connected to a particular term is the relation of denotation. Russell goes on to give a number of illustrative examples, one of which is our old friend the /any/-form proper content from the 'Analysis of Mathematical Reasoning':

---

[21] He immediately dismisses this sense of 'mean' as irrelevant to logic.

[T]he proposition 'any finite number is odd or even' is plainly true; yet the *concept* 'any finite number' is neither odd nor even. It is only particular numbers that are odd or even; there is not, in addition to these, another entity, *any number*,[22] which is either odd or even, and if there were, it is plain that it could not be odd and could not be even. (*ibid.*)

Russell's position, so far, may be summed up as follows: Certain phrases *indicate* concepts which *denote* terms. These phrases are called '*denoting phrases*' (*POM*, p. 56) and the concepts they indicate are called '*denoting concepts*'. Denoting phrases consist of a class name preceded by one of the following six words: 'all', 'every', 'any', 'a', 'some' and 'the' (*POM*, p. 55) or some synonym of one of them (*ibid.*, p. 56).

There is a tension in Russell's explicit account in *Principles* of those denoting concepts which are *not* expressed by definite descriptions. On the one hand, Russell defines denoting as a relation between a concept and a *term*. His examples also suggest that when the denoting concepts /a man/ and /any finite number/, or the class concept /man/, occur in a proposition the denotations are terms: a particular man, particular finite numbers, and particular men. The passage just quoted about /any finite number/ suggests that this denoting concept denotes all particular finite numbers. Similarly Russell writes:

If I say 'I met a man', the proposition is not about /a man/: this is a concept which does not walk the streets, but lives in the shadowy limbo of the logic-books. What I met was a thing, not a concept, an actual man

---

[22] There is, of course, another *object*, /any number/, the 'absolute peculiarity' of which is explained at *POM*, pp. 58–9. But this object (or combination), of course, is itself neither odd nor even.

with a tailor and a bank-account or a public-house
and a drunken wife. (*POM*, p. 53)

From this it certainly appears that the denoting concept
/a man/ denotes a particular man, namely the man
whom I met. But on the very next page, he gives a
different account: 'A *man*, we shall find, is neither a
concept nor a term, but a certain kind of combination
of certain terms, namely of those which are human'
(*ibid*., p. 54).[23] On the page after that, he introduces the
word 'object', with a broader extension than 'term',
precisely to cover what is denoted by denoting concepts
such as /a man/ and the ensuing discussion concerns
exclusively the relationship between denoting concepts
(those formed with /the/ now excluded) and the *objects*
they denote. On the account then given /a man/ denotes
what Russell calls 'a variable disjunction' of men, where
no man in particular may be taken to be denoted (*POM*,
p. 59). On this account /a man/ denotes, not a particular
man, but a certain type of combination of men.

It is tempting then to conclude that, for Russell in the
Principles, all denoting concepts (except those forms
with /the/) denote what Russell calls combinations. But
even this fails to accommodate the text. Let us consider
the individual cases: /All *a*'s/ denotes 'numerical
conjunction ... the terms of *a* taken all together'
(p. 58). /Every *a*/ denotes 'all the *a*'s, [but] denotes
them in a different manner, ie. severally instead of collec-
tively' (p. 58). But Russell's account of /any *a*/ is
different. /Any *a*/, Russell says 'denotes only one *a*; but
it is wholly irrelevant which it denotes' (p. 58). Similarly
with /some *a*/. This 'denotes just one term of the class

[23] Evidently Russell's italics in '*a man*' do not signify that a concept is what
is being talked about. The most plausible reading for the sentence,
supported in the following pages, is that Russell is here talking about what
/a man/ denotes.

a; but the term it denotes may be any term of the class' (p. 59). This certainly suggests an undue complexity of theory. However, a more probable explanation is carelessness. This material in the *Principles* was based on a draft written in May 1901 where he adopted a slightly different account of denoting from the one he published. In the 1901 version (*Papers*, vol. 3, pp. 196–8) only five types of quantifier are considered, those formed by /all/, /every/, /any/, /a/ and /some/.[24] Corresponding to each there is a different combination of terms, as in the *Principles* but in the 1901 theory the quantifiers are concepts which denote, not the combinations, but the terms which are combined. Since, for quantifiers formed on the same class, the same terms are combined in each of the five combinations (viz. the members of the class), the quantifiers have to denote them in five different ways. So in 1901 we have five different denotation relations, one for each type of quantification, whereas in the *Principles* we have a single relation of denotation and (with the inclusion of /the/) six different types of object to be denoted.[25] In 1901 the denoting concept, so to speak, penetrates the combination to denote the terms that make it up. In the published version, at least officially, it is the combination itself which is denoted. It is difficult to see why Russell came to prefer the second theory – except that on the first combinations, being neither denoting nor denoted, seem to have little role of play (cf. *POM*, pp. 61–2, where this is hinted at). It seems likely, however, that the inconsistencies in the *Principles* as to whether

---

[24] Definite denoting concepts are conspicuous by their absence.

[25] In *POM*, p. 56, Russell raises the question of whether there is one way of denoting six different kinds of object or whether the ways of denoting are different, deciding in favour of the former on p. 62. The question is apt to seem puzzling unless one knows of the earlier theory.

the combination or its constituent terms is (are) denoted, arise from his forgetting to reuse the old material in line with his new theory when he incorporated it into the book.

The difficulties Victoria Welby had with the *Principles* were not unlike those experienced by post-war linguistic philosophers, and they arose from a similar source. Both read their own interest in language into Russell's book. Welby's interest was in semiotics and she mistook chapters 4 and 5 of the *Principles* as being primarily about signs and what they signify. The bulk of Russell's letter is devoted to correcting this misconception.[26] In the course of doing so he is much more explicit about words and their senses than he had been in the *Principles* itself.

In the *Principles* he had said that all words have meaning 'in the simple sense that they are symbols which stand for something other than themselves' (*POM*, p. 47).[27] But it is clear that this linguistic view of meaning is a concession to ordinary usage. The main notion of meaning discussed on p. 47 of the *Principles* is one he got from Bradley: 'that all words stand for ideas having what [Bradley] calls *meaning*' (*ibid*.). It is ideas, rather than words, that have meaning in this sense. He tells Welby that, in this passage, meaning is 'whatever Mr Bradley intends to signify by *meaning*. This is what I contend to be a confused notion.' The

---

[26] B.R. letter to Victoria Welby, 3 February 1904 (Welby papers, York University, Toronto – copy in Russell Archives).

[27] cf. also p. 42: 'every word occurring in a sentence must have *some* meaning.' Russell subsequently characterized this view critically as the belief that 'if a word means something, there must be something that it means' (*PFM*, p. 63). cf. *PFM*, p. 41.

confusion arises, like the confusion in the concept of denotation, from a combination of psychological and logical elements.[28]

In the letter, he abandons 'meaning' altogether and uses 'sense' for what, in the book, he had called the meaning of a word. The sense of a word, he says, is 'that which should be expounded in a dictionary, or that which should be as far as possible unaltered in translating into another language'. The claim in the *Principles* that a word 'stands for' something other than itself is now considerably amplified in the letter:

> We have to distinguish (1) the relation of a word to the thought it *expresses*: this is the sense of a word as given in dictionaries and preserved in translation; (2) the relation of a thought (idea) to that of which it is the idea; (3) in certain cases, like that of the Prime Minister, a further relation of the object of the idea (which object, in such cases, I call a *concept*) to another object or collection of objects: it is this third relation that I call *denoting*. The object before the mind when we think 'the Prime Minister' is not the same as when we think 'Mr Arthur Balfour', or when an image of the man himself is before the mind. Yet the Prime Minister *is* Mr Arthur Balfour. This states the problem of denoting.

It seems plausible to assume that by the time he wrote the letter Russell had been influenced in his choice of terminology by his study of Frege. It might also be thought that Frege had influenced his account of 'the problem of denoting' but Russell arrived at this independently. In the *Principles*, for example, he appeals to denoting concepts in order to explain how true but

---

[28] cf. Moore, 1899, which begins with just such a critique of Bradley.

informative identity statements are possible (p. 64).

The full account, then, only part of which is supplied in the *Principles*, is as follows: The phrase 'the Prime Minister' *expresses* an idea which has as its *object* the denoting concept /the Prime Minister/[29] which in turn *denotes* a particular person. Russell's semantic theory in the *Principles* is thus not, as is usually supposed, a three-tier theory of words, concepts, and denotations, but a four-tier one of words, ideas, concepts and denotations. In the case of (ordinary) proper names, however, the tier occupied by concepts will presumably be omitted. (Though Russell is not explicit, I take it that the name 'Balfour' expresses an idea which has the man as its object.) In the *Principles* Russell says little about words on the ground, as he tells Welby, that 'logic is not concerned with words but what they stand for'. He says as much in the *Principles* as well (pp. 42, 47). Of the view that the sense of a word is given by the idea which it expresses, there is little trace in the *Principles*.

The relation between a word and its sense is an accidental and contingent matter, the result of linguistic convention or happenstance. We could, after all, have attached different senses to our words. The relation between a denoting concept and what it denotes, by contrast, is a matter of logic: '[T]he fact that description is possible – that we are able, by the employment of concepts, to designate a thing which is not a concept – is due to a logical relation between some concepts and

---

[29] The idea is an idea *of* the denoting concept /the Prime Minister/. It is not an idea of the man who is the Prime Minister. I suspect the reasons for this are very similar to those which Frege gave for introducing the notion of the sense of a Fregean proper name. On the one hand Russell's denoting concept, like Frege's *Sinn*, must be objective and publicly available (which the idea is not); on the other hand, it must be possible to distinguish the sense of sentences about the prime minister from sentences about Mr Balfour (hence the object of the idea cannot be the man). cp. Frege, 1892, pp. 56–7, 59–60.

some terms, in virtue of which such concepts inherently and logically *denote* such terms' (*POM*, p. 53).

Little of this detail appears in the (admittedly scant) secondary literature on the *Principles* until Chrystine Cassin's doctoral dissertation of 1968 (Cassin, 1968). To my knowledge Cassin's thesis is the first account of any exegetic sophistication of Russell's theory of denoting in the *Principles*. Cassin missed the role of ideas in Russell's theory – but only just. She quotes the passage in which Russell says that meaning, in the sense in which words have meaning, is a psychological notion. She finds the passage puzzling but perspicaciously comments: 'It is possible that he uses "psychological" to characterize Bradley's view that the meanings of words are ideas' (Cassin, 1968, p. 31). This, of course, is exactly right. That Cassin doesn't go further is hardly surprising, for Russell is not explicit about it in the *Principles*, but only in his letter to Welby. Cassin thus leaves ideas to one side and gives us the now-familiar three-tier account: words, concepts, denotations.

4. *Denotation Failure in the Principles*
Where Cassin goes wrong (along with almost everyone else) is in assuming that Russell in the *Principles* accepted 'a Meinongian universe' (Cassin, 1968, p. 32). Putting 'psychological meaning' to one side, she writes: 'the meaning of a word is the entity which it indicates, but the meaning of a denoting concept is the term, or terms, which it denotes. Denotation is "logical" meaning for Russell' (*ibid.*, p. 31). Adding to this Russell's claim that every word has meaning, leads her to accuse him of having failed to distinguish 'between meaning and reference, using "reference" to cover both indication and denotation' (*ibid.*). This 'hypostatizing of meanings' leads straight to the

Meinongian universe (*ibid.*, p. 32).

Cassin is certainly not alone in thinking this. In fact the claim that Russell identified meanings with references was part of the standard Oxford charge sheet against Russell. It was Russell whom Ryle thought had been guilty of perpetrating the 'Fido'-Fido theory of meaning. In fact, Cassin gives us rather better grounds – at least exegetically more subtle ones – for accepting the standard charge. Her error arose because, although she distinguished indication (the relation between words and their 'meanings') from denotation (the relation between denoting concepts and their 'meanings') and, noted (correctly) that, for Russell, every word had 'meaning' in the sense that there was some object (usually a term) which it meant, she jumped to the conclusion that for every denoting concept there must be some object (usually a combination) which it denotes. This last is false. It holds for most denoting concepts formed by quantifiers, but it fails for what I shall call 'descriptive denoting concepts', those denoting concepts which are indicated by definite descriptions. Not all descriptive denoting concepts denote.

In what follows, I shall ignore denoting concepts formed by means of quantifiers and consider only those expressed by means of definite descriptions. This is neither the time nor the place to go, any further than I already have done, into the fruitless complexities of Russell's early theory of quantification. Unlike the quantificational denoting concepts which denote various kinds of combination of the terms which we would today regard as members of the range of the bound variable, descriptive denoting concepts (those of the form /the u/, where /u/ is a class concept) denote a single term.

It has been generally assumed that, according to

Russell in the *Principles*, every descriptive denoting concept denoted a term. Thus while /the Prime Minister of England/ denoted Balfour, /the King of France/ denoted some non-existent term in the realm of being. Thus Russell's realm of being was thought to be occupied by a plethora of non-existent terms very much like Meinong's non-existent objects. This turns out to be a complete mistake. Geach, 1958, deserves credit for avoiding the mistake early on. More recently Cocchiarella, 1982, and to some extent also Hylton, 1990 (p. 212), have also rejected the quasi-Meinongian interpretation of the *Principles*.[30]

Although it was Cocchiarella who led me to see the failings of the quasi-Meinongian interpretation, it is important to note, that his interpretation is by no means the same as the one I present here. Cocchiarella does not mention denoting concepts at all. Instead he talks of denoting phrases which denote terms (or individuals). He claims that for Russell a definite description denotes that term which uniquely satisfies the description. Now the very important idea that I've taken from him is the view that *definite descriptions like 'the King of France' do not denote a term at all.* This conflicts with the conventional wisdom, but it is so thoroughly supported by textual evidence that it is hard now to see how it could have been missed.

Beyond this point, however, Cocchiarella's and my own interpretation differ. Cocchiarella holds that Russell countenances possible but non-existent objects, such as the present King of France, as occupants of

---

[30] Hylton claims that 'consistently with [Russell's] fundamental tenets', 'it is perfectly possible for there to be a denoting concept which denotes nothing'. However, he also claims that some of Russell's explicit statements exclude this possibility. In what follows, I shall try to reverse this emphasis claiming that Russell explicitly allows of this possibility (and the need to exploit it) but that occasionally he *appears* to exclude it.

other possible worlds. The reason he holds that this object is not denoted by the definite description 'the present King of France' is that the object does not (uniquely) satisfy the description: the present King of France is not, in fact, presently King of France. To satisfy the description, the present King of France would have to exist. This view certainly has its attractions – and it puts the early Russell happily close to the cutting-edge of Montague semantics. Yet it is not, I think, the right view. As I see it, Russell held that the denoting concept /the present King of France/ does not denote the term, the present King of France, because *there is no such term (either existent or merely possible) to be denoted.*[31]

Now whether Cocchiarella or I am right on the point on which we differ, we are certainly right (as against the standard view) on the point on which we agree – namely, that not all denoting concepts denote. Russell says as much in the *Principles* in a passage not frequently quoted:

> [A] concept may denote although it does not denote anything. This occurs when there are propositions in which the said concept occurs, and which are not about the said concept, but all such propositions are false ... . Consider, for example, the proposition 'chimaeras are animals' or 'even primes other than 2

---

[31] In 'The Existential Import of Propositions', written just before he discovered his theory of descriptions, Russell is, for the first time, quite explicit on the matter: "'The present King of England" is a complex concept denoting an individual; "the present King of France" is a similar complex concept denoting nothing. The phrase intends to point out an individual, but fails to do so: it does not point out an unreal individual, but no individual at all' (*EIP*, p. 487). This passage, however, gives only weak support for my interpretation of the *Principles*, since it is possible that Russell changed his position between writing the two works.

are numbers'. These propositions appear to be true, and it would seem that they are not concerned with the denoting concepts, but with what these concepts denote; yet that is impossible, for the concepts in question do not denote anything ... (*POM*, p. 73).

This passage occurs in the course of a discussion of the null class. Russell's treatment of the null class in the *Principles* is another point at which the quasi-Meinongian interpretation can be shown to be definitely mistaken. Russell defines the null class in several equivalent ways, one of which is 'the class of x's satisfying any propositional function ϕx which is false for all values of x' (*POM*, p. 23). Here ϕ is a class concept from which we can derive the denoting concepts /a ϕ/ and /the ϕ such that.../. If there is some term(s) which these concepts denote then the propositional function ϕx will be true for all such terms. The argument is worth a little elaboration. Russell himself is more explicit later on where he provides a 'complete definition' of a null class-concept a:

All denoting concepts ... are derived from class concepts; and a is a class-concept when 'x is an a' is a propositional function. The denoting concepts associated with a will not denote anything when and only when 'x is an a' is false for all values of x. (*POM*, p. 74)

Contraposing the right-to-left half of Russell's last claim, it follows that if the denoting concepts in question denote then 'x is an a' is true for some value of x. It follows, then, that if the denoting concepts associated with a denote anything, then a cannot be a null-class concept.

Against these passages, the best the quasi-Meinongian

interpretation can do is to complain that Russell has fallen into a confusion. There are certainly confusions in the *Principles of Mathematics* – and some, perhaps, even as egregious as these. But the 'plainly confused' ploy must be the last resort of any commentator (though it was the one I adopted in 1980). What makes it impossible to sustain in this case is the fact that Russell embraces essentially this account of the null class along with the theory of terms in 1898 (cf. *AMR*, p. 187). It is one thing to say that an author contradicted himself in a particular work, it is quite another to suggest that he maintained the same contradiction through work written over a five year span.

Russell's treatment of the null-class takes us to deeper reasons for rejecting the quasi-Meinongian interpretation of the *Principles*. Some of these concern key parts of Russell's logicist programme. The logicist project had two parts, the first was the derivation of mathematical principles deductively from principles of logic; the second was the definition of mathematical concepts in purely logical terms. The best known example of the second type of logicist reduction is Russell's definition of a cardinal number as the class of all equinumerous classes. Now such definitions are taken, quite rightly, to be reductions, that is, they permit the elimination of mathematical concepts in favour of purely logical (in this case, set theoretical) ones. If, as the quasi-Meinongian interpretation requires, Russell is still committed to the full range of cardinal numbers, considered as subsistent terms, it is difficult to see what the reductive definitions of logicism achieve and why Russell considered them to be important. It cannot be that existent terms are reduced to those that merely have being, for Russell never thought that numbers were existents. A main purpose of logicism was to eliminate our commitment to mathematical terms; the quasi-Meinongian interpretation requires us to make that commitment.

A closely related reason is given by Hylton (1990, pp. 211–12). In the *Principles* Russell frequently insists on the importance of existence proofs in mathematics. He complains, for example, that Dedekind's definition of irrational numbers simply postulates a limit for every converging infinite sequence of rationals instead of proving its existence (*POM*, pp. 280–82).[32] This, he later said, had all the advantages of theft over honest toil (*IMP*, p. 71). Now, as Hylton points out, if every denoting concept denotes, Russell's insistence on the importance of existence proofs becomes unintelligible. For given some mathematical item whose existence we wish to prove we need merely to form the descriptive denoting concept which denotes it and the (mathematical) existence of the term in question is guaranteed.

Not only does the quasi-Meinongian interpretation undermine Russell's efforts to develop mathematics out of logic, but it undermines the account of logic itself that Russell wants to give. In the *Principles* logic is marked by its extreme generality. Though Russell does not state it explicitly it seems that something like the following view of logic underlines the *Principles*.

A proposition p is logically true if (i) p is true and (ii) any proposition which results from p by replacing any constituent term in p (except for logical constants)

---

[32] It should be noted that in mathematical contexts 'existence' for Russell has a different meaning from that in which it is contrasted with being. The two senses, Russell says elsewhere (*EIP*, p. 486), are 'as different as stocks in a flower-garden and stocks on the Stock Exchange'. In the mathematical sense a class exists when it is not null. In the case in question, therefore, Russell is demanding a proof that the class in question have a (unique) member.

by any other term whatsoever is also true.

Logic can then be defined as the set of logically true propositions. None of this can stand if we take seriously the idea that every definite description indicates a denoting concept which denotes a term. For denoting concepts like /the round square/ or /the even prime other than 2/ will denote terms which cannot truth-preserving be substituted for other terms in logical principles. Thus, for example, the term denoted by $/(\iota x)(\phi x$ & $\sim\emptyset x)/$ cannot truth-preservingly be substituted for a in $\sim(Fa$ & $\sim Fa)$. Permitting such substitutions would do more than force Russell to redefine the boundary between logical and non-logical principles, it would destroy any account of logical principles that could be given along the substitution lines suggested above for the *Principles*. For suppose L is any putative law of logic, we can then form the denoting concept $(\iota x)\sim L$ which, then, on the standard interpretation, will then denote a term for which L is not true! It seems clear, then, that not only is the standard interpretation inconsistent with certain important passages in the *Principles*, but it is inconsistent with the entire philosophy of logic which underlines the book.

Nothing said so far, however, helps to adjudicate between Cocchiarella's interpretation and my own. Russell's use of 'even primes other that two' as an example, alongside 'chimaeras', tells against Cocchiarella's possibility interpretation, on which the two examples would receive radically different treatments. But maybe Russell's appeal to an even prime other than two merely tells in favour of a liberalization of Cocchiarella's position to admit a realm of impossible as well as possible terms. The real issue is whether these two denoting concepts do not denote because there is no term for them to denote, or because the terms in question, being non-existent, fail to satisfy the description 'even prime other than two' or 'chimaera'?

The main difficulty for Cocchiarella's interpretation seems to me that it leaves no role for denoting concepts to play. On Cocchiarella's view they would seem to be just supernumerary wheels within the semantic machinery.[33] Moreover, it is difficult to make out what role the non-existent objects themselves play in Cocchiarella's interpretation. It would seem that all descriptions are false of them – for if any description is true of a chimaera it is surely the description that it is a chimaera. So Cocchiarella's theory seems to require us to admit that there is a chimaera of which it is false to say that it is a chimaera. The problem is not just that we can't say true things about a chimaera, but that in the absence of truths about chimaeras we seem to be at a loss to identify or even talk about Cocchiarella's possible objects. It is not impossible to see ways in which this problem could be overcome, but it is impossible to find any trace of them in the *Principles of Mathematics*.

The difficulty for my own interpretation lies in dealing with Russell's lists of examples of terms. He writes:

A man, a moment, a number, a class, a relation, a chimaera, or anything else which can be mentioned, is sure to be a term; and to deny that such and such a thing is a term must always be false. (*POM*, p. 43)[34]

---

[33] This said, I should point out, in fairness to Cocchiarella, that he is not so much concerned as I am with what Russell's actual position was. He is more concerned with the viability of what he calls a 'reconstructed' Russellian view in contrast to the 'reconstructed' Meinongian view put forward by Terence Parsons. cf. Parsons, 1980.

[34] Note that the examples are given without underlining or any kind of quotational device, which he sometimes uses to indicate that he's talking about denoting concepts.

The passage, of course, gives no trouble to Cocchiarella, for his interpretation admits all such terms. On my interpretation, however, we must conclude that Russell is referring here to the denoting concepts themselves, not to the terms they appear to denote. For the denoting concept itself is always a term, though, in my view, there will often be no further term denoted by it. This reading of the passage will, I concede, seem strained in the absence of any explicit indication that Russell is mentioning denoting concepts. Yet it is in fact what I think he meant.

Earlier in the same paragraph from which I have just quoted he characterized terms as follows:

> Whatever may be an object of thought, or may occur in any true or false proposition, or can be counted as *one* is a term. (p. 43)

All three characterizations support the view that, in the list of examples which follow, he is thinking of denoting concepts. Objects of thought, for Russell, as we saw from his letter to Victoria Welby, are denoting concepts, not the terms those concepts denote.[35] So, too, are many of the constituents of true or false propositions. The proposition /The Prime Minister of Britain in 1905 had a moustache/ contains, not Mr Balfour, but the denoting concept /the Prime Minister of Britain in 1905/. Finally, denoting concepts are always countable. There

---

[35] The letter to Welby should be born in mind when construing the following passage: 'Every pair of terms... can be combined in the manner indicated by A *and* B, and if neither A nor B be many, then A and B are two. A and B may be any conceivable entities, any possible objects of thought... A teaspoon and the number 3, or a chimaera and a four-dimensional space, are certainly two' (*POM*, p. 71).

Once again, although Russell appears to be talking about a chimaera he is really talking about the denoting concept /a chimaera/, for it is the denoting concept that is an object of thought.

seems no ground for thinking it was Russell's view that chimaeras were countable, for example.

At least one of Russell's examples, however, clearly supports the view that, while he includes denoting concepts among terms, he does not include what they purport to denote, if what they purport to denote does not exist. He says: 'It is plain ... that in some sense nothing is something' (*POM*, p. 73). Moreover, if it is something, it is plainly a term. But obviously Russell does not intend that there is some term which /nothing/ denotes. As he goes on to explain, it is the denoting concept /nothing/ which is something.

It is important to note that my rejection of the quasi-Meinongian interpretation does not commit one to claiming that Russell held that there were no non-existent objects whatsoever. the evidence for this is less clear-cut, and there is certainly some evidence that he thought that there were non-existent fictional objects. At one point he refers to 'the pseudo-existents of a novel' (*POM*, p. 45) a remark which is hard to construe since he never uses the term 'pseudo-existent' elsewhere. But later on in the book he suggests that non-existent events may take place in real time:[36]

> It is hard to deny that Waverley's adventures occupied the time of the '45, or that the stories in the 1,001 Nights occupy the period of Harun al Raschid. (*POM*, p. 471)

Now Russell's verdict on this possibility is very far from clear – he concludes that 'non-existential occupation of time, if possible at all, is radically different from the existential kind of occupation' (*ibid.* p. 472) – and the problem itself is far from his main interest. Nonetheless,

---

[36] I'm grateful to Gideon Makin for reminding me of this passage.

in this case, at least, he must surely be talking about the events themselves and not the concepts which denote them.   It was not, after all, the denoting concepts associated with Waverley's adventures that took place at the time of the '45. Whether he envisaged other such cases is hard to determine. But the fact, if it is one, that he thought some denoting concepts denoted non-existent objects should not be taken to imply that he thought all denoting concepts must denote.

It is perhaps natural to ask, at this point, why, if Russell did not intend to admit non-existent objects like the King of France, he didn't say so. It seems to me that Russell never really considered this possibility until he encountered Meinong's theory of objects in *Über Annahmen* in 1904 (cf. *MTCA*). He hints as much in a letter to Meinong in December 1904:

> I have always believed until now that every object must in some sense have *being*, and I find it difficult to admit unreal objects.   In such a case as that of the golden mountain or the round square one must distinguish between *sense* and *reference* (to use Frege's terms): the sense is an object, and has being; the reference, however, is not an object.[37]

It is conceivable that this clear statement is of a different theory of denotation that Russell was working on after reading Frege. (His work in 1903 was heavily influenced by Frege, and took in attempts to develop a new theory of denotation.) However, had this been the case he would surely have explained how his view differed from the one he had recently published, especially since he goes on to recommend the *Principles* to Meinong for a fuller statement of his philosophy. What he tells

[37] Russell to Meinong, 15 December 1904 (Lackey, 1973, p. 16).

Meinong is I believe, entirely consistent with the position he had taken in the *Principles*.

The consequences of this reinterpretation of the theory of denoting in the *Principles of Mathematics* are somewhat radical. Most importantly, it means that, contrary to what until recently was the almost unanimous view of philosophers, Russell's reasons for adopting his new theory of definite descriptions in 1905 could have had *nothing whatsoever* to do with the need to prune back an unduly populous realm of being. The ontological situation remained very largely (though not exactly) the same on either side of the theory of descriptions. What forced Russell to the 1905 theory of description was not a need to prune a bloated ontology, but the discovery of an argument which convinced him that the notion of a denoting concept was incoherent.[38]

[38] Research supported by the Social Sciences and Humanities Research Council of Canada.

APPENDIX
RUSSELL TO VICTORIA WELBY:
3 February 1904[39]

14, CHEYNE WALK,
CHELSEA, S.W.

Feb. 3. '04

Dear Lady Welby

Please accept my best thanks for your kind letter, and for the notes on my book which you enclose. Since I wrote my book, I have come to think the questions connected with Meaning even more important than I then thought them: the logical nature of *description* seems to me now about the most fundamental and about the most difficult of all philosophical questions.

With regard to the ambiguities of usage which you note in my book, the word *sense* in Part IV has the special significance proper to mathematics, which has nothing whatever to do with our problem: in this significance, it means much the same as *direction* – up and down, right and left, etc. are opposite *senses*. This is such a totally different usage from the other that it seemed to me no confusion could result from the double employment of the word.

In the chapter headings, 'The meaning of order', etc., and also when I say 'Philosophy asks of mathematics: what does it mean?', the question is as to analysis of a complex idea employed by people who do not know how to analyze it – it is a question of *definition* in the philosophical sense, or of pointing out an indefinable

---

[39] The original is in the Welby Papers, York University, Toronto. The Russell Archives, McMaster University, has a copy. the letter is printed with permission of McMaster University.

when the term in question happens to be indefinable. In mathematics, the use of symbols makes it a common practice to draw deductions without knowing the definition of our symbols. People agree that $2+2 = 4$; here 2 and 4 and + and = are all definable, yet very few people know the definitions. It is in this sense that I ask what is the *meaning* of $2+2 = 4$?

On p. 47, *sense* is used linguistically, as that which should be expounded in a dictionary, or that which should be as far as possible unaltered in translating into another language. This is the sense of a *word*, or the meaning of a word in the sense which I dismiss as irrelevant to logic, on the ground that logic is not concerned with words but with what they stand for.

As for *meaning* on p. 47, it begins by being whatever Mr. Bradley intends to signify by *meaning*. This is what I contend to be a confused notion: my position is that (1) *all words* have a sense, but this is logically irrelevant, though it has influenced Bradley, (2) *some ideas (concepts)* denote, as 'the present Prime Minister of England' denotes the actual man Mr. Arthur Balfour. The concept which denotes is not mental: it is the *object* of an idea, not the idea itself. Thus denoting in this sense has nothing psychological about it.

We have to distinguish (1) the relation of a word to the thought which it *expresses*: this is the sense of a word as given in dictionaries and preserved in translation; (2) the relation of a thought (idea) to that of which it is the idea; (3) in certain cases, like that of the Prime Minister, a further relation of the object of the idea (which object, in such cases, I call a *concept*) to another object or collection of objects: it is this third relation that I call *denoting*. The object before the mind when we think 'the Prime Minister' is not the same as when we think 'Mr. Arthur Balfour', or when an image of the man himself is before us. Yet the Prime Minister *is* Mr. Arthur Balfour. This states the problem of denoting.

I agree entirely with what you say about language and making it do its work better. For definitely mathematical purposes, the symbolism which has been developed out of Peano gives an ideal of precision; but it will only express mathematical ideas. A similar work ought to be done for other ideas: but I feel that a technical language, without unphilosophical associations, is almost indispensable. E.g. verbs without tense are necessary to a right philosophy of Time.

Hoping to see you on the 10th

    I am

        Yours very truly

        Bertrand Russell

BIBLIOGRAPHY OF WORKS CITED

Works by Russell

The Collected Papers of Bertrand Russell

2. *Philosophical Papers. 1896–99*, ed. by Nicholas Griffin and Albert C. Lewis (London, Hyman Unwin, 1989).

3. *Towards the 'Principles of Mathematics'. 1900–1902*, ed. by G. H. Moore (London, Routledge, 1993).

4. *Foundations of Logic. 1903–1905*, ed. by Alasdair Urquhart (London, Routledge, 1994).

AMR, 1898. 'An Analysis of Mathematical Reasoning', in *Papers*, vol. 2, pp. 163–22.

EIP, 1905. 'The Existential Import of Propositions', in *Papers*, vol. 4, pp. 486–9.

IMP, [n.d.] *Introduction to Mathematical Philosophy* (New York, Simon and Schuster; 1st edn., 1919).

MPD, 1959. *My Philosophical Development* (London, Allen and Unwin).

MTCA, 1904. 'Meinong's Theory of Complexes and Assumptions', in *Essays in Analysis*, ed. by D. Lackey (London, Allen and Unwin, 1974), pp. 21–76.

OD, 1905. 'On Denoting', in *Logic and Knowledge,* ed. R. C. Marsh (London, Allen and Unwin, 1956), pp. 41–56.

PFM, *Portraits from Memory* (London, Allen and Unwin, 1958; 1st edn., 1956).

POM, *The Principles of Mathematics* (London, Allen and Unwin, 1964; 1st edn., 1903).

Works by Other Authors

Ayer, A. J., 1971. *Russell and Moore: The Analytical Heritage* (London, Macmillan).

Baldwin, Thomas, 1990. *G. E. Moore* (London, Routledge).

Bourgeois, Warren, 1981. 'Beyond Russell and Meinong', in *Canadian Journal of Philosophy*, vol. 11, pp. 653–66.

Cassin, Chrystine E., 1968. 'The Origin and Development of Russell's Theory of Descriptions' (Florida State University, unpublished Ph.D. thesis).

Cocchiarella, Nino B., 1982. 'Meinong Reconstructed versus Early Russell Reconstructed', *Journal of Philosophical Logic*, vol. 11, pp. 183–214.

Dau, Paolo, 1986. Russell's First Theory of Denoting and Quantification', *Notre Dame Journal of Formal Logic*, vol. 27, pp. 133–66.

Fine, Kit, 1985, *Reasoning with Arbitrary Objects*, Aristotelian Society Series, vol. 3 (Oxford, Blackwell).

Frege, Gottlob, 1891, 'Function and Concept', trans. by P. T. Geach in Frege, 1977, pp. 21–41.

—— 1892, 'On Sense and Reference', trans. by P. T. Geach in Frege, 1977, pp. 56–78.

—— 1977, *Translations from the Philosophical Writings of Gottlob Frege*, ed. by P. T. Geach and M. Black (Oxford, Blackwell; 2nd edn., 1977, 1st edn., 1952).

Geach, P. T., 1958. 'Russell on Meaning and Denoting', in *Analysis*, vol. 19, pp. 69–72; reprinted in E. D. Kemke (ed.), *Essays on Bertrand Russell* (Chicago, University of Illinois Press, 1970), pp. 209–12.

Geach, P. T., 1962. *Reference and Generality. An Examination of Some Medieval and Modern Theories*, (Ithaca, Cornell University Press; 3rd edn., 1980).

Griffin, Nicholas, 1977. 'Russell's "Horrible Travesty" of Meinong', *Russell: The Journal of the Bertrand Russell Archives*, nos. 25–8, pp. 39–50.

—— 1980. 'Russell on the Nature of Logic (1903 –1913)', *Synthese*, vol. 45, pp. 117–88.

—— 1985. 'Russell's Critique of Meinong's Theory of Objects', in *Grazer Philosophische Studien*, vols. 25–6, pp. 375–401.

—— 1991. *Russell's Idealist Apprenticeship* (Oxford, Oxford University Press).

Hilbert, David and Paul Bernays, 1934. *Grundlagen der Mathematik* (Berlin, Springer, 1934, 1939).

Hylton, Peter, 1990. *Russell, Idealism and the Emergence of Analytic Philosophy* (Oxford, Clarendon Press).

Jager, Ronald, 1972. *The Development of Bertrand Russell's Philosophy* (London, Allen and Unwin).

Kneale, William and Martha, 1962. *The Development of Logic* (Oxford, Oxford University Press)

Kneebone, G. T., 1963. *Mathematical Logic and The Foundations of Mathematics* (London, Van Nostrand).

Lackey, Douglas, 1973. 'Three Letters to Meinong: A Translation', *Russell: The Journal of the Bertrand Russell Archives*, vol. 9, pp. 15–18.

Montague, Richard, 1973. 'The Proper Treatment of Quantification in Ordinary English', in *Formal Philosophy*, ed. by R. H. Thomason (New Haven, Yale University Press).

Moore, G. E., 1899. 'The Nature of Judgment', *Mind*, vol. 8 ns, pp. 176–93; reprinted in G. E. Moore, *The Early Essays*, ed. by Tom Regan (Philadelphia, Temple University Press, 1986), pp. 59–80.

Parsons, Terence, 1980. *Nonexistent Objects* (New Haven, Yale University Press).

Pears, D. F., 1967. *Bertrand Russell and the British Tradition in Philosophy* (London, Collins).

Quine, W. V. O., 1967. 'Russell's Ontological Development', in R. Schrenmann (ed.), *Bertrand Russell: Philosopher of the Century* (London, Allen and Unwin).

Routley, Richard, 1980. *Exploring Meinong's Jungle and Beyond* (Canberra, Australian National University).

Urmson, J. O., 1956. *Philosophical Analysis: Its Development Between the Two World Wars* (Oxford, Oxford University Press).

THE 'GRAY'S ELEGY' ARGUMENT
– AND OTHERS

Harold Noonan
University of Birmingham

I

What is the argument about the first line of Gray's Elegy and the denoting concept 'C' in 'On Denoting'? What is its target? How effective is it against that target? These questions have exercised Russell scholars for many years, and despite significant advances in understanding the early Russell, and, in particular, the transition in his thought marked by 'On Denoting' there is yet no consensus about how they should be answered.

However, recent work has made it clear that understanding the Gray's Elegy argument is essential to understanding 'On Denoting', for, contrary to long-held opinion, it is the Gray's Elegy argument, and not some problem about the significance of empty denoting phrases, which provides the main consideration motivating Russell to develop the theory of descriptions of 'On Denoting'. That this is so is clear both from recently published material in the 4th volume of *The Collected Papers of Bertrand Russell* (Russell, 1994) and also from material that has long been available in the public domain, but has not received amongst philosophers in general, as opposed to Russell scholars in particular, the attention it deserves. The single most weighty piece of evidence that Russell's problem in 'On

Denoting' was not with empty denoting phrases, the proof-text, indeed, is, of course, the passage from 'The Existential Import of Propositions', first published in *Mind* in 1905, which reads as follows:

> There are no Centaurs; 'x is a Centaur' is false whatever value we give to x .... Similarly there are no round squares. The case of nectar and ambrosia is more difficult, since these seem to be individuals, not classes. But here we must presuppose definitions of nectar and ambrosia: they are substances having such and such properties, which, as a matter of fact, no substances do have. We have thus merely a defining concept for each, without any entity to which the concept applies. In this case the concept is an entity, but it does not denote anything. To take a simpler case: 'The present King of England' is a complex concept denoting an individual; 'the present King of France' is a similar complex concept denoting nothing. The phrase intends to pick out an individual, but fails to do so: it does not point out an unreal individual, but no individual at all. The same explanation applies to mythical personages, Apollo, Priam, etc. These words have a *meaning* which can be found by looking them up in a classical dictionary; but they have not a *denotation*: there is no entity, real or imaginary, which they point out. (Russell, 1994, p. 487)

Given this text, it cannot be claimed that Russell had any problem about the ontological commitments of empty denoting phrases to which he saw the theory of descriptions as providing the only possible solution. For the text makes it clear that he saw the theory of denoting presented in *Principles of Mathematics* (Russell, 1937) or, at any rate, some development from that which retained the distinction made in that book between the meaning and denotation of denoting phrases, and thus took it for granted that denoting phrases had meanings 'by themselves' in the sense in which this is denied in 'On Denoting', as enabling him to explain perfectly satisfactorily how empty descriptions could be meaningful even though nothing is denoted by them.

Another important passage occurs in 'On the Meaning and Denotation of Phrases', written in 1903 (printed in Russell, 1994 as item 11a), where Russell discusses the truth-value to be assigned to a subject-predicate sentence in which the subject is an empty definite description. In 'On Denoting', it will be remembered, this is a question to which Russell is quite certain of the answer. Such sentences, for example, 'the King of France is bald', are not, he declares, contrary to what, he suggests, Frege's theory would seem to imply, nonsense, since they are 'plainly false'. In 'On the Meaning and Denotation of Phrases' he writes:

> When a phrase, such as 'the instance of the concept a', which is of the form of those that denote, happens to denote nothing, what are we to say of phrases in which this phrase, in its capacity of denoting phrase, occurs? E.g. shall we say that 'the present King of France is bald', or 'the author of the Iliad was blind', are true or false or neither the one nor the other? Or better, shall we say that such phrases denote anything, or that they only have meaning, or that they have neither meaning nor denotation?
>
> In the first place, it is plain that 'the present King of France is bald' does not refer to the *meaning* of the phrase 'the present King of France'. The meaning is a complex concept, not capable of having hair or losing it; the concept does not have a head at all.

Thus although the concept is part of the *meaning* of 'the present King of France is bald', it is not part of the denotation (if any). Thus we shall have to say that 'the present King of France is bald' is neither true nor false; for truth and falsehood have to do with what a sentence *denotes*, not with what it *means*; and we must take it as axiomatic that the subject of a proposition is part of the denotation of the proposition. (Russell, 1994, p. 286)

These passages taken together make it quite clear that the view that Russell's chief aim in 'On Denoting' was to produce, what he had not before, a theory of descriptions which could accommodate the fact that sentences containing empty definite descriptions are meaningful without entailing bizarre ontological commitments does not fit the facts. In 1903 Russell already had a theory which satisfied this desideratum and had thought through its consequences at least as far as considering what truth-values should be assigned to sentences containing such descriptions.

Moreover, of course, we know now, with the publication of Russell's working papers from the period 1903–1905, in particular, 'On Fundamentals' (printed in Russell, 1994 as item 15), that the argument which did in fact cause Russell to abandon the theory of denoting he had previously accepted and to develop the theory of descriptions *was* the argument about the first line of Gray's Elegy and the denoting concept 'C'. For, it turns out, that argument simply consists of several of the crucial paragraphs from 'On Fundamentals' which immediately precede Russell's first formulation of the theory of descriptions. In fact, in 'On Fundamentals' Gray's Elegy is not mentioned; the argument proceeds in terms of 'the denoting concept "C"', but it is evidently the same argument minus a few additional sentences whose role we shall consider later.

The publication of 'On Fundamentals' also makes it clear, contrary to what some commentators on 'On Denoting' have suggested, that the theory of denoting Russell has in mind in the passage about the denoting concept 'C', is not primarily, at least, Frege's theory of sense and reference, but his own earlier theory of denoting concepts from *Principles of Mathematics*, or, at any rate, the theory into which that has evolved by the time of 'On Fundamentals' – for Frege's name is nowhere mentioned in the relevant parts of 'On Fundamentals'. Of course, given that Russell did not think that there was any significant difference between his own earlier theory of denoting and Frege's theory of sense and reference (as he says, in effect, in footnote 1 of 'On Denoting') he would doubtless have said that the Gray's Elegy argument was as good a refutation of Frege as it was of his own earlier self. But the fact remains that the target Russell has consciously in mind in the passage about the denoting concept 'C' in 'On Denoting' *is* his own earlier self rather than Frege; at this point in 'On Denoting' he no doubt thinks of himself as having said sufficient to indicate the unsatisfactoriness of Frege's theory in his earlier explicit discussion of it.

The question, therefore, remains: what *is* the argument about the first line of Gray's Elegy and the denoting concept 'C' which convinces Russell that his previous distinction between denoting concept and denotation cannot be retained and that denoting phrases, in general, and definite descriptions, in particular, must be regarded as incomplete symbols, having no meaning in themselves and only sometimes a denotation?

In this paper I shall be arguing for the following contentions:

(1) There are indeed arguments which ought to have convinced Russell that the theory of denoting presented in *Principles of Mathematics* and worked on and elaborated by him between 1903 and 1905 involved an untenable dualism of denoting concept and denotation. The arguments which show this are two. The first is that that theory is incompatible with the Principle of Acquaintance, which is formulated *before* 'On Denoting' and, in fact, is behind Russell's main argument for the necessity of distinguishing between denoting concept and denotation in *Principles of Mathematics*. The second is that it is a consequence of the theory that denoting concepts, if distinct from their denotations, cannot be made the subjects of propositions, ie. cannot be spoken of, and are thus not *terms* in the sense Russell gives to that expression in *Principles of Mathematics*; however, this is a contradiction, since it is part of Russell's (continuing) position that *all* concepts are terms.

(2) However, these arguments cannot plausibly be read into 'On Denoting', nor, in particular, into the passage about the first line of Gray's Elegy and the denoting concept 'C'.

(3) There is, nonetheless, a perfectly clear and unconfused argument that can plausibly be read into that passage, an argument that is, that neither manifests what has been called 'Russell's notorious inability to keep the distinction between use and mention straight' nor constitutes an 'inextricable tangle'. This is an argument to the effect that denoting concepts cannot be spoken of without *mentioning* the denoting phrases which express them. This is an entirely appropriate argument for Russell to use, given the ontological status denoting concepts are supposed to have, and would, if successful, refute the theory of denoting concepts. This

argument is not successful, but the only thing wrong with it is simply that it is incomplete; there are possible rejoinders to it which could be made by a defender of the distinction between denoting concept and denotation which Russell just does not consider. Perhaps this is because the responses to these rejoinders are so obvious to Russell that he thinks that they go without saying, but, as we shall see, it is not clear why he should have thought this if he did.

(4) Finally, whatever Russell thought, neither of the two arguments which *are* effective against the Russellian distinction between denoting concept and denotation nor, of course, the incomplete argument Russell himself presents in the Gray's Elegy passage, is effective against the Fregean distinction between sense and reference, so that, unless the explicit discussion of Frege's views in the earlier part of 'On Denoting' is regarded as refuting that distinction, which I take it, is not generally considered to be the case, it has to be said that Russell does not provide any good reason for accepting the theory of descriptions, when this is thought as a competitor to Frege's theory of sense and reference.

Having argued for these points I shall finish with some suggestions about how to interpret the passage in 'On Fundamentals' in which the theory of descriptions receives its first formulation.

II

Before considering the arguments against the distinction between denoting concept and denotation in 'On Denoting', however, we first need to look at how Russell conceived that distinction in *Principles of Mathematics*. The general features of Russell's position at that time are now quite familiar, so I shall highlight only the main points.

Central to Russell's philosophy at the time of *Principles of Mathematics* was the notion of a *term*. The word 'term', Russell states, is 'the widest word in the philosophical vocabulary' (*Principles of Mathematics*, sec. 47). Anything you can think of, or talk about, is a term and hence, Russell says, 'to deny that such and such a thing is a term must always be false'.

Terms include concrete objects, abstract objects and fictional objects. Russell gives as examples: a man, a moment, a number, a class, a relation, and a chimaera. Terms, are *not*, it cannot be stressed too greatly, the *words* which we use to speak of these things; they are the things themselves, whose being is quite independent of their being spoken of.

Terms unite to form propositions. Thus propositions also are not linguistic entities; nor are they psychological entities and their being is quite independent of their being expressed in language or grasped in thought.

In fact, at this time language is not a subject of interest to Russell, and when he mentions linguistic items at all he typically does so only to distinguish them from what he *is* interested in.

Thus, for example, he writes:

> *Words* have meaning in the simple sense that they are symbols which stand for something other than themselves. But a proposition, unless it happens to be linguistic [ie. *about* words] does not itself contain words; it contains the entities indicated by words. Thus meaning, in the sense in which words have meaning, is irrelevant to logic. (*Principles of Mathematics*, sec. 51)

The terms a proposition is about, ie. the terms which constitute the subject matter of a proposition, are typically, according to Russell, constituents of the proposition. Thus when Russell speaks of Socrates occurring in the proposition /Socrates is human/ he means it literally.[1] This is a proposition about Socrates because it contains Socrates, the man himself. Similarly, as Russell insists in a well-known exchange with Frege, it is Mont Blanc, with all its snowfields, that occurs in the proposition /Mont Blanc is 5,000 metres high/ (Frege 1980, p. 169). In general, in Russell's scheme of things, the entities a proposition is about are among its constituents. Exceptions to this occur, in fact, only in the case of propositions containing denoting concepts, to which we shall attend in a moment.

Terms unite to form propositions, but not just any terms can unite to form propositions, nor can any combination of given terms yield a proposition. There is no proposition composed just of Socrates and Plato, nor is there any proposition in which Socrates is attributed to mortality. There is, however, the proposition /Socrates is mortal/ in which mortality is attributed to Socrates.

Thus Russell draws a distinction between terms like Socrates, which can occur in a proposition only as subject, never as what is attributed to a subject and terms like mortality, which can occur both as subject and as attribute – albeit in different propositions. Terms of the former kind Russell calls 'things', terms of the latter kind he calls 'concepts' (concepts include both verbs and adjectives, which are therefore for Russell not linguistic classifications).

This terminology reminds one of Frege, but it is crucial to note that Russell's notion of a concept is quite different from Frege's. For Frege insists, of course, that

---

[1] I use the slashes to indicate that a proposition, or propositional constituent, is being spoken about. This is the convention introduced by Nicholas Griffin (1980).

the division between objects and concepts is not the division between those entities which can occur only as subjects and those which can occur both as subjects and as predicates, for just as objects cannot be referred to except by proper names, so concepts are essentially predicative.

Russell explicitly considers this Fregean view, which he expresses in the following way:

> a distinction ought to be drawn between a concept as such and a concept used as a term, between, eg. such pairs as *is* and *being, human* and *humanity*, one in such propositions as 'this is one' and 1 in '1 is a number'. (*Principles of Mathematics*, sec. 49)

However, he rejects it, for, he says, 'every term is a logical subject: it is, for example, the subject of the proposition that it itself is one'. His argument for this claim goes as follows:

> suppose that *one* as adjective differed from 1 as term. In this statement *one* as an adjective has been made into a term; hence either it has become 1, in which case the supposition is self-contradictory; or there is some other difference between *one* and 1 in addition to the fact that the first denotes a concept not a term whilst the second denotes a concept which is a term. But in this latter hypothesis there must be propositions concerning *one* as term and we shall still have to maintain propositions concerning *one* as adjective ... yet all such propositions must be false, since a proposition about *one* as adjective makes *one* the subject, and is therefore really about *one* as term ... . This state of things is self-contradictory. (*Principles of Mathematics*, sec. 49)

So, according to Russell at this time, the concept of

oneness, say, occurs both in the proposition /this is one/ and the proposition /1 is a number/. The difference is that it occurs as a term in the latter proposition, ie. it is there something the proposition is about, but it occurs merely attributively in the former proposition. It is, however, a term because it *can* occur in the way it does in the latter proposition, even though it does not do so always.

We now come to denoting concepts. Denoting concepts are concepts derived from a class concept (ie. one ordinarily meant by a common noun or noun phrase, like 'man' or 'man who loves women') by means of one of the operations associated with the words 'all', 'every', 'any', 'a', 'some' and 'the'. That is, they are the meanings of expressions of the forms , 'all n's', 'every n', 'any n', 'an n', 'some n' and 'the n'. What is special about denoting concepts is that they provide the only means by which we can speak about entities which are not constituents of the propositions we express. Whenever any other concept is a constituent of a proposition either it occurs as 1 does in /1 is a number/ and so is itself something the proposition is about, or it occurs as *one* does in /this is one/ and so is neither something the proposition is about nor, as it were, goes proxy for something the proposition is about. However, when a denoting concept occurs in a proposition where a thing can also occur (as the concept 1 does in the proposition /1 is a number/) then it does not *itself* become the subject matter of the proposition, but does somehow go proxy for something the proposition is about. In fact, this feature of denoting concepts enters into Russell's definition of the notion:

A concept *denotes* when, if it occurs in a proposition, the proposition is not *about* the concept, but about a term connected in a certain peculiar way with the concept. (*Principles of Mathematics*, sec. 56)

If denoting concepts did not exist, Russell believes, we could not speak about anything without giving expression to a proposition containing it; in particular, then, we could not speak about a *thing* without employing a proper name of that thing, ie. a proper name of which that thing was the meaning. But denoting concepts, which are the meanings of expressions of the forms listed above, themselves stand in a relation of meaning to things – they *denote* things (this is the peculiar connection referred to in the passage last quoted). It is this notion of meaning, Russell thinks, which is important for logic. Thus, in a passage already quoted in part, he states:

> To have meaning, it seems to me, is a notion confusedly compounded of logical and psychological elements. *Words* all have meaning, in the simple sense that they are symbols which stand for something other than themselves. But a proposition, unless it happens to be linguistic, does not contain words: it contains the entities indicated by words. Thus meaning, in the sense in which words have meaning, is irrelevant to logic. But such denoting concepts as *a man* have meaning in another sense: they are, so to speak, symbolic in their own logical nature because they have the property which I call *denoting* .... Thus concepts of this kind have meaning in a non-psychological sense. (*Principles of Mathematics*, sec. 51)

It is because denoting concepts denote that we can employ them, in description, to speak about things, and this possibility Russell thinks, is of fundamental importance. Indeed, the notion of denoting, he writes:

lies at the bottom (I think) of all theories of substance, of the subject-predicate logic, and of the opposition between things and ideas, discursive thought and immediate perception. (*Principles of Mathematics*, sec. 56)

One reason why Russell thinks denoting so important is that it enables us to understand how we can talk about the infinite. He writes:

With regard to infinite classes, say the class of numbers, it is to be observed that the concept *all numbers*, though not itself infinitely complex, yet denotes an infinitely complex object. This is the inmost secret of our power to deal with infinity. An infinitely complex concept, though there may be such, certainly cannot be manipulated by the human intelligence, but infinite collections, owing to the notion of denoting, can be manipulated without introducing any concepts of infinite complexity. (*Principles of Mathematics*, sec. 72)

In fact, Russell says later:

Indeed it may be said that the *logical purpose* which is served by the theory of denoting is, to enable propositions of finite complexity to deal with infinite classes of terms. (*Principles of Mathematics*, sec. 141)

The reason that propositions of infinite complexity pose such a problem, of course, is that it cannot be supposed that finite minds can be *acquainted with* an entity of infinite complexity; thus the theory of denoting concepts, by providing finitely complex proxies for such entities, with which it can be plausibly supposed that we can be acquainted, enables Russell to explain our grasp of such propositions consistently with what later came to be called 'the Principle of Acquaintance'.

The theory of denoting concepts also enables Russell to explain how identity statements can be both true and informative:

> If we say 'Edward VII is the King' we assert an identity; the reason why this assertion is worth making is, that in the one case the actual term occurs, while in the other a denoting concept takes its place... Often two denoting concepts occur, and the term itself is not mentioned.... When a term is given, the assertion of its identity with itself, though true, is perfectly futile, and is never made outside the logic books; but where denoting concepts are introduced, identity is at once seen to be significant. In this case, of course, there is involved, though not asserted, a relation of the denoting concept to the term, or of the two denoting concepts to each other. But the *is* which occurs in such propositions does not itself state this further relation, but states pure identity. (*Principles of Mathematics*, sec. 64)

Moreover, as we have seen, it also enables Russell to explain how sentences containing empty definite descriptions can be significant, although this is made explicit only after *Principles of Mathematics*.

These are two features of the theory of denoting concepts which show that theory to its best advantage. But there are, of course, other features of the theory which indicate that it is not wholly unproblematic. As we have seen, for Russell, 'term' is 'the widest word in the philosophical vocabulary', yet the denotations of the denoting concepts expressed by denoting phrases other than definite descriptions are *not* terms, but *objects* which are combinations of terms, non-relationally combined, which as such are essentially plural. 'The fact', Russell writes, 'that a word can be framed with a wider meaning than *term* raises grave logical problems' (*Principles of Mathematics*, sec. 58, footnote).

However, Russell does not go on to explore these problems, nor can they plausibly be supposed to lie behind his later rejection of the theory of denoting concepts, since that, of course, concentrates on the denoting concepts expressed by definite descriptions, whose denotations, when they exist, are unproblematically terms.

III

Let us now turn to the arguments against this theory of denoting concepts.

The first of these, I said, was that the theory was incompatible with the Principle of Acquaintance, and thus could not serve the main logical purpose for which Russell intended it. The point is a very straightforward one. Russell notes in 'On Denoting': 'the meaning [of a denoting phrase] cannot be got at except by means of denoting phrases' (Russell, 1994, p. 421), that is, denoting concepts can only be spoken of by using denoting phrases, in sentences expressing propositions in which occur what we might call 'second-level' denoting concepts, denoting the first-level denoting concepts we wish to speak about. In short, a denoting concept, unlike all other things and concepts, cannot be spoken of by using a *proper name* in the strict Russellian sense. For, if a Russellian proper name occurs in a sentence, the proposition expressed will contain the entity named, but then, if that is a denoting concept, the proposition will not be about that concept, but about what it denotes.

This point is not new in 'On Denoting', it occurs also in 'On Fundamentals' (Russell, 1994, p. 363) stated as: 'a denoting meaning can only be spoken of by means of denoting concepts which denote the meaning in question' and defended as follows:

> ... if we wish to ... say something about the meaning itself, we can only do so by means of a denoting concept, for if, instead of a denoting concept, we put the meaning ... we shall be talking unintentionally about the denotation of the meaning.

It also occurs in 'On Meaning and Denotation' (Russell, 1994, p. 322) where it is stated that 'direct inspection seems to show that if we wish to speak about the meaning of "the present Prime Minister of England", we can find no names for it except such as themselves have meaning; and these express something else and reach what we want only through the relation of denoting'. Russell goes on:

> ... 'the father of John', 'the number next after 1', or any other complex, seems incapable of being apprehended directly except by an idea expressing it: we cannot form an idea designating it directly in the kind of way in which our idea of whiteness designates whiteness. In such cases, if we invent a proper name for the complex (as opposed to what the complex denotes), the proper name qua name, does, of course, designate the complex, but the idea indicated by the proper name merely expresses 'the meaning of the complex so-called', which is a complex denoting the said complex. It is thus only through the medium of denoting that the concept can be dealt with at all as a subject.

Denoting concepts, then, cannot be spoken of using

Russellian proper names; and it follows directly from this that they cannot be possible objects of acquaintance – for if we could be acquainted with them we could name them, and use their names to express propositions about them. But, if so, the theory of denoting concepts is inconsistent with the Principle of Acquaintance and the explanation Russell thinks it provides of our ability to speak about the infinite is revealed as no explanation at all.[2]

Thus it seems that this argument shows very simply how the theory of denoting concepts fails to serve the purpose for which Russell intended it.

However, despite the fact that there seems to be no effective rejoinder a defender of the theory of denoting concepts could give to this argument, the matter remains puzzling. For, as noted, the argument is very straightforward, and Russell appears several times to be on the verge of stating it, yet he never does so. Moreover, in at least one place in 'On Fundamentals' (Russell, 1994, p. 369) he refers to 'acquaintance with a denoting concept', while elsewhere (Russell, 1994, p. 286) he speaks of 'a presentation of the meaning' of a phrase of the form 'an instance of *a*'. How could he have missed so obvious a point?

One possible response to this question, of course, is to say that Russell did not miss the point – not in the end, anyway – since it is precisely this reasoning which the Gray's Elegy passage puts forward.

However, I shall argue below, to read that passage as concerned with how we might come to be *acquainted*

---

[2] The point can be expressed as follows. There are four propositions, to each of which it looks as if Russell is committed, which are jointly inconsistent: 1) Any object of acquaintance can be given a logically proper name, 2) denoting concepts are objects of acquaintance, 3) whatever has a logically proper name can be spoken about by using that name, 4) denoting concepts cannot be spoken about except by using denoting phrases.

with denoting concepts is implausible, and it is even more implausible, given the convoluted character of the reasoning, to read it as an attempt to express the straightforward argument above. The puzzle how, if indeed the argument is valid, Russell could have failed to see it, thus remains.

The second argument against the theory of denoting concepts I wish to consider is more plausibly read into the Gray's Elegy passage (though this is still, I think, a misreading of the passage).

This is the argument that denoting concepts, if they are distinct from their denotations, cannot be terms, since they can never be spoken of at all, either by name or by description.

This argument is put forward, both as valid in its own right, and as an interpretation of the reasoning in the Gray's Elegy passage by Peter Hylton (1990, p. 209ff. and 251ff.) and Russell Wahl (1993).

It will be convenient to start with Hyltons's statement of the argument, which appeals to what he calls 'the Principle of Truth-Value Dependence'. This is the principle that for a proposition containing a denoting concept to be about some other entity, is for the truth-value of that proposition to be dependent upon the truth-value of the proposition obtained from it by replacing the denoting concept by the denoted entity (Hylton, 1990, p. 251). According to this principle what makes it true that the proposition /the teacher of Plato is wise/ is about Socrates, is that its truth-value depends on that of /Socrates is wise/, that is, the former proposition can be true if and only if the latter proposition is true.

Hylton introduces the Principle of Truth-Value Dependence to make sense of the idea of a proposition containing a denoting concept being *about* its denotation. His line of thought, a plausible one, goes something like this. With the introduction of denoting concepts into his ontology Russell is committed to there being two ways in which a proposition can be *about* Socrates: it can *contain* him, or it can contain a denoting concept which *denotes* him. However, *prima facie* these are two quite distinct relations which a proposition can bear to an entity. What, then, do they have in common which justifies us in regarding them as two species of aboutness? The Principle of Truth-Value Dependence provides an answer to this question. For, of course, the truth-value of the proposition /Socrates is wise/ depends trivially on the truth-value of a proposition containing Socrates, namely itself. But given the Principle of Truth-Value Dependence the same is true of the proposition /the teacher of Plato is wise/. This, then, is the common property of these two propositions which allows us to speak of them both as being *about* Socrates.

I shall come back in a moment to the question of whether one can legitimately appeal to the Principle of Truth-Value Dependence in arguing against Russell's theory of denoting concepts, but it is easy to see that if the Principle of Truth-Value Dependence *can* be appealed to as partly definitive of the notion of aboutness, Russell's distinction between denoting concept and denotation must collapse.

Consider the propositions:

(1) /the meaning of the description 'the teacher of Plato' is Socrates/

(2) /the teacher of Plato is Socrates/

(3) /Socrates is Socrates/.

Given the Principle of Truth-Value Dependence, these propositions must all have the same truth-value, ie.

must all be true. So there cannot be such a thing as the denoting concept expressed by the description 'the teacher of Plato', as distinct from its denotation, or if there is there cannot be such a proposition as (1), that is, the denoting concept expressed by the description 'the teacher of Plato' cannot be made the subject of a proposition and so cannot be a term. Obviously this argument generalizes.

There can be no doubt, then, that *if* the Principle of Truth-Value Dependence can be regarded as implicit in Russell's theory of denoting concepts, that theory is implicitly inconsistent. However, as Hylton notes, despite the plausibility of the argument given above for the Principle of Truth-Value Dependence, in fact:

> The truth or falsehood of one proposition depending upon that of another is clearly quite alien to Platonic Atomism [ie. to Russell's philosophy at the time of *Principles of Mathematics*]. It amounts, indeed, to the introduction of something like the correspondence theory of truth for the special case of those propositions which contain denoting concepts: whether such a proposition is true depends on whether there is a corresponding fact, where a fact is a true proposition which does not contain a denoting concept, or a combination of such propositions. The propositions (putative facts) which are the corresponding ones are presumably those which are obtained from the original by replacing the denoting concept by the denoted object(s). (Hylton, 1990, p. 209–10)

Hylton adds a little later:

> I should stress that the sort of considerations advanced in the three previous paragraphs [ie. in the argument for the Principle of Truth-Value Dependence] do not

occur explicitly in *Principles* .... For the most part ... Russell in *Principles* rests content with the notion of aboutness, without considering the implications of the notion. (Hylton, 1990, p. 211).

But if so it can hardly be legitimate to argue that the theory of denoting concepts is implicitly inconsistent by way of appeal to the Principle of Truth-Value Dependence.

All is not lost, however, for the argument for the implicit inconsistency of the theory of denoting concepts does not, in fact, need the Principle of Truth-Value Dependence. What it needs is merely, as it were, a truth-value *link* between propositions containing denoting concepts and propositions containing their denotations. But such a link is stated *explicitly* in Russell in 'On Fundamentals' in a passage that occurs before the occurrence of the argument about the denoting concept 'C' which *is* repeated in 'On Denoting' – where Russell is therefore still committed to the theory of denoting concepts.

Russell writes:

The following seem to be facts:
1. A complex has both *being* and meaning.
2. A complex may occur as being or as meaning.
3. When a complex is asserted, it occurs as meaning.
4. When a complex is said to be true, it occurs as being.
5. When a complex occurs as being, every other complex having the same denotation, or the denotation itself, may be substituted without altering the truth or non-truth of the complex in which the said complex occurs. (Russell, 1994, p. 369)

Here it is point (5), of course, which asserts the truth-value link. To get clear about this it is necessary to understand the distinction between 'occurring as being' and 'occurring as meaning'. This is the distinction (possible only for concepts) between occurring as a term in a proposition and occurring as a constituent but not a term; it is the distinction between the occurrence of one in ; '1 is a number' and the occurrence of one in 'this is one'.

Given this clarification it should now be obvious that if point (5) is an essential part of Russell's theory of denoting that theory is inconsistent. For in the propositions:

(1) /the meaning of 'the teacher of Plato' is Socrates/ and

(2) /the teacher of Plato is Socrates/
the denoting concepts expressed by the description 'the meaning of "the teacher of Plato"' and the description 'the teacher of Plato' occur as being. Thus, given point (5), in each of these, denotation can replace denoting concept *salva veritate* and so (1) and (2) must have the same truth-value as:

(3) Socrates is Socrates.

Russell Wahl draws attention to this argument in his article (1993) and, in fact, suggests that it is the argument implicit in the Gray's Elegy passage.

However, once again the theory of denoting concepts is not so easily refuted. For, as Wahl notes, Russell rejects point (5) almost immediately after stating it. Wahl insists, nonetheless, on his entitlement to appeal to it in his interpretation of the Gray's Elegy argument, since 'Point (5) is really the account of denoting: a complex denotes when, if it occurs in another complex, eg. a proposition, this complex is about the entity denoted, not the complex itself' (Wahl, 1993, p. 87). But what follows the colon in this sentence does not support what precedes it, unless an explication of 'aboutness' in terms of truth-value links is, question-beggingly, presupposed, and more importantly, it is presumably Russell, if anyone, who is entitled to say 'what is really the account of denoting'. However, since Russell rejects point (5) and proceeds to elaborate what he evidently still takes to be the theory of denoting, point (5) cannot legitimately be regarded as essential to it.

Russell's reasons for rejecting point (5) have to do with what he calls 'the occurrence of "the author of Waverley"' [ie. the denoting concept] in the proposition /People were surprised that Scott was the author of *Waverley*/. He first of all states, in point (10) (Russell, 1994, p. 370), that this denoting concept does not occur as entity in this proposition, since it is not replaceable without change of truth-value by its denotation, Scott, or by any other denoting concept which denotes Scott. Thus, for the moment he retains point (5). However, in the next point, (11), he states:

> The manner of occurrence of 'the author of *Waverley*' in the above case is peculiar. It has one of the marks of occurrence as entity, namely that any other entity can be substituted without loss of significance; but it has not the other mark, that a complex with the same denotation can be substituted without altering the truth or falsehood of the proposition concerned. Thus there would seem to be a third mode of occurrence of a complex, in which the occurrence is an entity-occurrence as regards significance, and a meaning-occurrence as regards truth. (Russell, 1994, p. 370)

Familiarity with Frege's theory of indirect reference makes it easy for us to question Russell's assumption that there is *any* occurrence of the denoting concept expressed by 'the author of *Waverley*' in the proposition /People were surprised Scott was the author of *Waverley*/. But Russell does not consider this line of thought. Instead after several intervening pages he distinguishes six pairs of kinds of occurrences of an entity in a complex (Russell, 1994, p. 374).

The first distinction to which he draws attention is once again the division between entity occurrences and meaning occurrences, but now defined in such a way that the denoting concept expressed by 'the author of *Waverley*' is said to have an entity occurrence *both* in /Scott was the author of *Waverley*/ and in /People were surprised that Scott was the author of *Waverley*/. Thus point (5) is now rejected. This new definition of the occurrence as entity/occurrence as meaning distinction is given in point (23), part (a) (1994, p. 374) as follows:

> An entity A may occur in a complex B in such a way that any entity, simple or complex, may be substituted for A in B without loss of significance; or A may occur in such a way that it can only be significantly replaced by an entity of a certain sort, eg. a proposition, or a type, or a relation. This is the most fundamental division of modes of occurrence. We will call the two modes concerned occurrence as *entity* and occurrence as *meaning* respectively, using other names for the other sorts of occurrence.

In point (23), part (b), the distinction between the two occurrences of the denoting complex expressed by 'the author of Waverley' in the proposition /Scott was the author of *Waverley*/ and the proposition /People were surprised that Scott was the author of *Waverley*/ is now drawn as follows:

> When a *denoting* complex A occurs in a complex B, it may occur in such a way that the truth-value of B is

unchanged by the substitution for A of anything having the same denotation. [For the sake of brevity, it is convenient to regard anything which is *not* a denoting complex as denoting itself.] This is the case with 'the author of *Waverley*' in 'Scott was the author of *Waverley*', but not in 'People were surprised that Scott was the author of *Waverley*' .... We will call A a *primary constituent* of B when only the denotation of A is relevant to the truth-value of B, and we will call the occurrence of A a *primary occurrence* in this case; otherwise we will speak of A as a *secondary constituent*, and of its occurrence as a *secondary occurrence*.

Thus the principle Russell now endorses can be stated as follows (using the rejected point (5) as a model):

When a complex both occurs as entity and has a primary occurrence in a proposition, any other complex having the same denotation, or the denotation itself, may be substituted without altering the truth or non-truth of the complex in which the said complex occurs.

The question that now arises is whether *this* principle makes Russell's theory of denoting concepts inconsistent. Of course, this depends on what occurrences of denoting complexes count as primary. But we have seen that Russell treats the occurrence of the denoting concept expressed by 'the author of *Waverley*' in /Scott was the author of *Waverley*/ as primary and a little later he states explicitly:

As regards '$x = \iota\text{'}u$', which is the general type of which 'Scott is the author of *Waverley*' is an instance, the occurrence of $\iota\text{'}u$ in this is

(a). as entity, not as meaning

(b). primary, not secondary (Russell, 1994, p. 377)[3]

This does indeed mean that the theory of denoting concepts as developed to this stage in 'On Fundamentals' is inconsistent. For now we can argue as follows. In the proposition:

/Scott is the author of *Waverley*/

the first level denoting concept expressed by 'the author of *Waverley*' has a primary occurrence. So in the proposition:

/Scott is the denoting concept expressed by the description 'the author of *Waverley*'/

the second-level denoting concept expressed by the description:

the denoting concept expressed by the description 'the author of *Waverley*'

also has a primary occurrence. But since the denotation of the second-level denoting concept is the first-level denoting concept these two propositions must have the same truth-value, and since Scott is the author of *Waverley* they must both have the same truth-value, ie. truth, as the proposition:

/Scott is Scott/.

Thus either denoting concepts cannot be spoken of at all, or the distinction between denoting concept and denotation collapses.

It may be said, in response to this argument, by a determined defender of the theory of denoting concepts, that all that this shows is that further refinements and distinctions need to be made to render the theory consistent. But it is important to note that an addition of further pairs of modes of occurrence to Russell's list of six will not serve. For as Russell uses the notion of a 'mode of occurrence', modes of occurrence are corre-

---

[3]   I use iota in place of inverted iota in quotations from Russell and elsewhere.

lated one-to-one with *positions* in propositions (Russell, 1994, pp. 369–70). Russell never considers the possibility that two complexes may have different modes of occurrence in the *same* position in a proposition, since he thinks that '[t]he way in which a complex occurs ... depends upon the nature of the complex in which it occurs' (1994, p. 369). To restore consistency to the theory of denoting concepts in the face of the above argument, therefore, what is needed is not any further distinction between modes of occurrence of denoting concepts in propositions, but an acknowledgement that second-level denoting concepts are differently related to their denotations than are first-level denoting concepts, in such a way that though both may be replaced without change of truth-value by any other denoting concepts having the same denotation when in primary position in a proposition (primary positions now being characterized as ones in which *first-level* denoting concepts have primary modes of occurrence) only first-level denoting concepts in such positions may be replaced without change of truth-value by their denotations. But now the unity of the concept of denoting is shattered; we no longer have a single relation which obtains between any denoting concept and its denotation. At this point we can surely say that the theory of denoting concepts, as Russell conceives it, has been abandoned in all but name.

III

So far I have claimed that there are two arguments, either of which, by itself, is sufficient to show that Russell was right to reject his earlier theory of denoting concepts in 'On Denoting'.

However, I do not think that we should be justified in

reading either argument into the passage about the first line of Gray's Elegy and the denoting concept 'C'.

Of the two arguments it is, perhaps, the first, concerning the incompatibility of the theory of denoting concepts with the Principle of Acquaintance which it is most implausible to read into the Gray's Elegy passage. For the Principle of Acquaintance is actually stated in 'On Denoting' (though not for the first time) and the notion of acquaintance figures prominently at the beginning and at the end of the article, yet in the Gray's Elegy passage the word 'acquaintance' does not occur once; nor does it occur in the corresponding part of 'On Fundamentals'.

The second argument, that if denoting concepts are capable of being spoken of at all they cannot be distinct from their denotations, is more plausibly read into the Gray's Elegy passage. The way in which denoting concepts can be spoken about clearly is a major concern of the passage. Nevertheless, Russell does not proceed in the way that would be expected if anything like this was his argument. For one thing he seems to allude to, and not to reject, the possibility of speaking about denoting concepts by *mentioning* denoting phrases. And his argument takes the form of a sort of proof by cases, which would be inappropriate if he had the general form of argument outlined above (whether thought of as based on Hylton's Principle of Truth-Value Dependence, or on point (5) from 'On Fundamentals' or on the principle modelled on point (5) stated above to which I have argued Russell is committed).

But what, then, is the argument of the Gray's Elegy passage?

Essentially, I think, Russell intends the following argument:

(1) If denoting concepts exist it must be possible to speak about them.

(2) Denoting concepts cannot be spoken of except by using denoting phrases; they cannot be referred to by name.

(3) Denoting phrases which contain *mention* of other denoting phrases *may* provide a way of speaking of denoting concepts, but given the ontological status of denoting concepts (qua concepts), this cannot be the *only* possibility if such concepts exist.

(4) A denoting concept cannot be spoken of by *using* the phrase which expresses it *unembedded* in a use of a larger denoting phrase.

(5) A denoting concept cannot be spoken of by *using* the phrase which expresses it *embedded* in a use of a larger denoting phrase.

(6) There are no other possibilities.

(7) Therefore, denoting concepts cannot exist.

If this is right there is no 'inextricable tangle' in the Gray's Elegy passage, nor a total confusion of use and mention, but a clear and straightforward argument. However, the argument is nonetheless flawed, since there are possible ways of speaking of denoting concepts which Russell does not consider. Consequently, he establishes neither point (5) nor point (6).

That Russell's concern is with how denoting concepts can be spoken of (point (1) above) is quite clear from the text of 'On Denoting', and, if anything, clearer still in the corresponding part of 'On Fundamentals', where the argument about the denoting complex 'C' follows a paragraph in which the use of inverted commas to speak about denoting concepts comes under scrutiny .

The paragraph, in fact, shows Russell's thought in the

making, for he begins quite confidently and then perceives a problem:

> The use of inverted commas may be explained as follows. When a concept has meaning and denotation, if we wish to say anything about the meaning we must put it in entity position, but if we put it itself in an entity position, we shall really be speaking about the denotation, not the meaning, for that is always the case when a denoting complex is put into any entity position. Thus in order to speak about the meaning we must substitute for the meaning something which *denotes* the meaning. Hence the meanings of denoting complexes can only be approached by means of complexes which denote those meanings. This is what complexes in inverted commas are. If we say '"any man" is a denoting complex', 'any man' stands for 'the meaning of the complex "any man"', which is a denoting complex. But this is circular, for we use 'any man' in explaining 'any man'. And the circle is unavoidable. For if we say, 'the meaning of any man', that will stand for the meaning of the denotation of any man, which is not what we want. (Russell, 1994, p. 382)

Russell continues:

> The endeavour to speak about the meanings of denoting complexes leads, if the above is correct, to the following dilemma. If we do not put the meaning in an entity position, we merely mean it, and do not say anything about it; if, on the contrary, we put it in an entity position, it stands for its denotation, and we get the meaning (if any) of what the complex denotes, not of what the complex means.

Here we see not only point (1) present in Russell's thought, but also points (2) and (4). We also see an argument repeated in 'On Denoting' in support of point (5): 'if we say "the meaning of any man", that will stand for the meaning of the denotation of any man, which is not what we want'.

It is for the purpose of stating this last argument, in fact, that Russell introduces the first line of Gray's Elegy into 'On Denoting', to make it clear that even when a denoting concepts denotes a linguistic entity, ie. something which does have a meaning, the meaning of that item cannot be identified with the denoting concept.

The further point Russell makes in support of point (5) in 'On Denoting' is that embedding a use of a denoting phrase in the context:

that which denotes ...

will not provide a way of identifying the denoting concept expressed by that phrase, since many denoting concepts will denote the same item, ie. 'there is no backward road from denotation to meaning'. This point is not made in 'On Fundamentals'.

Another point new in 'On Denoting' is that 'the relation of meaning and denotation is not merely linguistic through the phrase: there must be a logical relation involved, which we express by saying that the meaning denotes the denotation' (Russell, 1994, p. 421).

The purpose of this statement is to remind the reader that denoting concepts, like the propositions they compose, are language-independent entities which must therefore be identifiable without mentioning language, ie. Russell is making point (3) above.

The only point, then, in the reconstruction of Russell's argument suggested which cannot be found explicitly or implicitly made in either 'On Fundamentals' or 'On Denoting' is the sixth, that all the possible ways in which denoting concepts might be made the subjects of propositions have been considered. But, of course, this is just the sort of point that is likely to occur merely as a suppressed premiss.

That Russell's argument, as reconstructed, is incomplete should be obvious. First of all, if denoting concepts are complexes, then it would seem that they can be identified by listing their components and specifying the way that they are put together – unless there is some difficulty about speaking about their components, which Russell never suggests. And even if denoting concepts are simples they compose complexes, ie. propositions, and so can be identified, by subtraction as it were, if the complexes they compose and their other constituents can be identified. Of course, such an identification of a denoting concept will itself require the use of a denoting phrase, but that, in itself, is not an objection.

Secondly, Russell's argument does not even establish that one cannot identify a denoting concept by embedding a use of a phrase expressing that concept in a larger denoting phrase. For even though 'that which denotes ...' will not provide such a means of identification it does not follow that no such means is available. One might, for example, be able to identify a denoting concept as the simplest denoting a certain object. Of course, this will not provide a *general* procedure by which one can embed a use of a denoting phrase in a larger denoting phrase which will then denote the denoting concept expressed by the embedded phrase, as Russell's use of inverted commas suggests to be a possibility, but it is not obvious that this must be a genuine possibility if denoting concepts exist.

Given the incompleteness of Russell's argument, of course, it cannot be regarded as a refutation of Frege's distinction between sense and reference. However, neither of the arguments outlined earlier, which do seem to show Russell's theory of denoting concepts to be untenable, is effective against Frege's theory either. For the first simply shows that one cannot accept the theory of denoting concepts, or the theory of Fregean senses, if one accepts the Principle of Acquaintance, but there is no place in Frege's thought for the relation of acquaintance, which is supposed to give one *unmediated* access to the world. For Frege, *all* reference is mediated by sense. Secondly, of course, the premiss of the second argument against the theory of denoting concepts, that in certain positions in propositions denoting concepts can be replaced by their denotations without change of truth-value, has no true interpretation in Frege's theory, for whilst Mont Blanc is for Russell a component of certain propositions about Mont Blanc, there is for Frege no thought in which Mont Blanc occurs. Once again, the point is that for Frege all reference is mediated by sense.

What emerges is that the fatal flaw in Russell's theory of denoting concepts is precisely that feature of it which provides its sole rationale, namely, that it provides a class of exceptions to the general rule that whenever a proposition is about an entity it contains that entity. The lesson to be learned is that a successful theory of reference cannot make such an exception. It must treat all reference alike, either as mediated or unmediated.

IV

In conclusion I wish to make some comments on the passage in 'On Fundamentals' in which Russell gives his first statement of the theory of descriptions.

The passage reads as follows:

It might be supposed that the whole matter could be simplified by introducing a relation of denoting: instead of all the complications about 'C' and C, we might try to put 'x denotes y'. But we want to be able to speak of what x denotes and unfortunately 'what x denotes' is a denoting complex. We might avoid this as follows: Let C be an unambiguously denoting complex (we may now drop the inverted commas); then we have

$(\exists y)$: C denotes y: C denotes $z.\supset_z.z=y$.

Then what is commonly expressed by ø'C will be replaced by

$(\exists y)$: C denotes y: C denotes $z.\supset_z.z=y:\phi'y$

Thus eg. ϕ'(the author of *Waverley*) becomes

$(\exists y)$: 'the author of *Waverley*' denotes y: 'the author of *Waverley*' denotes $z.\supset_z.z=y:\phi'y$

Thus 'Scott is the author of *Waverley*' becomes:

$(\exists y)$: 'the author of *Waverley*' denotes y: 'the author of *Waverley*' denotes $\supset_z.z=y$: Scott=y.

This, then, was what surprised people, as well it might. On this view, we shall not introduce ɩ'u at all, but put

$\phi'\iota'u. = :(\exists y):y\in u:z\in u.\supset_z.z=y:\phi'y.$

This defines all propositions about ɩ'u, which is all we need. But now $\phi'\iota'u$ is a bad symbol; we shall have to substitute (say)

$(\phi\iota)'u$

On this view, 'the author of *Waverley*' has no significance at all by itself, but propositions in which it occurs have significance. Thus in regard to denoting phrases of this sort, the question of meaning and denotation ceases to exist. (Russell, 1994, pp. 384–5)

What is going on here? How does this transition to the theory of descriptions emerge from the attack on the theory of denoting concepts? The key to understanding the passage, I think, is the parenthetical remark 'we may now drop the inverted commas'. The purpose of the inverted commas device was to enable us to speak about denoting concepts. They were needed because, unlike all other concepts, a denoting concept was supposed to be such that a proposition containing it was not about that denoting concept, but about its denotation. Inverted commas can now be dropped because Russell has abandoned the assumption that denoting phrases, ie. phrases of the six familiar forms, do express *denoting* concepts. However, he has *not*, at the beginning of the passage, abandoned the assumption that they express concepts at all. That is, he is still treating them, at this point, as having meaning or signif-icance by themselves. But if in 'Scott is the author of *Waverley*' the phrase 'the author of *Waverley*' expresses an 'ordinary', non-denoting, concept, that sentence expresses a proposition, not about Scott (ignoring the occurrence of the name, which is an irrelevant feature of the example), but about the concept expressed by 'the author of *Waverley*'. What does it say about that concept? Of course, that it denotes some unique entity and that that entity is Scott, which can be expressed, if 'the author of *Waverley*' expresses an 'ordinary' concept, by saying

$(\exists y)$: the author of *Waverley*' denotes y: the author of *Waverley* denotes $z . \supset_z . z = y$: Scott$=y$,

in which the inverted commas have been omitted (Russell retains them, presumably out of habit).

But since 'the author of *Waverley*' is a definite description it would not denote at all if it did not denote uniquely. So an equivalent proposition would be expressed by

$(\exists y)$: the author of *Waverley* denotes y: Scott$=y$,

alternatively, an equivalent proposition can be obtained

by leaving in the uniqueness clause and using an indefinite denoting phrase instead of a definite denoting phrase: 'an author of *Waverley*' instead of 'the author of *Waverley*'.

Thus we get:

($\exists$y): an author of *Waverley* denotes y: an author of *Waverley* denotes z.$\supset_z$.z=y: Scott=y,

or equivalently:

($\exists$y): y is a member of the class of authors of *Waverley*: z is a member of the class of authors of *Waverley*. z.$\supset_z$.z=y: Scott=y.

But in the proposition expressed in this last way the concept expressed by 'the author of *Waverley*' does not occur (not, at least, if the structure of the sentence displayed is a faithful indication of the structure of the proposition expressed). Therefore if this *is* the proposition expressed by 'Scott is the author of *Waverley*' that also does not contain the concept expressed by 'the author of *Waverley*'. But this was just an example. Thus, in general, 'the author of *Waverley*' does not have corresponding to it in propositions expressed by using it any concept which it expresses. That is, 'it has no significance by itself, but only propositions in which it occurs have significance'.

Thus we see that, just as the popular interpretation suggests, the theory of descriptions comes about as a result of a movement of ontological simplification. It is a quite different movement of ontological simplification from that suggested by the popular view, however. According to that view, Russell trims his ontology by rejecting the view that there are subsistent entities denoted by empty definite descriptions like 'the King of France' and finds himself faced by the problem of explaining how sentences containing such denoting phrases can be meaningful. The theory of descriptions is the result. According to the view I am suggesting the process of ontological simplification takes place entirely *within* the class of concepts and it takes place in two stages. At the first stage of ontological simplification Russell abandons the assumption that there is a special sub-class of concepts, namely denoting concepts, which descriptions express, which have the peculiar property that they occur in propositions as, as it were, proxies for other entities. Then at the second stage of ontological simplification Russell abandons even the assumption that there are any concepts at all expressed by descriptions, an abandonment he expresses by saying that descriptions have no significance in themselves. This second abandonment is a result of his observing that the uniqueness condition whose satisfaction is required for the truth of a statement containing a definite description can be captured in a logically equivalent statement which does not contain that definite description, but a corresponding indefinite description. It therefore appears to be a sort of fortunate accident that when Russell starts to worry about the way in which inverted commas work to enable us to speak about denoting concepts, which is a worry about how we can speak about any denoting concepts at all, whether unambiguous or ambiguous, he narrows his gaze down to the *unambiguously* denoting concepts expressed by definite descriptions, for if he had not done so the crucial second stage in the transition to the theory of descriptions could not have taken place and we would be less one great paradigm of philosophy.

BIBLIOGRAPHY OF WORKS CITED

Frege G., 1980. *Philosophical and Mathematical Correspondence*, ed. by G. Gabriel et al. (Chicago, University of Chicago Press).

Griffin N., 1980. 'Russell on the Nature of Logic', *Synthese*, vol. 45, pp. 117–88.

Hylton P., 1990. *Russell, Idealism and the Emergence of Analytic Philosophy* (Oxford, Clarendon Press).

Russell B., 1937. *Principles of Mathematics* (London, George Allen and Unwin; 1st edn., Cambridge, Cambridge University Press, 1903).

—— 1994. *The Collected Papers of Bertrand Russell*, vol. 4, ed. by A. Urquhart with the assistance of Albert C. Lewis (London and New York, Routledge).

Wahl R., 1993. 'Russell's Theory of Meaning and Denotation and "On Denoting"', *Journal of the History of Philosophy*, vol. 31, no. 1, pp. 71–94.

THE UNITY OF THE PROPOSITION AND RUSSELL'S THEORIES OF JUDGEMENT

Stewart Candlish

The University of Western Australia

My purpose is to examine a little-recognized problem in the theories of judgement which Russell developed in the years 1903–1918. It is a problem which, sometimes in a rather subterranean fashion, was partly responsible for the rapid succession of those theories. I shall suggest that there were at the time two promising avenues to its solution, and mention how those avenues are being explored today.

1. *The 1903 Theory*

Russell's 1903 account of judgement is the merest sketch. Judgement is a single binary relation between two entities, a judging mind and a proposition. But the sketch is pregnant with consequences. A proposition does not consist of words; 'it contains the entities indicated by words' (Russell, 1903, sec. 51). These Russell called 'terms', and they include, eg. men, chimaeras, and relations (sec. 47).[1] 'Every term', he says, '... is a logical subject ... possessed of all the

---

[1] The reason Russell takes this view of constituents of propositions as being the things the propositions are *about* appears to be that the sole alternative is to regard them as ideas, which are 'constituents of the mind of the person judging' and 'a veil between us and outside things' (Russell, 1911; *CP6*, p. 155; *ML*, p. 160).

properties commonly assigned to substances' (sec. 47). This idea that everything is at bottom an object, and of the same sort, is, Russell thinks, unavoidable: the attempt to deny it leads to self-contradiction (sec. 49).

Why did he think of propositions as entities? Because he held that they were unities (sec. 54), and he subscribed to the principle *ens et unum convertuntur* (sec. 47 and *CP6*, p. 350).

What makes a proposition a unity? His answer is that its constituents are related by the proposition's verb: 'the true logical verb in a proposition may be always regarded as asserting a relation' (sec. 53).[2] The verb, he says, 'when used as a verb, embodies the unity of the proposition' (sec. 54).[3]

What, then, is the unity of the proposition? It is what distinguishes a proposition from a list of its constituents, so that it says something. But this seemingly undeniable unity, when combined with Russell's principle that 'Every constituent of every proposition must, on pain of self-contradiction, be capable of being made a logical subject' (sec. 52), generates a difficulty. On pain of contradiction, the verb must itself be a term, something capable of appearing as a logical subject. But it must be a very unusual kind of term, for it must simultaneously be the source of the proposition's unity, relating all its constituents while itself being one of the related items. That is, the verb is unlike other terms in that it has, he

---

[2]   Russell gets round the apparent exceptions posed by intransitive verbs such as 'breathes' by claiming that in such cases the verb expresses a complex notion which 'usually asserts a definite relation to an indefinite relatum' (sec. 48).

[3]   We should not take this to mean that a proposition is a matter of words: with a few exceptions, he thinks of English as a transparent medium through which reality's ingredients may be inspected, and talks indifferently of 'verbs' whether he means words or the 'entites indicated by words' (sec. 51), ie. terms.

says, a 'twofold nature ..., as actual verb and verbal noun, [which] may be expressed ... as the difference between a relation in itself and a relation actually relating' (sec. 54). Yet as soon as we make the verb a logical subject, we are forced to identify it as 'a relation in itself' rather than as 'a relation actually relating', destroying the unity of the original proposition in which it was the source of that unity. He illustrates the point like this (sec. 54):

> Consider, for example, the proposition 'A differs from B.' The constituents of this proposition, if we analyze it, appear to be only A, difference, B. Yet these constituents, thus placed side by side, do not reconstitute the proposition. The difference which occurs in the proposition actually relates A and B, whereas the difference after analysis is a notion which has no connection with A and B ....
>
> A proposition, in fact, is essentially a unity, and when analysis has destroyed the unity, no enumeration of constituents will restore the proposition. The verb, when used as a verb, embodies the unity of the proposition, and is thus distinguishable from the verb considered as a term, though I do not know how to give a clear account of the precise nature of the distinction.

Russell's problem, then, is that while he cannot deny propositional unity, he can find no account of the proposition which can do justice to it. Opinions differ over how serious that problem is.[4] But a related difficulty is certainly serious: whether true or false, a proposition is a unity, hence an entity. In fact it is a complex entity whose constituents are the things it is about, which

---

[4] Palmer (1988) thinks it extremely serious. Sainsbury (1979) seems inclined to think it just the result of a muddle.

makes it hard to see how it can differ from what in Russell's later vocabulary would be called a fact. This makes it difficult for him to give a sensible account of truth, and the correspondence theory is noticeably absent from *The Principles of Mathematics*. He says merely that truth is an unanalysable property: true propositions just have it, false ones just lack it (sec. 52).[5] The world contains both objective falsehoods and objective truths: 'objective', here, meaning that they are entities in no sense mind dependent. His difficulty, in disguise, is just the perennial conundrum: how is false judgement possible? But the source of the problem is new, or at least makes explicit what is concealed in older versions: it is the combination of an attachment to the unity of the proposition and the idea that propositional constituents are the things the proposition is about.

2. *The 1910 Theory*

When Russell introduces his new multiple relation theory of judgement (Russell, 1910), he does so against the background of its 1903 predecessor (though he does not mention *Principles* and appears to attribute the earlier theory, rightly or wrongly, to Meinong, by reading whose works he seems to have become more aware of the difficulties it generates). But the 1903 theory's commitment to the existence of objective falsehoods, which had been clear to him all along, now appears as his principal reason for rejecting it. He now finds it impossible to believe in the existence of these objective falsehoods, and can no longer bring himself to

---

[5] By 1904 the theory becomes one in which true propositions have one property and false another. I do not think this difference matters in the present context.

maintain that the world contains such things as *that Charles I died in his bed* even though Charles I died on the scaffold. And he holds this incredibility of objective falsehoods to provide sufficient reason for not believing in the existence of their counterparts in the case of truths.

Interestingly enough, he contemplates the possibility of an asymmetric theory in which true propositions are complex objects but false ones are not, only to reject this, not on the grounds that false propositions would disintegrate altogether, but rather because there would then be an intrinsic difference between true and false propositions which would be visible on inspection. This, he says, is obviously impossible: and indeed it is obvious that we cannot in general tell truths from falsehoods by sheer inspection. But Russell forgets the radical nature of the 1903 theory here, and helps himself to the common sense which it appears to preclude, for on his theory he is not entitled to the obviousness of the impossibility: the constituents of judgments are real things, and actually related in the way the judgement claims. Hence inspecting the proposition cannot be distinguished from inspecting the world, and inspecting the world is just how we should go about distinguishing truths from falsehoods. (This looks like an instance of a common phenomenon: helping oneself to the data and treating them as part of the theory so that the theory can gain a spurious plausibility by its being surreptitiously self-authenticating. The usual source of this error is the employment of the same expression, eg. 'proposition', to designate both explanandum and explanans. More recent philosophers can also plead the malign influence of the idea that theories should be closed under implication.) Lacking the possibility of a retreat to his property theory of truth (which of course he is now arguing against), and only dubiously entitled to the idea that propositions may be inspected introspectively or by the study of sentences (only dubiously, because he holds their constituents to be real things, not representatives of them, and because by 1910 he has moved a long way from his 1903 idea that logical form is nearly always reflected in grammatical form), Russell has got himself into a position where it might reasonably be said that only if false propositions were not there to be found would the difference between them and the true ones be visible on inspection. And only if one thought this an introspectively determinable matter should one find it surprising.[6]

Russell's rejection of the 1903 theory has two notable consequences. One is that its associated property theory of truth is likewise rejected in favour of a correspondence theory in which a fact, to which a true judgement corresponds, is supposed to be something quite different from that judgement itself. The other is that he no longer treats judgement as a binary relation between the judging mind and a single entity, the proposition, but rather as 'a multiple relation of the mind to the various other terms with which the judgement is concerned' (Russell, 1910; *CP6*, p. 122; *PE*, p. 155). Propositions, in the 1903 sense, have disappeared from the scene altogether.

The full account of the 1910 theory, together with its version of the correspondence theory of truth, can be summarized as follows (using some of Russell's own

---

[6] The considerations in this paragraph suggest that Russell should have considered the possibility of there being false sentences without false propositions (in his 1903 sense of 'proposition'). His (largely post-1903) idea that logical form may not be reflected in surface grammar is suggestive of this idea. But his insistence on a univocal account of meaning closes off the possibility, which clearly requires some distinction like Frege's within the realm of meaning that can account for the intelligibility of falsehoods.

words). When we judge that, say, A loves B, we have not a two-place relation between the mind and the whole proposition as a unit but a multiple relation between the mind and the individual constituents of the proposition, so that there is 'before the mind', separately, the person A, the person B, and the relation of loving, in such a way that the relation is not present 'abstractly' but 'as proceeding from A to B'. The judgement is true when there is a corresponding complex object, A's loving B, and false when there is not.

Thus in the 1910 theory the existence in the world of objective falsehoods is – apparently – avoided by sacrificing propositions: the unity of the proposition is consequently sacrificed in favour of the unity of what one might (following the lead of Claudio de Almeida)[7] call the propositional act which brings together in thought things which may not be so related in the world. In other words, the unity is imposed by the mind. But these sacrifices are illusory.

To see this, consider the exposition of the theory. If all it means is merely that we can think that A loves B, and that it is really A and B and loving and not some representational substitutes that we are thinking about, then of course it is true; but then this is what the theory is supposed to be explaining. If, however, it is meant to be an account of how we can think that A loves B, it collapses judgement and judged fact. Let me explain what I mean.

On Russell's 1903 view of the constituents of propositions, the difficulty about judgement was that the unity of the proposition requires that either the world contain peculiar entities such as *that Charles I died in his bed*, or false judgement is impossible. The 1903 theory opts

---

[7] Acknowledged in Griffin, 1993.

for the first horn of this dilemma. Russell held the 1910 theory, which retained this view of constituents but as constituents of propositional acts rather than of the 1903 propositions, to avoid both: 'We therefore escape the necessity of admitting objective falsehoods, or of admitting that in judging falsely we have nothing before the mind' (*ibid.*: *CP6*, p. 120; *PE*, p. 153); and, re-inforcing the latter point, 'the possibility of false judge-ments is fully allowed for' (*ibid.*: *CP6*, p. 122; *PE*, p. 155). I think it is fair to say that although critics from Wittgenstein onwards have subjected the theory to devastating objections, this last claim has been allowed to stand: the impression has been that if the theory worked, it would account for false judgement. But as we shall see, this claim collapses too.

In expounding the 1910 theory, Russell recognizes one of the shortcomings of the 1903 theory to which we have already drawn attention: that it could give no account of how relations, which figure in all proposi-tions, manage to combine the rules of being proposi-tional constituents and of being the sources of proposi-tional unity. He tries to overcome this problem in the 1910 theory by insisting that there is no propositional unity: one of the inconsistent roles disappears in favour of the unity of the propositional act, a unity provided by the different relation of judging, leaving the other to be filled without difficulty. But then he remembers that he must also account for the 'sense' or 'direction' of non-symmetrical relational judgments, which he tries to manage by his already-noted specification that 'the relation must not be abstractly before the mind, but must be before it as proceeding from *A* to *B* rather than from *B* to *A*' (*ibid.*: *GP6*, p. 123; *PE*, p. 158). This is clearly a repetition of the requirement that, after all, the relation must be more than just another constituent, though so far it looks as if we have no more than a re-statement of the problem masquerading as a solution of it. And in this explanation of what 'not being abstractly before the mind' means, a commitment to the propositional unity he has been denying re-emerges in a compound with his solution to the problem of accounting for the direction of a non-symmetrical relation.[8] It is at least clear that both present genuine requirements: unity is needed for the relation to provide a judgement, as opposed to a mere list, so that we can distinguish the mind's mere simultaneous acquaintance with A and love and B on the one hand from, on the other, any judgement at all involving these; direction is needed for the relation to distinguish the judgement that A loves B from the judgement that B loves A. It is unsurprising that Russell did not consistently keep the two requirements separate: anything that enables the direction requirement to be met would normally enable the meeting of the unity requirement as well. (Though not the other way about, as Russell realized in 1913.) It is also unsurprising that the 1910 theory should get into trouble. It effectively separates unity from direction, attributing the former to the propositional act, unified by the relating relation of judgement, and the latter to the judged material, the order of whose constituents is determined by the sense of the related relation; but then it explains direction in a way which involves unity. The two requirements must indeed be simultaneously satisfied, but without being confused with one another.

---

[8] This appears to be a longstanding, if intermittent, conflation. It is present in Russell, 1904 (*CP4*, p. 437; *EA*, p. 28); and, as we shall see, is still dogging him in 1913. According to Mark Sainsbury (Sainsbury, 1979, p. 225), the problem of the unity of the proposition is still interfering with Russell's discussion of other problems as late as 1918.

Can the confusion be sorted out?   Because of this compounding of two different (albeit connected) problems, there are two ways in which we might interpret the theory's requirement that the relation not be present 'abstractly'. We might think (and some of Russell's own words might encourage us in this) that it should be understood as meaning merely that the relation's direction must figure in the judgement. This would allow us to express the different directions involved in non-symmetrical relations, so that the theory can distinguish the judgement that *A* loves *B* from the judgement that *B* loves *A*. But if this is all that is meant, the 1910 theory remains vulnerable to one of Bradley's criticisms of *The Principles of Mathematics*, that it lacks the resources to account for the unity of the proposition: all we get is two ordered lists, *A*, love, and *B*, on the one hand, and *B*, love, and *A* on the other, plus the idea that these orderings are somehow significant. (This significance cannot consist in the different orderings being themselves further constituents, for familiar reasons involving infinite regress.) Even if we respond to this by saying that the theory shows propositional unity to be unnecessary, with the unity of the propositional act being a perfectly adequate substitute, there is still no account of the unity of the act: the theory cannot account for the distinction between an ordered list and a judgement except by attributing the ability to form both and distinguish them from each other to an otherwise mysterious power of the mind.

In the face of this objection, we might take the requirement that the relation not be present 'abstractly' to mean, not that the relation's direction must figure in the judgement, but that the relation is to really relate *A* and *B* and thus supply unity to the proposition judged, a unity additional to that of the propositional act. On this interpretation, the actual objects are before the mind in their actual relation, with that relation actually relating them. This, one supposes (as Russell himself seems to have supposed), would have to include the ordering as well for there to be unity: ie. the imposition of unity automatically imposes direction. (Unity without direction would result in the creation of a logical monster: a unified proposition – with Russellian constituents, not some mere symbolic construct – that remained ambiguous between 'A loves B' and 'B loves A'.) But if that is so, the combination involved in the judging cannot after all differ from the actual fact which is being judged to obtain.

It might not yet be clear that this consequence is damaging: what is wrong with the idea that the combination involved in the judging cannot differ from the actual fact which is being judged to obtain? Isn't this just what Russell wanted? But in fact the results are dramatic. The immediate consequence is that the theory of judgement is after all incompatible with its companion correspondence theory of truth, for when the judgement is true, judgement and judged fact coalesce, the former absorbing the latter as a proper part. The point may be illustrated by the use of a 'map' of the complex corresponding to a binary judgement, a map whose justification is that it is derived from the one which, as we shall see, Russell himself used to illustrate the application of the 1913 theory. (Russell refers to these problems again through the notion of a map in his 1918 lectures 'The Philosophy of Logical Atomism'.) It is immediately apparent from this map that the larger fact of the judgement illegitimately includes the judged fact 'A loves B' as an existing unity (look at the directions of the arrows, which are essential for the map to incorporate the expression of direction and unity) and cannot be formally distinguished, within the resources of the 1910 theory, from a case where the larger fact, in Russell's view, really does include the smaller as a proper part, as when S perceives *A*'s loving *B*.[9]

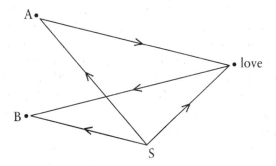

This is bad enough, but worse is to come. There are two forms this 'worse' might take, depending on our starting point.

We might begin from the position that any proposition at all can be judged to be true. (There are of course exceptions, but they are not relevant to the seriousness of the difficulty I am identifying.) This has the consequence that the old dilemma reappears but with a different outcome: where the 1903 theory required the existence of objective falsehoods, the 1910 theory makes, despite Russell's claims to the contrary, false judgement impossible. Not, though, because it makes false judgements disintegrate, but because any

---

[9] Another way of putting this point would be to ask the question why S rather than judging appears as a constituent of the diagram. This question shows something of the pressure on Russell to drop the ego from his ontology, a pressure to which he succumbed in 1919. (Adding judging to the diagram, rather than replacing S with it, brings with it a return of the relational regress of which Bradley made so much and which Russell was also trying to avoid.)

coherent judgement at all will make itself true in the act of formulation. The theory seems committed to attributing a kind of psychokinetic power to the mind, in that simply by judging that *A* loves *B* I bring *A* and *B* into the relation of love. If I fail to do this, then I fail to achieve the unified proposition without which there can be no judgement. So false judgement is impossible, because any judging creates the fact that makes the judgement true. (Indeed, the difficulty is still more fundamental than this. Mere formulation of a proposition suffices to pose the problem: propositional unity is required for understanding just as it is for judgement, as Russell realized in 1913. Thus even formulating a proposition, let alone judging it true, will create the fact which makes it true.)

The other possible starting point is the recognition that psychokinesis is impossible, that we cannot – of course – bring objects into a non-mental relation with each other merely by taking thought. But this, in combination with the 1910 theory of judgement, restricts our judgemental capacity to the passive recognition of truths; again, false judgement turns out to be impossible, though for a different reason: that false judgements resist formulation.

Russell clearly would not have owned to attributing psychokinetic powers to the mind; yet in 1910 he thought the mind to have the capacity to bring objects into a non-mental relation with each other in the propositional act, in such a way as to meet the requirement of the unity of the proposition. But this had to be accomplished without the creation of the judged fact. It is as if he was committed not only to a psychokinetic power, but one counterbalanced by what one might call a psychoinertial power. For the mind, in judging that, say, *A* loves *B*, is supposed to be able to bring the real things

A and *B* and love, not just mental or linguistic proxies, into the appropriate relation without actually making *A* love *B*. These powers are not only magical but mutually inconsistent.

3. *The 1912 Theory*

It is not always noticed that the theory of judgement presented in *The Problems of Philosophy* (1912) is different from the 1910 theory. The 1912 theory is only a modification of its predecessor, but the modification is significant. It arose in response to criticisms, related to those I made in the previous section, which Russell received from G. F. Stout. Russell wrote in reply:

> As regards the sense of R in judging aRb, you make a point, which had already occurred to me, but is met by a slight re-wording of the account of sense in judgement, & this re-wording is in any case necessary to my theory. There must never, so I now perceive, be any relation having sense in a complex except the relating relation of that complex; hence in the act of judging, the sense must be confined to the judging, & must not appear in the R. But, judging being a multiple relation, its sense is not merely twofold like that of a dual relation, & the judging alone may arrange our terms in the order 'Mind, a, R, b' as opposed to 'Mind, b, R, a'. This has the same effect as if R had a sense in the judgement, & gives all one wants without being obnoxious to your objections. (Original MS; rewritten by Stout, 1911, p. 350)

Russell refers to the change as 'a slight re-wording', but it is clear that it is far more. In the 1910 theory, Russell had tried (but, as we saw, failed) to separate unity and direction ('sense'), transferring the former from the judged relation (ie. the relation belonging to what was judged) to the propositional act but leaving the latter where it was. But he soon noticed the difficulties this attempt created: how could a relation have direction without relating and thereby imposing unity? And he dealt with it in the 1912 multiple relation theory by re-uniting direction and unity, transferring direction also to the propositional act so that 'sense' belonged to the relation of judging rather than to the judged relation. The sole relating relation, in the 1912 theory, is that of judging.

Russell's satisfaction with the 1912 theory did not last long, as we shall see. But was it an improvement on the 1910 theory? And, in particular, did it meet the difficulties we have identified here?

The theory works like this. When I judge that *A* loves *B*, the relation *love* appears purely as a relation in itself – a related relation, one might say – not as a relating one. What then makes this into a *judgement*? Suppose my mind leaps from *A* to love to *B*, or groups them in that order: this is not a judgement that *A* loves *B*. It will not be a judgement unless *love* is allowed to appear as a relating relation itself.[10] And once that is allowed, all the old difficulties of the 1910 theory re-emerge. The sole alternative to allowing the appearance of *love* as a relating relation is to specify that the relation *judgement* is special: it is the sole relation which combines its *relata* into a judgement, rather than a mere collection, even an ordered collection. No doubt this is correct. But it is an idea which we criticized in the previous section as appealing to 'an otherwise mysterious power of the mind', with the relation of judgement taking the place

---

[10] Stout himself, in the article just cited, percipiently fixed on the 1912 theory's plausibility as deriving from a confusion between the view that A and love B have no unity of their own in the judgement at all and the view that they form a subordinate unity.

of the mind. In other words, it is not a *theory* of judgement at all: it merely imposes a new jargon on the expression of what we knew already.[11]

4. *The 1913 Theory*

Russell's post-1910 unease over the idea that his theory of judgement has a problem keeping judgement distinct from judged fact surfaces again in the 1913 *Theory of Knowledge*, albeit in a different though related version. There are a couple of things to sort out before I can display this version clearly. I begin by noting that his response to the problem is to try a further modification: his revised theory[12] is that judgement requires (while the corresponding fact does not) an ingredient additional to the mind and the constituents of the judgement, a logical form. However, Russell's attempt at a 'proof that we must understand the "form" before we can understand

---

[11] This criticism was anticipated by Geach, and earlier by Ramsey (Geach, 1957, p. 51; Ramsey, 1927, p. 142). Though Ramsey was talking about the 1910 theory, his verdict still applies here:

> We are driven, therefore, to Mr Russell's conclusion that a judgement has not one object but many, to which the mental factor is multiply related; but to leave it at that, as he did, cannot be regarded as satisfactory. ... Similarly, a theory of descriptions which contented itself with observing that 'The King of France is wise' could be regarded as asserting a possibly complex multiple relation between kingship, France, and wisdom, would be miserably inferior to Mr Russell's theory, which explains exactly what relation it is.

[12] The 1913 theory is one way importantly different from the 1910 and 1912 theories: in what it is a theory of. It focuses on understanding rather than belief (as he is now inclined to refer to judgement). For this reason it is strictly incorrect to present it as a theory of judgement. But such presentation does no harm: it makes the theory slightly simpler to expound, and easier to compare with its predecessors. And of course the theory applies to judging as well as to understanding.

The revised theory is an improvement because, as Russell says (Russell, 1913, pp. 108, 110), understanding is more fundamental than belief. But it tends to obscure the problem of false judgement, which motivated its predecessor. (Of course one could re-pose this problem as one of avoiding making all falsehoods unintelligible.)

the proposition' (Russell, 1913, p. 116) is introduced with a complication arising from a confusing presentation of the matter, a complication we must first set on one side. He begins the proof by referring to the 1912 theory thus:

> I held formerly that the objects alone sufficed [for understanding the proposition], and that the 'sense' of the relation of understanding would put them in the right order; this, however, no longer seems to me to be the case.

What does he mean by this talk of getting the objects 'in the right order'? From his own words it would seem that he is talking about getting objects into the right places with respect to non-symmetrical relations like *loves*, for this was the difficulty he had previously talked of with the expression 'sense'. But in fact Russell has already ruled this out himself; on p. 112 he has said:

> Thus if our analysis has been correct, the proposition '*A* precedes *B*', which seemed fairly simple, is really complicated owing to difficulties concerned with 'sense'. These difficulties are not an essential part of the difficulty of discovering what is meant by 'understanding a proposition'. We shall do well, therefore, to take examples which do not introduce 'sense'.

Peter Hylton, after noticing this potential muddle, comments about his actual practice (Hylton, 1990, pp. 344–5),

> Russell treats the order of constituents as a separate problem, one that is not solved by the notion of form.
> He also makes it clear that form is required for all judgements, including subject-predicate judgements and those involving symmetrical relations.

The example which Russell chooses to consider in his proof is accordingly one which does not involve 'sense': it is the symmetrical relation of similarity, and the problem he illustrates with it is that of uniting objects in thought, that is, in what we have called the propositional act. In fact, despite Russell's beginning the proof with talk of 'order', the problem actually uppermost in his mind is, as we shall see in a moment, that of unity.

So let us put on one side as a mere distraction the problem of direction, and concentrate on the problem of unity. Russell's main proof of the necessity of form runs like this (Russell, 1913, p. 116; there is another on p. 99):

Suppose we wish to understand 'A and B are similar'. It is essential that our thought should, as is said, 'unite' or 'synthesize' the two terms and the relation; but we cannot *actually* 'unite' them, since either A and B are similar, in which case they are already united, or they are dissimilar, in which case no amount of thinking can force them to become united. The process of 'uniting' which we *can* effect in thought is the process of bringing them into relation with the general form of dual complexes. The form being 'something and something have a certain relation', our understanding of the proposition might he expressed in the words 'something, namely A, and something, namely B, have a certain relation, namely similarity' .... In an actual complex, the general form is not presupposed; but when we are concerned with a proposition which may be false, and where, therefore, the actual complex is not given, we have only, as it were, the 'idea' or 'suggestion' of the terms being united in such a complex; and this, evidently, requires that the general form of the merely supposed complex should be given.

The difficulty for an account of judgements which holds actual objects to be their constituents, as Russell sees it, is that either the objects and relation are already united (in actual fact, whether judged to be the case or not), or they are not. In the latter case, nothing can be done in the way of uniting them in judgement; and in the former, nothing remains to be done. This is just another way of recognizing the problem with the 1910 theory's requirement that the unifying relation be present not merely 'abstractly'. And his solution is that judgement differs from fact in that its unification proceeds via the inclusion of a logical form: in the case of his chosen example, the general form of dual complexes is what is supposed to enable the mind to provide that sort of unity which makes possible the understanding of '*A* and *B* are similar', without delivering the kind that creates the corresponding fact too. Hylton appears to accept this (Hylton, 1990, p. 346):

> How can we give a meaning to 'unite in thought' which keeps this notion clearly distinct from uniting in reality? Russell's answer is that the judgement represents the constituents as combined in the right way not by so combining them but by including 'the way they are to be combined' as a further entity. And the mode of combination of all these entities (*including* the form) clearly need not be (and in fact cannot be) the same as that of the fact corresponding to the judgement, so we are in no danger of having to identify uniting in thought with bringing about the corresponding fact.

And later Russell gives a 'map' of the five-term complex involved in the understanding of his exemplary proposition 'S judges that *A* is similar to *B*',[13] where the form of the particular proposition understood is symbolized by '*R(x,y)*':

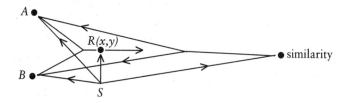

This is different from a map of the proposition '*A* is similar to *B*', in which neither *S* nor the form of dual complexes would figure. Does this difference solve the problem?

That question amounts to: can the 1913 introduction of the form into the apparatus of the 1910 theory do the job demanded of it? This job is, in effect, to enable the mind to do what it was meant (but failed) to achieve on its own in the earlier theory: unify the judgement without creating the judged fact. Let us for the moment postpone answering this question directly, and concentrate upon the question of what happens if the answer is no. In that event, according to Russell's own statement in the passage quoted, where something is *not* the case it will be impossible to judge that it is the case; and where something *is* the case, the judged proposition will be indistinguishable from the actual fact. But this will make a correspondence theory of truth impossible, and ensure that we have no account of falsehood

[13] Russell, 1913, p. 118. As was said, strictly this proposition should be 'S understands the proposition that A is similar to B'. But this makes no difference here.

at all. As with the 1910 theory interpreted on the assumption that psychokinesis is impossible – an assumption now supposedly rendered unnecessary by the form's satisfying its job-description – judgement will be restricted to the passive recognition of truths.

This had not been clear to Russell in 1910. It was this kind of unclarity, perhaps, which made him think the 1910 theory compatible with a correspondence theory of truth. In 1913 he recognizes the problem over unity that he had missed in 1910, but he does not see that in his attempt at a solution all that happens is that what we identified previously as an inconsistent combination of magical powers is transferred from the mind alone to the mind with access to logical forms (on which further inconsistent demands are made, as we shall see in the next paragraph). Nor does he see that his solution still forces him away from the correspondence theory of truth, and for the same reason that there was a problem with the 1910 theory. He seems to imagine that the form's presence in the judgement but absence from the fact allows him to account for the truth of a judgement in terms of a correspondence between two complexes. This, though, is an illusion, as can be seen from the map: only its relative complexity disguises the fact that *A is similar to B* still appears in it as a unified whole, now attached to the form as well as to the judging mind though the addition of this second extra object, the form, can help matters no more than did the original addition of the mind.

Furthermore, this second extra 'object' turns out, on Russell's own admission, not to be a mere form, but an actual proposition, 'Something has some relation to something', and thus an entity which merely re-poses the difficulties over unity in its own case which it is brought in to solve in the case of the original proposition.

Russell sees this objection (Russell, 1913, p. 130) and attempts to answer it by alleging that in this special case the proposition is both simple and a fact, and that by introspection one finds understanding it to be just acquaintance with it. But this response which, as even Russell acknowledges, bristles with difficulties, is to be valued more for its curiosity than its credibility.

There are more difficulties yet with the 1913 theory. For example, one might ask, why should only the judgement and not the fact require in addition to the objects this 'way they are to be combined' as an ingredient? This is a serious question, because on Russell's theory of forms, as Hylton points out (1990, p. 345), 'the logical form which figures in the judgement is the form of the corresponding fact'. But it is a question to which the theory has no answer.[14]

5. *The 1918 Non-Theory*

It was, of course, Wittgenstein's criticism, and not these difficulties, which as a matter of historical fact led to Russell's abandoning the 1913 theory. For some time, though, he seems to have lived in the hope that his theory of judgement might just need some sort of philosophical epicycle to deal with that criticism, as his 1917 description of the 1910 theory as 'somewhat unduly simple' testifies.[15] But in the discussion of belief (as he

---

[14] Two other problems with Russell's accounts of judgement which have been largely neglected in the literature are these: first, it is hard to see how to extend the accounts to general propositions; secondly, the logic of *Principia Mathematica* requires an infinite number of propositions whose existence cannot wait upon the contingent inclinations of human minds to formulate them. I say nothing about them here because the neglect has recently been remedied. The former problem is well discussed by Leonard Linsky (Linksy, 1992, pp. 257–9), and the latter by Peter Hylton (Hylton, 1990, pp. 355–6). Other problems are indentified by Mark Sainsbury (Sainsbury, 1979, pp. 64, 225), and by David Pears (Pears, 1977, pp. 177–83).

[15] See the second footnote, added in 1917, to Russell, 1911 (CP6, p. 154; ML, p. 159).

is now consistently calling judgement) in the 1918 lectures 'The Philosophy of Logical Atomism', although he is still describing the 1910 (or 1912)[16] theory as being 'a little unduly simple', he is clearly close to despairing of it, and makes no attempt at offering a solution of its problems.

There are two problems with belief identified in these lectures (*CP8*, p. 199; *LK*, p. 226). One is the objection to the *Principles of Mathematics* account of propositions which inspired the 1910 theory in the first place. The 1910/1912 theory, as we saw, attempted to deal with it by sacrificing the unity of the proposition in favour of the unity of the propositional act. Despite his describing this theory as just 'a little unduly simple', Russell's treatment of the second problem shows that by this stage, under Wittgenstein's influence, he has come to appreciate that the problem is of a difficulty that no mere addition of an epicycle could hope to overcome. The admission of the second problem is an implicit concession to Bradley (that it was such a concession is made explicit only in their private correspondence, never in print): that in giving an account of belief (or judgement; or, more fundamentally, understanding), the subordinate verb (ie. the one other than 'believe') has to occur *as a verb* – whereas in the 1912 theory Russell treated it as a term like any other. And yet despite its occurring as a verb, it cannot *really* relate, for otherwise there would be no false judgement. In what is doubtless a conscious harking back to the unfinished *Theory of Knowledge*, Russell makes the point in terms of the impossibility of making a map in space which is

---

[16] Given that he described the 1912 theory as 'slight re-wording' of the 1910, he probably thought of them as one theory and at this point it does no harm to let this pass.

'logically of the same form as belief' (*CP8*, p. 198; *LK*, p. 225), and says of the 1912 theory that it made the error of 'putting the subordinate verb [sc. relation] on a level with its terms as an object term in the belief' (*CP8*, p. 199; *LK*, p. 226). This is quite right. But it is clear that he has nothing better to offer in response to the problems.

And he is not even much closer to full clarity about them. He says (*CP8*, p. 198; *LK*, p. 225):

> I mean that when A believes that B loves C, you have to have a verb in the place where 'loves' occurs. You cannot put a substantive in its place. Therefore it is clear that the subordinate verb (ie. the verb other than believing) is functioning as a verb, and seems to be relating two terms, but as a matter of fact does not when a judgement happens to be false.

In other words, the problem is still perceived as one of false judgement. Although he hovers on the verge of recognition, he does not seem quite to see that the problem concerns true judgement as well, for one cannot specify what is believed, truly or falsely, without invoking the very propositions whose existence Russell has denied.[17] He says that the verb 'as a matter of fact does not [relate two terms] when a judgement happens to be false'. The conversational implicature here is that when a judgement happens to be true, it does so relate. This all seems innocent enough: the problem is that it is

---

[17] This is the deeper of the two explanations of Russell's apparent inconsistency in the logical atomism lectures. On some pages, Russell talks about our believing propositions (*CP8*, pp. 191, 199; *LK*, pp. 218, 226); on other pages, he says we don't (*CP8*, pp. 197 and 200; *LK*, pp. 224, 227). The superficial explanation is that he talks carelessly in an ordinary language way when he talks about believing propositions, whereas when he denies explanation reveals that the 'careless talk' is in fact unavoidable, as emerges at *CP8*, p. 198 (*LK*, p. 225).

inconsistent with the correspondence theory of truth, for he still thinks of the judgement as distinguished from the fact only by the addition of the mind as an extra ingredient – there is nothing for the fact to correspond with other than itself, and even the way in which he describes the problem, let alone canvasses solutions, means that judgement is always going to include the fact judged.

6. *Subsequent Developments*

For there to arise a theory of judgement which stood a chance of being workable within the framework of doctrine which characterized logical atomism, at least one of two historically crucial steps had to be taken.

Russell took one of them when in 1919 he eventually exchanged real objects for their symbols as constituents of propositions.[18] But this was preliminary to his moving away from logical atomism altogether in the direction of neutral monism. And while it provides for the unity of the proposition, on its own it still has no account of this unity, no answer to the question of what differentiates a proposition from a list.

To find both steps taken within the atomist framework, one has to look at the *Tractatus Logico-Philosophicus*. There the constituents of propositions are not the Objects which compose the facts which make up the world, but representations of those Objects, their Names, which go proxy for them in propositions. This provides the possibility of having the unity of the proposition without each judgement's self-fulfillingly creating the judged fact, and a proposition could now be regarded as a mental or linguistic entity. That is the first step, the one shared with Russell. The second step, which Wittgenstein took alone (though followed shortly

---

[18] See Russell, 1919.

by Ramsey) was the more important idea that propositions are able to represent facts because the propositional signs are themselves facts: this allowed the proposition the unity required for saying something without
the addition of an explicitly represented relation to bind
the proposition's constituents together while at the same
time being one of those constituents itself.[19] It was that
addition which had been the primary source of such
problems as the creation of Bradleian infinite regresses,
and the need to make the implausible distinction
between the relation as it is in itself and the relation as
relating. Neither the relation which unifies the proposition, nor anything that could be called its Name, is
itself a constituent of that proposition; and that relation
is not necessarily the one which would unify the corresponding fact if there happened to be one. And only
Names, not Objects, are unified within the proposition.

In this way Wittgenstein was able to acknowledge the
unity of the proposition by eliminating the idea of the
relating relation's (or some symbol thereof) being itself
a constituent of the proposition, without this elimination's appearing to be, as Russell had feared, the
beginning of the slippery slope to monism. But an interesting feature of this latter move is that it is independent
of the former. (That is, the former, though sufficient, is
not necessary for the avoidance of the elimination of the
correspondence theory of truth by the unity of the
proposition.) It makes no difference whether one thinks
of the proposition as being a (quasi-) linguistic, representing entity or, on Russellian lines, as something

---

[19] Again, Ramsey observed this (1927, p. 145). He noticed, too, the fact that
Wittgenstein's idea also allows the solution to the problem of representing
a non-symmetrical relation's direction ('sense'). It was obviously a
desirable feature of a solution to one of these problems that it should also
provide a solution to the other without blurring the distinction between
them.

whose constituents are the things represented: in the first case, any conventional expression for the relation will not function as the name of an object and is, as is shown at *Tractatus* 3.1432, in principle eliminable from the propositional sign; in the second case, the problem Russell faced, of one thing's having to do double duty as both a constituent to be linked to other constituents and as the linking principle itself, is solved by the elimination of the first duty altogether and assigning the other to a different (presumably mental) relation between non-relational constituents. Russell, had he only realized it, had been given by Wittgenstein (what had previously though less transparently been available to him from Bradley) the materials which would have enabled him to have retained much of the 1910/1912 theory of judgement without the difficulties which led to the formulation of the 1913 theory. For on this view the relation which unifies the propositional constituents into a representation of a fact is not the relation which unifies those constituents into the represented fact (if there be one, which there does not have to be). Objects can be their own Names, as befits Russell's earlier account of propositional constituents, but can form two different facts, one of which can represent the other. A correspondence theory can, after all, be combined with Russell's view that the constituents of representations are the constituents of the represented. Of course, there remain other better-known objections at least as serious as those which we have just seen may perhaps be overcome. One of these, which may now loom large again, is Wittgenstein's. But even were these objections to be surmounted, what we would have so far is still merely the sketch of a possible theory and thereby, as Ramsey said, 'miserably inferior' to the Theory of Descriptions.

Nevertheless, what we have uncovered are some of the historical roots or at least anticipations of at least three of the more widely canvassed current approaches to the study of what we now prefer to call 'belief'. Some of these evolved from the taking of what I called 'the first step'. As Russell's thinking developed through what we can call his 1919 theory of judgement, this step was combined with a tendency to behaviourism; and it gave rise to two initially competing ideas. One of these two ideas, that of an internal symbolism, can be developed into, eg. Fodor's methodological solipsism and the hypothesis of a language of thought. The other idea, reflecting the influence of behaviourism, produced the suggestion that a belief can be explicated as a causal function from desire to action. This latter line of development goes through Ramsey; a recent manifestation is 'success semantics' (Whyte, 1990). Another of the current approaches, which arises from the 1910 theory and implicitly exploits what I called 'the second step', takes seriously the idea that thought encompasses the extra-mental. This line can be traced through the views of Gareth Evans and Hilary Putnam to the notion of 'broad content'.[20]

[20] This paper is considerably improved as a result of discussion at and after presentations in Perth and Southampton. I am particularly indebted to Nicholas Griffin, Peter Hylton, and Hartley Slater. I also owe Mark Sainsbury thanks for a great deal of earlier discussion.

BIBLIOGRAPHY OF WORKS CITED

Russell's Writings

CP4, 1994. *The Collected Papers of Bertrand Russell, Foundations of Logic, 1903–05*, vol. 4 (London, Routledge).

CP6, 1992. *The Collected Papers of Bertrand Russell, Logical and Philosophical Papers, 1909–13*, vol. 6 (London, Routledge).

CP8, 1986. *The Collected Papers of Bertrand Russell, The Philosophy of Logical Atomism and Other Essays, 1914–19*, vol. 8 (London, Allen and Unwin).

EA, 1973. *Essays in Analysis*, ed. by Douglas Lackey (London, Allen and Unwin).

LK, 1956. *Logic and Knowledge*, ed. by Robert Marsh (London, Allen and Unwin).

ML, 1963. *Mysticism and Logic* (London, Allen and Unwin).

PE, 1966. *Philosophical Essays* (London, Allen and Unwin).

Russell, 1903. *The Principles of Mathematics* (London, Allen and Unwin, 1937).

—— 1904. 'Meinong's Theory of Complexes and Assumptions', in *CP4* and *EA*.

—— 1910. 'On the Nature of Truth and Falsehood', in *CP6* and *PE*.

—— 1911. 'Knowledge by Acquaintance and Knowledge by Description', in *CP6* and *ML*.

—— 1912. *The Problems of Philosophy* (London, Oxford University Press, 1946).

—— 1913, *Theory of Knowledge: The 1913 Manuscript* (London, Routledge, 1992).

—— 1918. 'The Philosophy of Logical Atomism', in *CP8* and *LK*.

—— 1919, 'On propositions: what they are and how they mean', in *CP8* and *LK*.

Other Writings

Candlish, S., 1989. 'The Truth About F. H. Bradley', *Mind*, vol. 98.

Geach, P. T., 1957. *Mental Acts* (London, Routledge and Kegan Paul; reprinted Thoemmes Press, 1992).

Griffin, N., 1993. 'Terms, Relations, Complexes', in A. D. Irvine and G. A. Wedeking (eds.), *Russell and Analytic Philosophy* (Toronto, University of Toronto Press).

Hylton, Peter, 1984. 'The Nature of the Proposition', in R. Rorty, J. Schneewind and Q. Skinner (eds.), *Philosophy in History* (Cambridge, Cambridge University Press).

—— 1990. *Russell, Idealism, and the Emergence of Analytic Philosophy* (Oxford, Clarendon Press).

Linsky, Leonard, 1992. 'The Unity of the Proposition', *Journal of the History of Philosophy*, vol. 30.

Palmer, A., 1988. *Concept and Object* (London, Routledge, 1988).

Pears, David, 1977. 'The Relation between Wittgenstein's Picture Theory of Propositions and Russell's Theories of Judgement', *The Philosophical Review*, vol. 86.

Ramsey, F. P., 1927. 'Facts and Propositions', in *The Foundations of Mathematics* (London, Routledge and Kegan Paul, 1931).

Sainsbury, R. M., 1979. *Russell* (London, Routledge).

Stout, G. F., 1911. 'Real Being and Being for Thought', in *Studies in Philosophy and Psychology* (London, Macmillan, 1930).

Whyte, J. T., 1990. 'Success Semantics', *Analysis*, vol. 50.

APPENDIX: REPLY TO SAINSBURY[21]

In Part 2 of his response to my paper at our symposium, Mark Sainsbury said, 'Candlish suggests that either of two moves made by Wittgenstein in the Tractatus would have resolved Russell's problem.... I think it is questionable whether either move is necessary or sufficient for a solution to the problem.'

Although I have made some changes to the final version of my paper in the light of discussion on the occasion of its presentation, I have left untouched the suggestions to which Sainsbury refers. The interested reader may compare the first sentence of my section 6 with Sainsbury's remarks (though I was much less careful in a parenthetical remark two paragraphs later), a sentence which is concerned with the opening up of an historical possibility. I am grateful to have been given the chance to make clear that my talk of 'sufficiency' should be interpreted in this light, as concerning what enabled the avoidance of a blind alley. It is of course quite right to say, as Sainsbury does, that merely treating the propositional sign as itself a fact is insufficient to resolve all three of the problems he properly distinguishes as involved in the question of the unity of the proposition. Wittgenstein himself brought the picture theory and the notion of a method of projection into play here, this method of projection being a matter of the use to which propositional signs are put. But the relevant point in this context is that Wittgenstein made a complete break with Russell's attempts to find solutions either by inventing special entities ('logical forms') with inconsistent properties or by just assigning inconsistent powers to the mind.

---

[21] Mark Sainsbury's article follows on from this article, see p. 137–53.

In his Part 3, Sainsbury courageously offered a
Davidsonian solution to the problem in terms of a
'special propositional way' of concatenating signs which
solves all three of his unity-problems, a way which he
identifies via the device of curly brackets. As presented
at the symposium, this device seems to combine Russell's
alternative solutions together with their problems.
Sainsbury, as one would expect, denied this, appealing
to recursion as the means of evading those problems. It
is not clear how it does this. And given that, in
explaining what the recursive procedure is, Sainsbury
appeals to a prior understanding of the distinction
between names and predicates, one might reasonably
suspect that propositional unity has been implicitly
appealed to in the explanation of its achievement.

HOW CAN WE SAY SOMETHING?

Mark Sainsbury
King's College London

1. *Background*

Russell's multiple relation theory of judgement (*MRTJ*) brings to the fore two related matters, more general than judgement itself, which Russell found perplexing in the first decade of the century and beyond: the nature of complexes and the twofold nature of verbs.[1] The problem of the unity of the proposition, which in turn lies at the heart of the difficulties Russell encountered with *MRTJ*, are special cases of these more general ones. The general ones arise whether or not we are concerned to find an account of judgement.

Must we regard complexes as something 'over and above' their constituents? Russell answered negatively in the case of what he calls aggregates. 'Such a whole', he says, 'is completely specified when all its simple constituents are specified' (*POM*, p. 140). Some wholes do not meet this condition, and are to be called 'unities'. For example, the unity *A differs from B* cannot be completely specified by its constituents, since these may form simply an aggregate of the terms, A, difference and B, or alternatively the proposition that B differs from A. In *POM*, he claims that 'such a whole [sc. a unity] is

---

[1] The importance of these two problems was brought home to me by Griffin (1993).

137

always a proposition' (*POM*, p. 139); in other words, all unities are propositions.[2] If we hold to this, two potential problems fuse into one: how can meanings form any kind of unity? And how can they form the distinctively propositional kind of unity?

However, Russell does not, and should not, hold that all unities are propositions. For example, a fact will count as a unity, by the test of not being exhausted by its components; so, in particular, will Othello's judging that Desdemona loves Cassio.

The other general problem is discussed in *POM* in terms of the 'twofold nature of the verb' (*POM*, p. 49): on the one hand it may be a relating relation and, on the other, a relation in itself (*POM*, p. 100). 'A relation is one thing when it relates, and another when it is merely enumerated as a term in a collection' (*POM*, p. 140). When we say that music is the food of love, the verb or relation *love* appears in itself. When we say that Desdemona loves Cassio, *love* appears in such a way as to relate Desdemona and Cassio.

Russell makes plain that the two problems are connected: 'Owing to the way in which the verb actually relates the terms of a proposition, every proposition has a unity which renders it distinct from the sum of its constituents' (*POM*, p. 52). In itemizing the constituents, the verb or relation appears 'in itself' as opposed to 'as relating'; so the proposition is more than just its constituents.

Various difficulties supposedly emerge from the phenomena mentioned.

1) An adequate account of the phenomena involves

---

[2] This appears inconsistent with his discussion of denoting complexes, which meet the test for being unities rather than aggregates but which are not propositions.

contradiction (*POM*, p. 48).

2) We are at a loss to say what a proposition is.

3) Unities which are not aggregates pose a threat to pluralism.

4) There's a special problem about falsehood, quite independently of any theory of judgement: it seems that if, in the unity *Desdemona loves Cassio*, love really relates Desdemona and Cassio, then Desdemona loves Cassio.

5) There's a problem for the *MRTJ*.

Russell's rather casual remark in 'Lectures on the Philosophy of Logical Atomism' that the *MRTJ*'s treatment of the verb was 'a little unduly simple' seems a little unduly disappointing. Had no progress been made in fifteen years? On what would nowadays seem the central topic, the nature of propositions, I think the answer is no.[3] We understand better how Russell failed to address this problem when we see that his primary concern was the consistency of the existence of unities with pluralism (number 3 in the list above). He was less concerned to say what a unity is, than to show that allowing them was consistent with his overall philosophy, in which pluralism is underpinned by analysis. This is brought out by a comparison of his response to Bradley with his positional statement of the nature of 'analytic realism'. He writes:

---

[3] I do not mean to imply that he had not tried to make progress. But it is not clear in his modifications of *MRTJ*, chronicled by Candlish (1996) and by Griffin (1985, 1996) that he had grasped that the root of his problems lay not with judgement but with propositions. I am not aware of any evidence for the view that it would have been obvious to Russell that Wittgenstein was right in writing to him in 1913 that the problems with the theory of judgement 'can only be removed by a correct theory of propositions' (Wittgenstein, 1974, p. 13).

Mr Bradley finds an inconsistency in my simultaneous advocacy of a strict pluralism and of 'unities which are complex and which cannot be analysed into terms and relations'. It would seem that everything here turns upon the sense in which such unities cannot be analysed. What I admit is that no enumeration of their constituents will reconstitute them, since any such enumeration gives us a plurality, not a unity. But I do not admit that they are not composed of their constituents; and what is more to the purpose, I do not admit that their constituents cannot be considered truly unless we remember that they are their constituents. (Russell, 1910, p. 354)

No hint here of a positive account of what a unity is. The consistency of unities with the overall project is given pride of place in this passage from 'Le realisme analytique':

Elle [cette philosophie] est analytique, puisqu'elle soutient que l'existence du complexe dépend de l'existence du simple, et non pas *vice versa*, et que le constituant d'un complexe est absolument identique, comme constituant, a ce qu'il est en lui-meme quand on ne considere pas ses relations. Cette philosophie est donc une philosophie atomique. (Russell, 1911, p. 410)

Concern with the admissibility of unities might distract from concern with their nature.

2. *How to solve the problem: Candlish's suggestions*
One could think of 'the' problem of the unity of the proposition as composed of several related sub-problems:

(i) how does one distinguish, among collections of meanings, between those which can be arranged so as to say something (eg. Desdemona, love and Cassio) and those which cannot be so arranged (eg. Desdemona and Cassio)?

(ii) given a collection of meanings (eg. Desdemona, love and Cassio), how does one distinguish between those arrangements of that collection which do say something (eg. that Desdemona loves Cassio) and those that do not (eg. that love Desdemona Cassio)?

(iii) given a collection of meanings which can be arranged so as to say more than one thing (eg. Desdemona, love and Cassio), how does one distinguish between the things (eg. between saying that Desdemona loves Cassio and saying that Cassio loves Desdemona)?

(iv) given a collection of meanings arranged so as to say just one thing, what cements the meanings together in the required way? What is the nature of the further ingredient or entity involved, here referred to as 'arrangement', over and above the meanings themselves?

I think the central puzle is located in (iv) and that the others serve to illustrate that (iv) is genuinely puzzling.

Candlish (1996), following Russell, gives central place to a special case of (iii), the case I employed in illustrating (iii). He suggests that either of two moves made by Wittgenstein in the *Tractatus* would have resolved this problem. One is to think of propositions as linguistic rather than non-linguistic, for then unity can be acknowledged without automatic creation of the represented fact. The other is to think of propositional signs as themselves facts, so that there is no need for an explicitly represented relation to be both a propositional constituent and the source of propositional unity.

I think it is questionable whether either move is necessary or sufficient for a solution.

Consider the first of these suggestions: the unity of a sentence (ie. of a proposition thought of as something linguistic) can be acknowledged without automatic creation of the represented fact. Perhaps the thought is that one can allow that the sentence 'Cassio loves Desdemona' is a unity, in that it says something, without being obliged to say that Cassio loves Desdemona. But if a sentence can say something false, why should not a collection of meanings? Perhaps it is easy to think of a sentence as ordered, and order can play a special role in connection with problem (iii). But if order is allowed in the story, it can also play a special role in ordering the meanings themselves, a role well adapted to solving problem (iii). I can find only one relevant difference between the level of meanings and the level of language. At the former, Russell seems to have been tempted to explain what it is for a collection of meanings to say something by the fact that its verb 'really relates' its terms; it is not tempting to explain what it is for a collection of words to says something by the fact that the verb really relates the names or their referents. However, since Russell realized that the temptation had to be resisted, on pain of making falsehood impossible, this does not appear to be a difference which matters.

Merely moving to the level of language does not seem to make a significant difference, let alone to suffice for a solution. It seems clear that the linguistic analogues of the four problems above are to be resolved, to the extent that they are well posed, by grammar and semantics. It is not clear why such theories should not be mirrored as theories about meanings, rather than about the words which mean them. For example, a rule which would contribute to answering the linguistic analogue of question (i) is that an atomic sentence, a species of word collection which says something, consists in an *n*-place predicate and *n* names, in a certain order. This could be mirrored at the non-linguistic level: an atomic non-linguistic collection of meanings which says something consists in an *n*-place property and *n* individuals, in a certain order.

Candlish's other Wittgensteinian suggestion is that 'propositions are able to represent facts because the propositional signs are themselves facts' (Candlish, 1996, p. 128). If we had a conception of facts which allows for false facts, or for which we can make a distinction between whether the fact exists and whether it is instantiated, then we make some progress towards a solution.[4] On this view, any appropriately assembled collection of meanings would be a fact. Truth would be a matter of the fact being instantiated; falsehood is not being instantiated. Wittgenstein does indeed have such a conception (standardly translated as 'state of affairs'); but it is not to this conception that Candlish draws attention. Rather, what is supposed to do the trick is that the propositional sign itself is a fact.

The fact '*that* "a" stands to "b" in a certain relation says that aRb' (*Tractatus* 3.1432). What is this 'certain relation', and how is it expressed? In the standard example, it can't be the relation of loving, since signs do not love one another. A better candidate would be the relation of flanking an occurrence of 'loves'. But now it is mysterious why the *fact* that 'Desdemona' and 'Cassio' are related by this relation should be a better candidate for meaning than just the sentence 'Desdemona loves Cassio'. To put the worry another

---

[4] We don't get all the way, since there is still a question about what makes for the difference between a fact (eg. that Desdemona loves Cassio) and a collection of meanings (eg. Desdemona, love and Cassio).

way, if it is acceptable to introduce this special syntactic relation (flanking 'loves', in the 'Desdemona' then 'Cassio' order), why would it not be acceptable to introduce an analogous relation at the level of meanings (flanking love, in the Desdemona then Cassio order)? This is just what Othello's thought does to Desdemona and Cassio: it places them in the relation of 'flanking' love, ie. of being thought by Othello to be love-related (in the Desdemona then Cassio order). So it doesn't seem to me that shifting to regarding the propositional sign as a fact is sufficient to resolve the problem.

I have not explicitly addressed the question of whether either moving to language, or moving to regarding the propositional sign as a fact is necessary for a solution. My view is that neither move is necessary. This will emerge in the light of what I think is required.

3. *Another approach to the solution*
Are the problems of the unity of the proposition special to Russell's philosophy, or are they still visible from our contemporary perspective? If so, have they been solved, or simply ignored? I think that the problems remain visible, but they are not often explicitly addressed, despite the fact that, or perhaps because, an adequate solution is available within contemporary received wisdom.

Given the amount of criticism Russell's *MRTJ* has received,[5] it is surprising to find apparently similar theories being advanced, or at least taken seriously, by many influential contemporary writers (for example

---

[5] Not just by my fellow symposiast (Candlish, 1996) but by Wittgenstein (as chronicled in Griffin, 1985), Geach (1957, p. 50), Mackie (1973, p. 28) and many others.

David Kaplan),[6] who do not indicate that such theories bring into prominence any problem of propositional unity. Admittedly, contemporary theorists unify the meanings as a sequence, rather than taking them individually. This removes certain difficulties: it enables the belief relation to be invariably dyadic, rather than having to have variable adicity; and it addresses problem (iii), the problem of distinguishing the different things which could be said by a collection of meanings as a function of their order. Russell could not have tolerated sequences in a complete analysis, consistently with the no-class theory of classes. But it would be a mistake to suppose that allowing sequences would have resolved his problems. Merely ordering meanings, without further devices, cannot be guaranteed to resolve more than special cases of problem (iii), leaving untouched some issues to do with scope;[7] and it does not so much as address problems (i), (ii) and (iv). Do those who are happy to roll out accounts of judgement in which people are related to sequences of entities have up their sleeves an answer to these problems?

Perhaps some look to the Fregean notion of functional application. However, there is no solution in this quarter. The question of what makes the difference between a collection consisting of a function and its potential arguments, on the one hand, and the 'insertion'

---

[6]   eg. Kaplan (1977). The recent symposium between François Recanati (1995) and Mark Crimmins (held just a week before the Southampton conference at which this paper was delivered) takes a version of *MRTJ* seriously without manifesting any sense that it raises a problem of propositional unity.

[7]   For example, the ambiguity in 'Harry is a dirty window cleaner' is not resolved by linking the meaning to the sequence <Harry, dirty, window, cleaner>, as opposed to some other sequence each of whose members is one of these elements. More complex set-theoretic constructions, sequences with sequences as members, arguably could resolve all these ambiguities.

of these arguments into the function, and their insertion in one rather than another order, is of essentially the same kind as our original question. Argument-function unity is of a piece with propositional unity.[8]

One current orthodoxy is that a proposition can be thought of as a set of possible worlds. In its more plausible and cautious form, the set of worlds is not identified with the proposition, but simply specifies truth and identity conditions: a proposition p is true if the actual world is included in p's associated set, and propositions are identical if associated with the same set. This theory faces a problem analogous to that of unity: what is the difference between the proposition and the associated set? A proposition manages to say something, to have truth conditions; the set is some kind of model of these. A set cannot be identified with a truth condition, since a condition, unlike a set, is something which can be satisfied (met, fulfilled) or not.

On another version of the possible worlds theory, propositions are simply identical with sets of worlds. This view confronts another problem resembling that of unity: what is it to employ the contemplation of a set of worlds to entertain a thought, rather than simply contemplating it? If we could answer this question, we could solve the problems of unity. This is not the only way in which, in principle, the problems of unity could be solved, since we might also try to solve them by focusing on some non-set-theoretic mode of combination. This alternative approach would claim that to contemplate anything thus combined is eo ipso to entertain a proposition, rather than merely to contemplate some collection of entities.

---

[8]   Only an erroneous interpretation of Frege (in my opinion) would attribute to him an attempt to explain (as opposed to label) this unity in terms of unsaturatedness.

My view is that a problem deserving the name of that of the unity of the proposition remains for many philosophers; all those, at least, who place sets of worlds at the centre of their semantic theorizing. But not all philosophers do this, and not all face a unity problem. The problem is absent from, for example, a Davidsonian approach to meaning. This is an account of the meaning of sentences which dispenses with meanings as entities, although we will see that this feature is inessential to the approach's capacity to solve the problems of unity.

In a Davidsonian theory, concatenation of the relevant kind is by definition a way of arranging expressions so that the result has a truth condition; which truth condition depends upon the words concatenated and their mode of concatenation. To contemplate an appropriate concatenation of words with understanding is to appreciate its truth condition. There is no unanswered question about how the sentence manages to say something.

The account would not be satisfying unless the way in which concatenation achieves a truth condition were spelled out. In Davidson's approach, this is achieved by a recursive specification of truth conditions. Names are given reference clauses, predicates satisfaction clauses, a general account is given of how names and predicates combine, and in the light of these one can deduce not only that the result of concatenating an n-ary predicate with n names says something, but what it says.

In Davidson's hands, the approach assumes that we are concerned with language, and that meanings as entities are not required. This feature is inessential. One could borrow the recursive approach in order to specify special truth-condition-conferring ways of concatenating Russellian meanings; in doing this one would solve the problems of the unity of the proposition in more or less the terms in which Russell stated them.

Let us use curly brackets to indicate the truth-condition-conferring mode of concatenating meanings (regarded as non-linguistic entities). An expression like '{Desdemona, love, Cassio}' will refer to the result of concatenating the meanings in the list in the special way. The theory will say that this result is true if Desdemona loves Cassio. In general, for any n objects, $o_1 \ldots o_n$, and any n-ary universal, φ^n, φ^n, $o_1 \ldots o_n\}$ is true if $o_1 \ldots o_n$ are φ^n-related. Providing the truth condition displays the cement, as demanded by problem (iv): the cement consists in the possession of a truth condition, where this is systematically specified. This also resolves which thing is said, as demanded by problem (iii). Problems (i) and (ii) are resolved (for the atomic cases) by dividing the world into individuals and universals, and subdividing universals according to their degree.

I conclude with five observations.

First, the approach is firmly non-reductive. What it is for a concatenation of meanings to say something is explained by the systematic provision of the saying in question. What else could one expect? In Russell's terms, it might be said that we are treating the relevant kind of concatenation as primitive and indefinable. It is not a relation which exists anyhow, ready to be appealed to by the theorist of propositions or judgements. In this sense, it is sui generis.

Russell was quite clear, in the unpublished paper 'On Functions' (cited in Griffin, 1993), about some necessary conditions for solving the problems: we need to find a distinctive mode of combination (my 'concatenation'), which, together with the constituents, determines the complex without itself being a constituent; yet the mode of combination must also be capable, on other occasions, of being a constituent of complexes; on such occasions, it will not be exercising its unifying role. If Russell had borne these points firmly in mind in 1913, his attempt at that time to make use of the notion of logical form in the *MRTJ* might have taken a different, and Davidsonian, turn: rather than trying to make logical form a constituent of what is judged, each logical form should be seen as one way of concatenating meanings so that something is said. It is the systematic, recursive, progress through the totality of logical forms that makes the Davidsonian account possible.

Second, my suggested approach returns us sharply to Russell's problem of the dual nature of the verb. A constituent of a concatenation is a universal. We need to extract from it something more relational for the truth condition. I did this by keeping 'φ^n' unequivocal, and tacking on '-related' to reveal its role in the truth condition. This just is the shift from relation in itself to relation as really relating. In this setting, 'really relating' can unproblematically be understood in the way that Russell feared would lead to objective falsehoods, since the real relating features only on one side of a biconditional. As we might express the unity: the meaning complex {Desdemona, love Cassio} is true iff *love* really relates Desdemona to Cassio.

It may well be an essential feature of this approach that full homophony cannot be achieved, though we can approach it more closely by dividing classes of concatenations more finely. Thus for unary atoms, we can say {*a*, the property of being *F*} is true iff *a* has the property of being *F*. However, I think homophony may well be not completely attainable, on account of the following tendency. If you think of a proposition as a collection of meanings, and think of meanings as, in the first instance, individuals and properties, then it is hard to resist the thought that a unary atom, for example, is most properly described as attributing a property to an individual. The atom is apparently unary in nature, and not just in name; the truth condition binary (involving an individual, a property, and the attribution relation between them). So there's a tendency to see an extra argument place in every proposition. Although this 'extra place' conception is, in my view, incorrect, it does not threaten to generate Bradley's regress.

The third matter is a question: would this apparatus entitle us to Russell's *MRTJ*? Russell wanted a multiple relation theory because he thought that if judgement related one who judged falsely to a single thing, it would have to be an unpalatable 'objective falsehood'. On my proposal, there is no such problem, so the most obvious theory of judgement would relate thinkers to concatenations of meanings. However, there might be other reasons for preferring a theory upon which the mind is related simply to the constituents of the concatenations, where to think of these constituents in a certain way is to concatenate them. Given that we can say recursively what it is to concatenate, this need not be regarded as a mysterious mental power. As far as I know, provided we are happy with multigrade relations, there is no obstacle to this development of the theory I offer Russell.

Fourth, I have considered only atomic concatenations of meanings. For those who, like Wittgenstein and Russell at some periods, think that the logical constants do not denote meanings, it will not be obvious how to extend this approach to non-atomic cases. On this view of the logical constants, the very form of the problems would have to be different, since the constants would supply no meanings (regarded as entities) to be concatenated.

Fifth, and finally, the present concerns raise a further question, not yet mentioned. How can mere lifeless words or meanings (understood in Russell's way, as ordinary individuals and properties), however well selected and arranged, say anything at all? If 'mere' is supposed to make us focus on the intrinsic and non-relational properties of words or meanings, then they cannot say anything. They can say something only in virtue of their relational properties, their use. It would be another project to consider the extent to which Russell and Wittgenstein's difficulties about the nature of propositions in the early part of the century can be traced to their not in that period finding room for this crucial notion.

BIBLIOGRAPHY OF WORKS CITED

Candlish, Stewart, 1966. 'The Unity of the Proposition and Russell's Theories of Judgement', this volume, pp. 101–133.

Geach, Peter, 1957. *Mental Acts* (London, Routledge and Kegan Paul; reprinted Thoemmes Press, 1992).

Griffin, Nicholas, 1985. 'Russell's Multiple Relation Theory of Judgement', *Philosophical Studies*, vol. 47, pp. 213–47.

—— 1985. 'Wittgenstein's Criticism of Russell's Theory of Judgement', *Russell*, vol. 5, no. 2, pp. 132–5.

—— 1993. 'Terms, Relations, Complexes', in Irvine, A. D. and G. A. Wedeking (eds.), *Russell and Analytic Philolsophy*, pp. 159–92 (Toronto, University of Toronto Press).

Kaplan, David, 1977. 'Demonstratives', reprinted in Joseph Almog, John Perry and Howard Wettstein (eds.), 1989, *Themes from Kaplan*, pp. 481–14 (Oxford, Oxford University Press).

Mackie, J. L., 1973. Truth, Probability and Paradox (Oxford, Oxford University Press).

Recanati, François, 1995. 'Quasi-singular Propositions: the Semantics of Belief Reports', *Supplementary Proceedings of the Aristotelian Society*, pp. 175–93.

Russell, Bertrand, 1903 (*POM*). *The Principles of Mathematics* (Cambridge, Cambridge University Press).

—— 1910. 'Some explanations in reply to Mr Bradley' *Mind*, vol. 19, pp. 373–8. Reprinted in John G. Slater (ed.), 1992, *The Collected Papers of Bertrand Russell*, pp. 354–8, page reference to reprint (London, Routledge).

Russell, Bertrand, 1911. 'Le Realisme Analytique', *Bulletin de la Societe Francaise de Philosophie*, vol. 11, pp. 282–91. Reprinted in John G. Slater (ed.), 1992, *The Collected Papers of Bertrand Russell*, vol. 6, page reference to reprint (London, Routledge).

—— 1918–19. 'Lectures on the Philosophy of Logical Atomism', *Monist*, 28, 29. Reprinted in R. C. Marsh, (ed.), 1956, *Logic and Knowledge Knowledge*, pp. 177–281 (London, George Allen and Unwin).

Wittgenstein, Ludwig, 1921. *Tractatus Logico-Philosophicus* (London, Routledge and Kegan Paul).

—— 1974. *Letters to Russell, Keynes and Moore* (Oxford, Basil Blackwell).

THE COMPLEX PROBLEM AND THE
THEORY OF SYMBOLISM

Anthony Palmer
University of Southampton

Every proposition is essentially true-false. Thus a proposition has two poles (corresponding to the case of its truth and the case of its falsity). We call this the sense of a proposition. (Wittgenstein, 1969, p. 94)

Logical indefinables cannot be predicates or relations, because propositions, owing to sense, cannot have predicates or relations. (Wittgenstein, 1969, p. 101)

Introduction
In a paper entitled 'Early Wittgenstein and Middle Russell' Kenneth Blackwell tells us that in October 1912 Russell told Ottiline Morell that his mind was full of a paper on 'What is logic' and that he thought it might be really important. The next day he told her that he 'couldn't get on with it' and 'felt strongly inclined to leave it to Wittgenstein' (Bloch, 1981, p. 10). There is a five-page manuscript amongst Russell's papers from that period entitled 'What is Logic'. In it logic is defined as the study of the forms of complexes. Blackwell also tells us that Wittgenstein's 'letters to Russell in the next few months show him hard at work upon what he calls "the complex problem" and the theory of symbolism'. This gives me the title of my paper in which I argue that

the 'Notes on Logic' and the 'Notes Dictated to Moore' show us that Wittgenstein did not think that these were unrelated problems.

I

Negation and Bipolarity

The 'Notes on Logic' and the 'Notes Dictated to Moore' expound what I consider to be Wittgenstein's first great insight into the nature of logic: the doctrine of the bipolarity of the proposition. It is a doctrine which is difficult to explain just because it is so easily confused with a doctrine to which it is in reality in stark opposition. The doctrine with which it is easily confused is Russell's. More confusingly still it is a doctrine which Russell thinks he has been taught by Wittgenstein! This is the doctrine that 'the essence of a proposition considered as a symbol is its duality of possible relation to fact'. In other words, a proposition is a symbol which is either true or false.

I can find no indication in Russell's writings that he ever recognized any difference between this doctrine and the doctrine of bipolarity. Most commentators on Wittgenstein follow Russell in drawing no such distinction either. For Wittgenstein, however, as I shall try to show, the distinction was of the utmost importance.

The theory of bipolarity is first expressed in the 'Notes on Logic' as follows:

> Every proposition is essentially true-false. Thus a proposition has two poles (corresponding to the case of its truth and the case of its falsity). We call this the *sense* of a proposition. (Wittgenstein, 1969, p. 94)

In the paragraph which follows in Russell's own organization of Wittgenstein's notes, the doctrine of bipolarity is carefully distinguished from the doctrine that a proposition is either true or false.

> I understand the proposition 'aRb' when I know that either the fact that aRb or the fact that not aRb corresponds to it; *but this is not to be confused with the false opinion that I understand 'aRb' when I know that 'aRb or not aRb' is the case.* (My italics)

Even after his close study of the 'Notes on Logic' there is no evidence that Russell ever made this distinction. He constantly introduces the notion of a proposition by saying that it is what is either true or false. So, for example, in his *Introduction to Mathematical Philosophy*, which we know infuriated Wittgenstein, he writes: 'we mean by "proposition" primarily a form of words which expresses what is either true or false' (p. 155).

Why then should Wittgenstein have been so concerned to stress the difference between a proposition having two poles and a proposition being something which is either true or false?

The 'Notes on Logic' show that the doctrine of bipolarity arises out of reflection on the proper notation for negation. 'One reason for thinking that the old notation is wrong' he argued 'is that it is very unlikely that from every proposition p an infinite number of propositions not-not-p, not-not-not-not-P should follow.' The way to prevent this is to recognize that 'not-p' means the same, ie. has the same reference as, 'p'. 'The meaning (bedeutung) of a proposition is the fact which actually corresponds to it.' If it is the case that Caesar crossed the Rubicon then this fact is the meaning of both the proposition 'Caesar crossed the Rubicon' and of the proposition 'Caesar did not cross the

Rubicon' just because it is this fact which makes the first proposition true and the second proposition false. That is why we should resist the temptation to think of 'not p' as meaning everything else only not p. All the facts other than the fact that p do not make 'not-p' true. If all those facts were listed we would still not be able to conclude 'not-p' from them since they would not tell us what was being negated by 'not p'. And 'however ... "not-p" is explained the question what is negated must have meaning'.

Of course the sense of 'p' is not the same as the sense of 'not-p', 'p' and 'not-p' have opposite sense, nevertheless the fact that makes each of them true or false is the same and unless we understand this we do not understand 'p'.

> To understand a proposition p it is not enough to know that p implies '"p" is true' but we must also know that not-p implies '"p" is false'. This shows the bipolarity of the proposition. (Wittgenstein, 1969, p. 94)

Once we understand that 'p' and 'not-p' mean the same, we shall realize that any correct propositional notation will bring this out. It is this realization which generates the symbolism by which Wittgenstein set such store, viz. the ab notation. Instead of writing 'p' we should write 'a-p-b' which makes clear that a proposition is bipolar. The point that generates the doctrine of bipolarity, ie. the point about 'p' and 'not-p' having the same meaning, will then be brought out by merely reversing the poles in order to symbolize 'not-p'. 'Not-p' now becomes 'b-a-p-b-a'. If we now reverse the poles of that proposition we get 'a-b-a-p-b-a-b' and it now becomes obvious that this is the same as 'a-p-b'.

The point is that the process of reasoning by which we arrive at the result that a-b-a-p-b-a-b is the same symbol as a-p-b, is exactly the same as that by which we discover that its meaning is the same, viz where we reason if b-a-p-b-a, then not a-p-b, if a-b-a-p-b-a-b then *not* b-a-p-b-a, therefore if a-b-a-p-b-a-b, then a-p-b. (Wittgenstein, 1969, pp. 113–4)

What the ab notation does is to enable us to see *without going beyond the symbolism itself* that p is equivalent to not-not p is a tautology. Actually it does not quite say this since you would have to stipulate first of all which pole is which, but once that is done the point holds good that tautologies and contradictions can be recognized without looking beyond the symbols themselves. The point holds generally for all molecular propositions. When we symbolize molecular propositions in the ab way what we in effect do is to show how the poles of the inner propositions, when they are arranged in a particular way stand in relation to the poles of the proposition as a whole. If the arrangement of the inner poles is such that they correlate with only one of the poles of the whole proposition then we know that we are dealing either with a tautology or a contradiction. Hence, whether we are dealing with a tautology or a contradiction can be ascertained merely by inspecting the symbol for the whole proposition. Whether what we are dealing with is actually a tautology or a contradiction cannot, of course, be gained from such an inspection but that it is either a tautology or contradiction can be so ascertained. The symbolism will become perspicuous once it is arbitrarily stipulated which is which, and once that stipulation has been made which further arrangements of propositions to form molecular propositions are tautologies or contradictions will no longer be arbitrary.

These ideas about symbolism, which arise out of the recognition that 'p' means the same as 'not-p' are expounded in the notes dictated at Russell's insistence in 1913. Russell rearranged them and discussed them at Harvard. Meanwhile Moore visited Wittgenstein in Norway and Wittgenstein dictated to him what, in effect, is a continuation of the same line of thinking.

What the notes dictated to Moore do is to tease out the consequences of the idea of the bipolarity of the proposition in relation to the notions of tautology and contradiction. If it is the case that we can ascertain whether a proposition is a tautology or contradiction merely by inspecting the symbol for it then it follows that whether a proposition is a tautology or contradiction can have nothing whatsoever to do with what its elementary propositions say. We do however learn something about the nature of elementary propositions once we understand that propositional symbols can be arranged in such a way that it will be obvious on inspection that they are either tautologies or contradictions. What we have learned is precisely that, ie. *that propositions are such that symbols for them can be arranged in such a way that whether the arrangement results in a tautology or contradiction can be ascertained merely by an inspection of the symbol for the arrangement.* As the *Notebooks* have it 'The ab function does not stop short of the elementary proposition but penetrates it.' Moreover, since it follows from this that whether a particular arrangement of propositional symbols symbolizes is a tautology or a contradiction has nothing to do with what the propositions so symbolized in such an arrangement say, it now becomes obvious that you cannot say what there is about those propositions which makes such an arrangement possible. If you could say what there was about these propositions which makes the tautological or contradictory arrangement of the symbols for them possible it would be clear that this could not be gleaned merely from a consideration of the symbols themselves. This is the idea with which the 'Notes Dictated to Moore' begin.

> Logical so-called propositions *shew* the logical properties of language, and therefore of the universe, but *say* nothing./ This means that merely by looking at them you can see the properties; whereas in a proposition proper, you cannot see what is true by looking at it. (Wittgenstein, 1969, p. 107)

From the fact that the propositional symbols can be combined in such a way that it will be obvious on inspection whether the combination is a tautology or contradiction we learn something about propositions. We learn that

> Every *real* proposition *shews* something besides what it says about the universe. (Wittgenstein, 1969, p. 107)

This whole line of reasoning eventually gets its definitive statement in the *Tractatus*.

> 6.113 It is the particular mark of logical propositions that one can recognise that they are true from the symbol alone, and this fact contains in itself the whole of the philosophy of logic. And so too it is a very important fact that the truth or falsity of non-logical propositions cannot be recognised from the propositions alone.

> 6.12 The fact that the propositions of logic are tautologies *shows* the formal – logical – properties of

language and the world.

The fact that a tautology is yielded by *this particular way* of connecting its constituents characterises the logic of its constituents.

If propositions are to yield a tautology when they are connected in a certain way, they must have certain structural properties. So their yielding a tautology when combined *in this way* shows that they possess these structural properties

Wittgenstein's thought has moved from the attempt to find a correct notation for negation through the doctrine of the bipolarity of the proposition to a conception of tautology and contradiction and from that to the doctrine that propositions, as well as saying something, also show something which cannot be said. In the 'Notes on Logic' and the 'Notes dictated to Moore' Wittgenstein, from a search for a correct notation for negation, had already in 1913 arrived at what was to become the central plank of his *Tractatus Logico-Philosophicus*, the distinction between what can be said and what can be shown but not said.

It was this central plank which Russell, while pretending to expound the *Tractatus* in the introduction he wrote for it at Wittgenstein's request, is concerned to oppose. It is as though he thought that Wittgenstein's central contention might in the end turn out to be no more than a local difficulty which might be overcome while leaving an overall structure intact. One of the most striking facts about Russell's introduction to the *Tractatus* is that the argument which Wittgenstein takes to contain 'the whole of the philosophy of logic' and which leads directly to the saying/ showing distinction, ie. the point that 'it is peculiar mark of logical propositions that one can recognise that they are true from the symbol alone', is not even mentioned in it. Moreover, the saying/showing distinction is itself treated with scorn.

> After all, Mr Wittgenstein manages to say a good deal about what cannot be said, thus suggesting to the sceptical reader that possibly there may be some loophole through a hierarchy of languages, or by some other exit. (Wittgenstein, 1961, p. xxi)

There are, indeed, passages in Russell's work in which we can see him seeking to come to terms with these insights into the nature of symbolism, but it is equally clear from these passages that he did not understand them.

One such passage occurs in his 'Lectures on Logical Atomism' delivered in 1918.

> It is very important to realise ... that *propositions are not the names of facts*. It is quite obvious as soon as it is pointed out to you, but as a matter of fact I never realised it until it was pointed out to me by a former pupil of mine, Wittgenstein. It is perfectly evident, as soon as you think of it, that a proposition is not a name for a fact from the mere circumstance that there are two propositions corresponding to each fact. Suppose it is a fact that Socrates is dead. You have two propositions: 'Socrates is dead' and 'Socrates is not dead'. And those two propositions correspond to the same fact, there is one fact in the world which makes one true and one false .... For each fact there are two propositions, one true and one false, and there is nothing in the nature of the symbol to show us which is the true one and which is the false one. (Russell, 1956, p. 187)

Now, you can certainly see here the influence of

Wittgenstein's claim that 'p' and 'not-p' have the same meaning, but instead of following Wittgenstein's development of the doctrine of the bipolarity of propositions from this, Russell goes on to do precisely the opposite. He argues that because to one fact p there correspond two propositions 'p' and 'not-p' we must conclude that a proposition *has two ways of being related to a reality*, a true way or a false way. Being either true or false gives you the possible relations of a symbol to reality which makes it a proposition.

This failure on Russell's part to understand the doctrine of bipolarity and to think instead of a proposition as being a symbol that is capable of being related to reality in two ways, a true way and a false way, is ultimately what accounts for his inability to understand Wittgenstein doctrine of tautology and contradiction. If a proposition is thought of as a symbol that is capable of being related to reality in two ways it will not follow from this that we can recognize tautologies of contradictions from an inspection of the symbols alone.

The difference between the idea of a proposition being essentially either true or false and the idea of a proposition being bipolar also accounts for the difference between Russell and Wittgenstein on the importance of negative facts. Because Russell thought that the hallmark of a propositional symbol was its possible dual relation to reality the postulation of negative facts *which are as ultimate as positive facts* becomes unavoidable. There just have to be negative facts for negative propositions to be related to in a true way otherwise there could never be true negative propositions: true negative propositions ultimately require negative facts. In the 'Lectures on Logical Atomism' Russell tells us that when he proposed this idea in his Harvard lectures it caused a riot, and in a late paper he bemoans the fact that 'there is implanted in the human breast an almost unquenchable desire to find some way of avoiding the admission that negative facts are as ultimate as those that are positive' (Russell, 1986, p. 280).

The Harvard students were surely right. Instead of defending their ultimate existence against all comers, Russell should have taken their universal execration as an indication that there was something wrong with the theory that a proposition is essentially an expression that can be related to a fact in two ways, a true way and a false way. It is in this respect that Wittgenstein's doctrine of bipolarity most clearly distinguishes itself from Russell's 'either true or false' doctrine, just because Wittgenstein's doctrine arises out of concern for a correct notation for negation.

II

Complexes, Facts and Propositions
The doctrine of bipolarity is Wittgenstein's doctrine of sense, and it is from this doctrine of sense that some of the more startling doctrines of the *Tractatus* flow. They are encapsulated in the second remark from 'The Notes on Logic' which I have placed at the head of this paper.

> Logical indefinables cannot be predicates or relations, because propositions, owing to sense, cannot have predicates or relations. (Wittgenstein, 1969, p. 101)

Once more we need to look at this remark in relation to Russell's concerns and in particular what Russell has to say about facts and complexes. Russell thought of facts as complexes whereas Wittgenstein insisted on distinguishing between facts and complexes. This difference becomes central at the point at which propositions are themselves thought of as facts by both Wittgenstein and

Russell.

The reason for differentiating between facts and complexes is most clearly brought out in a series of remarks Wittgenstein wrote much later than the period we are now considering. They can be found both in his *Philosophical Grammar* and in his *Philosophical Remarks* and were written round about 1931. The central idea I want to concentrate on is contained in the following passages.

> A complex is composed of its parts, the things of a kind which go to make it up. (This is of course a grammatical proposition concerning the words 'complex', 'part' and 'compose'.)
>
> To say that a red circle is *composed* of redness and circularity, or is a complex with these component parts, is a misuse of these words and is misleading. (Frege was aware of this and told me.)
>
> It is just as misleading to say the fact that this circle is red (that I am tired) is a complex whose components are a circle and redness (myself and tiredness).
>
> Neither is a house a complex of bricks and their spatial relation; i.e. that too goes against a correct use of the word.
>
> A chain, too, is composed of its links, not of these and their spatial relations.
>
> The fact that these links are so concatenated, isn't *composed* of anything at all. (Wittgenstein, 1975, pp. 302–303)

So a complex is composed of its parts while a fact is not composed of anything at all. Moreover, while it is true that for anything that is rightly regarded as being composed of parts, ie. as a complex, there will be a fact that corresponds to it, viz. the fact that its constituents, its component parts, are arranged in a certain way, nevertheless a fact is not itself a complex; a fact is not composed of parts.

Now we know that in the 'Notes on Logic' Wittgenstein was already insisting that

> Only facts can express a sense, a class of names cannot. This is easily shown. In aRb it is not the complex that symbolizes but the fact that the symbol a stands in a certain relation to the symbol b. Thus facts are symbolized by facts, or more correctly; that a certain thing is the case in the symbol says that a certain thing is the case in the case in the world. (Wittgenstein, 1969, p. 105)

Moreover, the point holds good of the ab notation. 'The symbolizing fact in "a-p-b" is that *say* a is on the left of p and b is on the right of p.'

Now, if it is the case that the fact that the symbol 'a' stands in a certain relation to the symbol 'b' that enables 'aRb' to say that aRb then this can only be so if 'a' stands for a and 'b' stands for b. And here we must take quite literally the idea of a symbol standing for what it symbolizes. It quite literally has to *take the place of* or *go proxy for* what it symbolizes. If it did not then the fact that one symbol stood in a certain relation to another symbol *by itself* could say nothing whatsoever about the relation in which things other than the symbols stand. Moreover, it should be equally clear that outside of the business of using facts to say something, no sense whatsoever could be made of the idea of one thing standing for, or going proxy for, another. I cannot make one thing stand for another simply by saying, for example, let this pen go proxy for Palmer, or let this table go proxy for a chair. I have not made anything go proxy for anything until I have used the fact that the pen is on the table to represent that – say – Palmer is on the chair. The idea that 'The possibility of the proposition is founded on the principle of signs going proxy for objects' (Wittgenstein, 1969, p. 47) leads directly to the idea that 'only in the nexus of a proposition does a name have meaning' (*Tractatus* 3.3).

There was a time when Russell thought of propositions as facts (no doubt under Wittgenstein's influence) but, unlike Wittgenstein he also thought of facts as complexes. When we put these two views together a logical disaster is generated. It is a disaster which becomes most apparent at the point at which we ask the question could the fact which is a proposition be a negative fact? Could the fact that something is not the case in the symbol be used to say that something is not the case in the world? Could we use the fact that 'a' does not stand in the relation R to 'b' to say that a does not stand in the relation R to b? The answer is clearly No. If we tried to construe a symbolizing fact as negative we will inevitably fail. For example, suppose that instead of the 'aRb' we tried the symbol 'a-Rb' as the symbol for a negative fact. Could we then say, in Wittgenstein's fashion, that what symbolizes in 'a-Rb' is that'-R' stands between 'a' and 'b'. Clearly not since that '-R' stands between 'a' and 'b' is no longer a negative fact. So, in the *Tractatus*, Wittgenstein argues

> 5.1511 Why should it not be possible to express a negative proposition by means of a negative fact? (Eg. suppose that 'a' does not stand in a certain relation to 'b'; then this might be used to say that aRb was not the case.
>
>   But even in this case the negative proposition is constructed by an indirect use of the positive.

There is a point in the 1918 manuscripts where Russell comes close to seeing this point, but because of his

weddedness to negative facts as the ultimate *relata* of
true negative propositions he can only see a danger and
hope, sometime, to discover a defence.

> 'xRy', 'x-Ry': these two symbols are each of them a
> *fact*. Each consists in a certain relation between x and
> y, the first, that 'R' stands between them, the second
> that '-R' stands between them. If x has the relation R
> to y there is a correspondence between this fact and
> the fact 'xRy'; ie. if x is replaced by 'x', y by 'y' and R
> by 'R' xRy becomes 'xRy'. This suggests a way in
> which a complex symbol may be 'true'; it may result
> from the fact symbolized by mere substitution. This
> won't do for *negative* facts. The fact that 'R' does not
> appear between 'x' and 'y' would be a very inconve-
> nient symbol for the fact that x and y do not have the
> relation R ... hence we invent the symbol '-R' for the
> purpose ... But 'z-Rw' is itself a positive fact, not of
> the same form as the fact it symbolizes. Negative facts
> are unsuitable as symbols. (Russell, 1986, p. 269)

Russell's problem now is this. If negative facts are
unsuitable as symbols how can negative facts themselves
be correctly symbolized? While Wittgenstein's reply
would be that 'p' and 'not p' have the same meaning
since the p in 'not p' is the same as the p in 'p' and that
this shows the bipolarity of the proposition, for Russell
this avenue is closed. For him a proposition is
something which is capable of a dual relation with
reality, ie. it can be related to reality in the true way or
the false way, and since negative propositions can be
related to reality in a true way there must in reality be
negative facts, which is why the difficulty in symbolizing
them becomes acute.

We are now beginning to see the difference that a
correct notation for negation, and therefore for propo-

sitions, makes to our conception of logic. If we take one route we are led to a philosophy of logical atomism as Russell conceived it, but if we take the other route, Wittgenstein's route, what we are led to is precisely the rejection of this. Russell's route regards propositions as complexes: they are complex symbols, and facts are complexes also. The essential thing about complexes is that they have components or constituents, and the problem for logic becomes one of the relation of complex symbols to facts. Russell needs to know just what complex facts there are for our complex symbols to be related to in a true way or a false way. What complex facts there are will depend upon what constituents there are so we need a means of identifying simples which constitute complexes. A simple symbol can only have one relation to reality. The possibility of a complex symbol having a dual relation to reality depends upon whether the simples of reality are related to each other in the way in which our simple symbols are related *or not*. So, in the lectures on logical atomism Russell systematically investigates the complexity of propositions and thereby the corresponding complexity of the facts which correspond to them. He thought he had developed a tool by which this analysis could be conducted in his theory of definite descriptions, a tool which generated a method which he called the method of logical fictions.

For Wittgenstein, on the other hand, while facts and propositions which are also facts are complex, neither should be regarded as a complexes. Unlike either simples or complexes, propositions do not have relations to each other, or to anything else. '[p]ropositions, by virtue of sense, cannot have predicates or relations.' A proposition is not something that can be related to reality in a true or false way just because facts are not capable of being related to anything at all.

III

Facts and States of Affairs in the 'Tractatus'
We can now tease out the consequences of what has so far been argued for the way in which we read the *Tractatus*. Although many of the deficiencies of Russell's introduction to it have long been recognized, it has not, to the best of my knowledge ever been recognized that if we read it in Russell's fashion we are likely to misconstrue it from the very beginning.

In the background of what we might have learned from the two sets of dictated Notes it should come as no surprise that the *Tractatus* begins with reflection on the nature of Facts.

1. The World is all that is the case.
1.1 It is the totality of Facts not things.

Wittgenstein then goes on to tell us what facts are. What they are, he says is the holding (or the obtaining) of states of affairs.

> Was der Fall ist, die Tatsache, ist das Bestehen von Sachverhalten.

In translating 'das Bestehen von Sachverhalten' as 'the holding (or obtaining) of states of affairs' I have departed from both of the official translations. Ogden translates it as 'the existence of atomic facts' and Pears and McGuinness translate it as 'the existence of states of affairs'. The Ogden translation, whether or not it was sanctioned by Wittgenstein, carries all of Russell's logical baggage with it, and in any case just does not make sense. If you are trying to tell someone what facts are, or what a fact is, not much enlightenment is provided by saying that a fact is the existence of other facts even if these other facts are qualified by the adjective 'atomic'. Eric Stenius pointed this out in 1960.

> The English version of the *Tractatus* translates *Sachverhalt* as 'atomic fact', *bestehen* as 'exist', and *Tatsache* as 'fact' ... this terminology leads to the absurdity in the formulation of 2 that 'the fact' is said to be 'the existence of ... facts. A corresponding absurdity is not, of course, found in the original. (Stenius, 1960, p. 31)

The Pears and McGuinness translation is from this point of view much better. In fact I am inclined to think it is not actually wrong at all. I do however think that it can be, and in fact has been, misleading. For it is easy to move from 'The existence of states of affairs' to 'existing states of affairs' and then to think of facts as existing things or combinations of things, and thereby go in Russell's direction and think of facts as complexes. A good example of such a move can be found on the first page of Norman Malcolm's book *Wittgenstein; Nothing is Hidden*.

> A configuration of objects is a possible state of affairs. A possible configuration is a possible state of affairs; an actual configuration is an existing state of affairs. The actual world (at a certain time) is just the totality of existing states of affairs (at that time). (Malcolm, 1986, p. 1)

This, as we have already seen from the two sets of dictated notes, is to take the wrong route. It is in effect to take Russell's route. It marks the wrong sort of difference between 'Tatsache' and 'Sachverhalt'. That is why it is better to translate 'das Bestehen von Sach-verhalten' as 'the holding (or obtaining) of states of affairs', rather than 'the existence of states of affairs', since there is no temptation whatsoever to think of the holding of states of affairs as existing things or existing complexes. It is interesting to note that G. E. M. Anscombe, both in her introduction to the *Tractatus*, and in her translation of Wittgenstein's 1914–18 *Notebooks* does indeed occasionally translate the expression 'bestehen' in that way. Witness, for example, her translation of the last sentence of the following passage from the *Notebooks*.

> Ein Name repräsentiert ein Ding, ein anderer ein anderes Ding und selbst sind sie verbunden; so stellt das Ganze – wie ein lebendes Bild – den Sachverhalt vor.
> Die logische Verbindung muss naturlict unter den repräsentierten Dingen möglich sein, und dies vird immer der Fall sein, wenn die Dinge wirklich repräsentiert sind. Wohlgemerkt, jene Verbindung ist keine Relation, sondern nur das *Bestehen* einer Relation. (Wittgenstein, 1969, p. 26)

Anscombe translates the last sentence of this passage as

> N.B. that connection is not a relation but only the *holding* of a relation.

The whole passage which throws a great deal of light on proposition 2 of the *Tractatus* as well as on the picturing theory of propositions, she translates as follows.

> One name is representative of one thing, another of another thing, and they themselves are connected. In this way the whole images the situation – like a *tableau vivant*.
> The logical connexion must, of course, be one that is possible as between the things that the names are representatives of, and this will always be the case if

the names are really representatives of things. N.B.
that connection is not a relation but only the *holding*
of a relation.

Having explained facts as the holding of states of affairs,
Wittgenstein then goes on to explain what states of
affairs are. With them we are indeed in the realm of
Russell's complexes. A state of affairs Wittgenstein tells
us is a 'Verbindung von Gegenstanden' a combination
of objects. If we have understood the 'Notes on Logic'
and the 'Notes Dictated to Moore' we cannot help
noticing that Wittgenstein has already on the first page
of the *Tractatus* made the distinction between facts and
complexes which Russell found so difficult to understand and which are once more spelled out in the 1931
passages entitled 'Fact and Complex'. It might be added
at this point that Russell was not the only one who
found this distinction difficult to understand. Witness
Frege's response to the first page of the *Tractatus*.

> What is the case, a fact, is the existence of *Sach-
> verhalte*. I take this to mean that every fact is the
> existence of a *Sachverhalt*, so that another fact is the
> existence of another *Sachverhalt*. Couldn't one delete
> the words 'existence of' and say 'Every fact is a
> *Sachverhalt*, every other fact is another *Sachverhalt*'.
> Couldn't one perhaps also say 'Every *Sachverhalt* is
> the existence of a fact'? (Monk, 1990, p. 163)

But before going on to exploit the difference between
fact and state of affairs Wittgenstein has more to say
about states of affairs themselves. And what he has to
say relies on the distinction between facts and complexes
having been already made. The best way to read the
comments on 2.01 'A state of affairs (a state of things)
is a combination of objects (things)' ie. 2.011–2.0141,

is to think of them as a commentary on the notion of a complex *once the distinction between complex and fact has been made.* When they are read in that light most of the claims of obscurity that have been levelled against them disappear.

If we have not already distinguished between fact and complex, ie. if we think of facts as complexes then the very notion of a complex presents us with difficulties. Russell's theory of knowledge manuscript which was never completed because of Wittgenstein's criticism is thoroughly enmeshed in these difficulties.

The first comment that Wittgenstein makes is that

2.01. It is essential to things that they should be possible constituents of states of affairs.

Now why should this be thought to be essential to things? If we have not already distinguished between facts and complexes this will not seem obvious at all. The theory of knowledge manuscript, for example, shows that it was not at all obvious to Russell.

Let us suppose that it is a fact that there is an inkwell on a table. If we have distinguished between facts and complexes then we can use the fact that the inkwell is on the table to give us the complex with two constituents, the inkwell and the table.

2.0201. Every statement about complexes can be resolved into a statement about their constituents and into the propositions that describe the complexes completely.

However if we have not distinguished between fact and complex and regard facts as themselves complexes we cannot do this. The fact that the inkwell is on the table will itself have to be regarded as having constituents, now not two constituents but three, the inkwell, the table and the relation between them, and with regard to this complex with these constituents we will now, if we are deprived of facts which are not complexes, need a further complex which gives us the way in which these constituents are arranged. This situation is quite clearly hopeless. It is this which led Russell to invent the idea of the form of a complex which is not a constituent of the complex.

> It is obvious, in fact, that when all the constituents of a complex have been enumerated, there remains something which can be called the form of the complex, which is the way in which the constituents are combined in the complex. (Russell, 1984, p. 98)

This demand for the form of a complex is generated by Russell's failure to distinguish facts from complexes or facts from combinations of objects. Because he fails to make that distinction and thinks of facts as themselves combinations of objects he needed the apparatus not only of the constituents of complexes but of forms of complexes which are not constituents of complexes together with the idea that acquaintance with such a form is involved in the understanding of a sentence.

> Suppose that someone tells us that Socrates precedes Plato. How do we know what he means? It is plain that his statement does not give us acquaintance with the complex 'Socrates precedes Plato'. What we understand is that Socrates and Plato and 'precedes' are united in a complex of the form 'xRy' where Socrates has the x place and Plato has the y place. It is difficult to see how we could possibly understand how Socrates and Plato and 'precedes' are combined unless we had acquaintance with the form of the complex. (Russell, 1984, p. 99)

We now have complexes, constituents of complexes, and forms of complexes. Yet even given this apparatus of constituents together with form it will still seem an accident that particular things can be the constituents of a complex which has a particular logical form. Deprived of facts that are not complexes Russell has no way out. But equally if like Wittgenstein we insist from the beginning that facts are distinguished from complexes or combinations of things, nevertheless the fact that things are combined in a certain way entails that it is possible for things to be combined in that way. It follows from this that possibility must be built into the idea of the constituents of complexes themselves. There can be no distinction between constituents of complexes and forms of complexes. Hence

> 2.011 It is essential to things that they should be possible constituents of states of affairs.

and

> 2.0121 If things can occur in a state of affairs, this possibility must be in them from the beginning.

and

> 2.014 Objects contain the possibility of all situations.

A state of affairs is a combination of objects, but it can only be a combination of objects that *can* be combined in that way. No sense can be made of a way of combining objects which does not take into account the objects that are to be combined in that way. Such a way of combining objects which is independent of the objects so to be combined would just be Russell's form of a complex, and it is clear that such an idea gets us nowhere. So, having distinguished between fact and complex, or between fact and state of affairs in proposition 2 of the *Tractatus* Wittgenstein goes on to tease out the consequences for the idea of a complex and its constituents *in the light of that distinction*. The first consequence we have already noticed. The idea of form belongs to the concept of an object since

> If things can occur in states of affairs, this possibility must be in them from the beginning. (2.0121)

It is not incidental to objects that there can be combinations of them. It is not that we are first of all given objects and then somehow notice that they can combine in certain ways. What we begin with is the fact that objects are combined in a certain way. If we begin with facts then we already know about possible combinations of objects. We are given possible combinations of objects just because we are first of all given facts. Given objects we are simultaneously given possible combinations of objects ie. we are simultaneously given the possible structures of complexes. If form is the possible structure of a complex then objects are not only the contents or constituents of complexes they are also the forms of complexes. They are, as Wittgenstein says, 'both form and content'.

Because Wittgenstein insists that objects are both form and content, ie. that their possible combination with other objects is in them from the beginning, it has sometimes seemed puzzling that he insists at 2.02 that 'objects are simple'. This comment, as the numbering system of the *Tractatus* makes clear, is the second major comment on proposition 2, where, as I am arguing, the distinction between fact and complex is first made. We have already seen how if, like Russell, we have not drawn that distinction, and think of facts as existing combinations of things, or existing complexes, the simplicity of objects would actually rule out of court the idea that objects themselves give us the possibility of the combinations in which they can occur. Form, on that view, cannot belong to the constituents of complexes. But, if like Wittgenstein, you have made the distinction between fact and complex then the possibility of being a constituent in a complex (the possibility of occurring in a state of affairs) *will be precisely what being simple consists in.* The line of thought that proposition 2 of the *Tractatus* and its corollaries present moves from the holding of states of affairs to states of affairs themselves and thence to the objects of which states of affairs are said to be combinations and then back to the holding of states of affairs once more. Wittgenstein's numbering system actually makes this clear. The first four major comments between proposition 2 and 2.1 read as follows.

> 2. What is the case – a fact – is the holding of states of affairs.
> 2.01 A state of affairs (a state of things) is a combination of objects.
> 2.02 Objects are simple.
> 2.03 In a state of affairs objects fit into one another like links of a chain.
> 2.04 The totality of obtaining states of affairs is the world.

This movement of thought is exactly the reverse of the movement of thought which Russell presented to us. Russell wished to begin with objects and end up with facts, ie. existing complexes, whereas Wittgenstein begins with facts and allows reflection upon facts to dictate the way in which we think about objects.

It is this distinction between fact and complex, between the holding of states of affairs and states of affairs themselves, which should settle once and for all the controversy which has raged ever since the publication of the *Tractatus* about the nature of its objects.

It has been a commonplace among commentators on the *Tractatus* to point out that Wittgenstein gives us no examples of objects, and because of that no examples of elementary propositions either. For example David Pears in a book on Wittgenstein published in 1971 writes:

> It is mystifying to introduce elementary propositions without explaining what they are. But there is a real difficulty here. Wittgenstein did not claim to be able to give any examples of elementary propositions, because he thought that neither he nor any philosopher had yet got down to the ultimate components of factual propositions. (Pears, 1971, p. 59)

Three years later Anthony Kenny in his book on Wittgenstein wrote in much the same vein.

> We are given no information in the *Tractatus* as to what kind of things simple objects are ... It is not even clear whether the simples would be particular individuals or universal types ... But this lack of clarity accords with Wittgenstein's insistence that it is only *a priori* that he knows of the existence of simples, not that he can give any examples. (Kenny, 1974, p. 85)

The controversy, as David Pears points out, has been about the validity of two entirely opposed views about the nature of objects in the *Tractatus*. The one view holds that it makes sense to ask for examples of objects even though Wittgenstein does not himself provide us with any examples. The extreme version of this is the Hintikkas' view that they turn out in the end to be the same as Russell's viz. sense-data. The other associated with Hide Ishiguro, Cora Diamond and Brian

McGuinness denies that this makes sense. Now it should be clear that the distinction between fact and complex, which I have argued is made in proposition 2 of the *Tractatus*, should make us come down decisively in favour of the second interpretation.

BIBLIOGRAPHY OF WORKS CITED

Bloch, I., 1981. *Perspectives on the Philosophy of Wittgenstein* (Oxford, Blackwell).

Kenny, A., 1974. *Wittgenstein* (London, Allen Lane the Penguin Press).

Malcolm, N., 1986. *Wittgenstein: Nothing is Hidden* (Oxford, Basil Blackwell).

Monk, R., 1990. *Ludwig Wittgenstein: The Duty of Genius* (London, Jonathan Cape).

Pears, D. F., 1971. *Wittgenstein* (London, Fontana/ Collins).

Russell, B., 1956. *Logic and Knowledge,* ed. by R. C. Marsh (London, George Allen and Unwin).

—— 1984. *The Collected Papers of Bertrand Russell,* vol. 7, ed. by J. G. Slater (London, George Allen and Unwin).

—— 1986. *The Collected Papers of Bertrand Russell,* vol. 8, ed. by J. G. Slater (London, George Allen and Unwin).

Wittgenstein, L., 1969. *1914–1916 Notebooks,* ed. by G. H. Von Wright and G. E. M. Anscombe (Oxford, Blackwell).

—— 1961. *Tractatus Logico-Philosophicus*, trans. by D. F. Pears and B. F. McGuinness (London, Routledge and Kegan Paul).

—— 1975. *Philosophical Remarks,* ed. by R. Rhees, trans. by R. Hargreaves and R. White (Oxford, Basil Blackwell).

Stenius, E., 1960. *Wittgenstein's Tractatus: A Critical Exposition of its Main Lines of Thought* (Oxford, Basil Blackwell).

BEGINNING WITH ANALYSIS[1]

Peter Hylton
University of Illinois

In a book published in 1900, based on a series of lectures given in the previous year, Russell says: 'That all sound philosophy should begin with an analysis of propositions, is a truth too evident, perhaps, to demand a proof' (Russell, 1937a, p. 8). Like many appeals to self-evidence (or, in more recent jargon, to 'intuition'), this is a highly tendentious assertion. It suggests that the ideas of a proposition and of analysis are obvious and straightforward notions, which can thus serve as a starting point of philosophy. These views have had significant influence in the subsequent development of analytic philosophy – as the very name of that tradition suggests. The idea of a proposition, and of the analysis of propositions, has often been treated as if they were quite uncontroversial, no more than common sense. This attitude, I think, is quite wrong. Any given conception of propositions and analysis, is in fact inextricably tangled in metaphysics. The idea of 'finding and analysing the proposition expressed' by a given sentence is one that makes sense only within a given

[1] This essay overlaps a significantly shorter essay published under the title 'Russell: Propositions and Analysis', in *Proceedings of the 1994 International Wittgenstein Symposium* (Vienna, Hoelder-Pichler-Tempsky Verlag, 1995), ed. Klaus Puhl. I am grateful to the editor and to the publishers of that volume for permission to publish an overlapping essay.

philosophical context, which imposes constraints on the process; the philosophical context cannot itself, therefore, be based on a neutral or uncontroversial notion of analysis.

My thesis is thus a very general claim about the role of propositions and analysis in analytic philosophy. My subject, of course, is much narrower, and can only suggest the plausibility of the thesis. What I shall chiefly discuss are Russell's changing views about propositions, and also the correlative idea of analysis, in the period, roughly, from 1900 to 1914. Those views illustrate my thesis with great clarity, because Russell seldom completely covers up or smooths over the difficulties which face his view at any given time; he simply treats them as problems to be solved, and moves on. His views change quite markedly over time, because at each point he encounters difficulties which require shifts, which in turn throw up further difficulties, so that a stable view remains as remote at the end as at the beginning. It is not that there is a knock-down argument against any of Russell's views, or that his views are in any very straightforward sense incoherent; it is rather that in Russell's hands the notion of a proposition simply begins to collapse of its own weight.

I shall start by talking about the notion of a proposition very generally, and then about the views that Russell puts forward in *The Principles of Mathematics*; (Russell, 1937b) later Russellian doctrines will emerge as we go.

It should strike us as noteworthy that each of Frege and Russell has as central to his thought the idea of an abstract entity which represents, or perhaps *is*, the content of a declarative sentence. For Russell, of course, this is the notion of a proposition; for Frege it is that of a *Gedanke*. Part of the reason for this may be that both Frege and Russell were mathematicians, and began their serious philosophical careers by attempting to give an account of mathematics, where the idea of the abstract content of a sentence seems to be at home.[2] As W. D. Hart puts it: 'Frege ... may have drawn on his mathematical education for some of his philosophical ideals. The theorem is an ideal of mathematical statement. It is typically a single sentence meant to be strong enough to stand by itself: what it says should be impersonal, unambiguous and impervious to context; above all, it should be true utterly without qualification' (Hart, 1990, p. 199). Although my focus is on Russellian propositions, I shall mention points of contrast with Fregean *Gedanken*. The fact that these contrasts exist, and are significant, suggests that articulating what may seem to be the commonsensical notion of the content of a declarative sentence is by no means a straightforward task.

As a first step in articulating the notion of a proposition we may say that it is to be an abstract entity which is, so to speak, like a sentence only more so. The properties of a proposition are to be those properties which might be thought to characterize declarative sentences, except that where a sentence has those properties in a messy or unclear way, the proposition has them in a purified form. Truth or falsehood is the most obvious of these properties. Declarative sentences, one might suppose, are what have truth-values. But a declarative sentence may be vague or ambiguous, and so of uncertain truth-value; it may be true only approxi-

---

[2] I do not, of course, want to claim that *only* a mathematician could have had the idea of the content of a sentence as an independent abstract entity. Indeed Russell attributes it to Moore (see the Preface to *The Principles of Mathematics*; and see Moore's 'The Nature of Judgement', *Mind*, 1898, pp. 176–93). It is, however, in the context of views about mathematics that this conception of a proposition seems most natural, and most powerful.

mately, or to some extent; it may change its truth value from one occasion of utterance to the next. A proposition, by contrast, is true or false eternally and without qualification. It is, we might say, a bearer of truth-values suitable for the theorems of mathematics. Similarly, a sentence is the object of understanding, but may be misunderstood, or only more or less understood. A proposition, by contrast, if grasped, is grasped completely. The metaphor of grasping here is Frege's. Russell, as we shall see, speaks of being acquainted with a proposition or – slightly later – of being acquainted with the constituents of the proposition and uniting them into a judgement by means of a mental act of judging. The point, however, is the same: the vagueness and unclarity which we might associate with understanding sentences is replaced by a definite, clear-cut, all-or-nothing idea. So sentences come to be seen as simply the more or less defective expressions of propositions, abstract entities which are the real bearers of content and vehicles of truth-values; propositions lie behind our sentences, and give them such meaning as they have.

One immediate presupposition of the idea of a proposition is that we can usefully and significantly talk of a proposition as an entity, which may be considered in isolation. This is a sort of atomism of sentences or propositions: that a sentence conveys what it conveys as a discrete unit, independent of the discourse with which it is surrounded. Taken as a quite general claim about sentences, this seems to me quite implausible. It is, of course, open to someone to claim that this sort of atomism holds of propositions, even though it does not hold of sentences. I shall not, however, try to argue these points here; my focus will be on issues more relevant to Russell's attempt to find a conception of the proposition which would satisfy him.

To this point I have been talking about the origin of the idea of a proposition as a sort of abstract super-sentence. And just as sentences have a grammatical structure, so propositions too, at least on Russell's conception, have a structure. A proposition, as Russell conceives the notion, contains constituent parts; it consists, indeed, of certain constituents in a certain, definite arrangement.[3] He seems, indeed, to think of a proposition as made up of its constituents in a quite literal sense, almost as a wall is made up of bricks. Now one crucial point about Russell's conception of propositions in *The Principles of Mathematics* is that he assumes that in most cases the structure of a proposition very closely reflects the structure of the sentence which expresses it. Thus in section 46 of *Principles* he says, for example:

> The correctness of our philosophical analysis of a proposition may be checked by the exercise of assigning the meaning of each word in the sentence expressing the proposition. On the whole, grammar seems to bring us much nearer to a correct logic than the current opinions of philosophers....

---

[3] There is a contrast here even with Frege, whose views are close to Russell on these matters. A Fregean *Gedanke* does not appear to consist of definite constituents in a definite arrangement. Frege is not wholly consistent on this point, but he sometimes puts forward the view that a *Gedanke* can be analysed in different ways, equally correct. Thus the *Gedanke* expressed by a subject-predicate sentence (or perhaps by a given utterance of the sentence) might on one occasion by analysed as made up of the sense of a proper name and the sense of a first-level predicate, and on another occasion as made up of the sense of a first-level predicate and the sense of a second-level predicate. On this view, to ask: but which are the real constituents of the *Gedanke*? would be to ask a misleading question. Thus Frege says explicitly: 'We must notice, however, that one and the same thought (*Gedanke*) can be split up in different ways and so can be seen as put together out of parts in different ways.' – 'A Brief Survey of my Logical Doctrines', in *Posthumous Writings*, ed. H. Hermes, et al. (Oxford, Blackwell, 1979), pp. 201–202.

A potential problem here is seen in the phrase '*the sentence*' expressing a given proposition. Russell individuates propositions extremely finely, but even on his view a given proposition can be expressed by more than one sentence. Nothing rules out the possibility that one proposition should be expressed by two sentences with different grammatical structures. And what then of the assumption that the structure of a proposition is more or less isomorphic to that of the sentence which expresses it? At the time of *Principles*, however, this problem does not seem to occur to Russell; on his later view, as we shall see, the problem does not arise, because he abandons the assumption that there is generally an isomorphism between a sentence and the proposition which it expresses.

Let us now take up another fundamental feature of Russellian propositions, which is shared by Fregean *Gedanke*. Even from our brief sketch, it is clear that propositions are context-independent; they do not depend for their content or their truth-values upon their context of utterance. Indeed this feature is so fundamental that the way I expressed it is misleading. A proposition, as an abstract entity, *has* no context of utterance. A more accurate way to put the point is that Russell assumes that our utterances are not propositions, vehicles of content and bearers of truth-values, which are abstract, independent of context. A sentence which expresses a given proposition is spoken or written in a given context, and may express the proposition that it expresses only because of that context; but nothing analogous can be said of propositions themselves.

The sentences of mathematics, as we have seen, seem to lend themselves naturally to Russell's way of thinking: it is not hard to see how one might take such a sentence as expressing a content which is eternal, context-independent, and free of the contingencies of our means of expressing it. This is true also of theoretical sentences of the more abstract natural sciences. But such sentences are more the exception than the rule. Very few of the sentences that we actually utter say what they say, and have the truth-values that they have, independent of the contexts in which they are uttered. Most are dependent for their contents and their truth-values upon their contexts of utterance. This is most obviously true of sentences containing so-called indexical or token-reflexive expressions, such as 'I', 'here', 'now', and 'this'; sentences containing such expressions are obviously dependent, for their truth-values, upon the identity of the utterer and the time and place and circumstances of utterance. Sentences of this sort are sometimes treated by philosophers as a sort of oddity, but in fact they account for most of the sentences actually uttered. The phenomenon of indexicality, however, is more widespread than our examples perhaps suggest. Clearly sentences containing tensed verbs also fall under this heading; so do sentences containing proper names, for many people may share a single name, with uses of the name being disambiguated by the context of utterance.

The phenomenon of indexicality has often been treated as posing special difficulties or puzzles, or at any rate as requiring discussion additional to that afforded the general nature of language. This is one aspect of the influence that the notion of a proposition has had on much subsequent analytic philosophy. Context-independent utterances are in fact quite unusual, especially in the spoken language. Yet very often that type of utterance is, so to speak, treated as the norm, so that deviations from it are what require special explanation and treatment.   In particular, the issue is often one of finding a systematic way of representing the context-dependent as context-independent, ie. finding systematic rules to indicate what context-independent contents our context-dependent sentences in fact express.   The assumption here is that each of our sentences can be thought of as expressing a context-independent content, and perhaps also that we only fully understand the workings of a sentence when we see how to convert it into a context-independent equivalent.

There are, however, arguments which suggest that except in quite special cases the notion of the content of a sentence cannot be peeled off from the context of utterance of the sentence; consideration of these arguments will lead us to a feature of Russellian propositions which we have not yet mentioned, a feature which also distinguishes them from Fregean *Gedanke*. These arguments, at least in the form that I shall discuss them, are to be found in the work of F. H. Bradley,[4] the idealist against whom much of Russell's polemic is directed.   Although the point can be made more generally, I shall indicate how the argument goes by talking about sentences that make reference to particular parts of time.   The claim here is that such sentences are in fact dependent for their meaning and their truth-value on their contexts of utterance, even if they do not contain any overtly indexical expressions.

Consider an example such as 'It is raining at Heathrow at 1600 GMT on 23 February, 1974'.   The sentence is Quine's, nearly enough, and it is intended as an example

---

[4]   See F. H. Bradley, *Principles of Logic* (Oxford, Oxford University Press, 1922; 1st edn. 1883), especially book 1, chapter 2; see also P. F. Strawson, *Individuals* (London, Methuen, 1959), especially chaps. 2 and 3.

of what Quine calls a standing sentence – one that is not dependent for its truth-value on the occasion of its utterance.[5] We have familiar ways of keeping track of the years: we say how many years have elapsed from some notable event, the accession of an emperor, perhaps, or the birth of a saviour. But how, from a more distant perspective, is that notable event itself to be located in time? Given that the same system is still in use, there is no problem, for we can locate the starting point indexically, relative to me-here-now: we begin our system of numbering years with a year which is one thousand nine hundred and ninety-three years before the year in which I am writing *this*. For the same reason, once the system is established it does not in fact matter if the given event did not take place in the year that is supposed – the system functions because it is in general use, not because of distant history. But if a given system were no longer in use, and if we did not know the relation of that system to the one we use, we should have to rely on a description of the event, and we have no guarantee that such a description would suffice to identify it uniquely.

Still, it may be said, the system that we have for keeping track of time is perfectly adequate. Given not only its intended audience, but anyone who is ever at all likely to read it, surely Quine's sentence will do perfectly well to convey what it conveys independent of time and circumstances of utterance. This is correct; for all human purposes, we can achieve context-independence. But it is far from clear that the qualification, 'for all human purposes', is one that we can assume when talking about Russellian propositions, for these are

[5] W. V. Quine, 'The Nature of Natural Knowledge', in *Mind and Language*, ed. Samuel Gutenplan (Oxford, Oxford University Press, 1975), pp. 67–81; see especially p. 75.

abstract eternal entities, altogether independent of human beings. By those standards, it may seem that any sentence referring to a particular part of time or of space is unavoidably context-dependent (nothing here counts against *Quine's* use of the notion of a standing sentence, which has no such metaphysical pretensions or ambitions as Russell's notion of a proposition).

The claim that this argument points towards is that *none* of our sentences, except perhaps for the abstract sentences of mathematics and theoretical science, are in fact context-independent. But then how can we think of the notion of content, in such a way that it avoids these difficulties? The argument suggests that we cannot, and hence that for most sentences it is incoherent to think in terms of the content of the sentence, as something that can be wholly abstracted from the context in which the sentence is used, and treated as an independent abstract object.

Now in *The Principles of Mathematics* the notion of a proposition which Russell takes as paradigmatic is in fact not vulnerable to this sort of argument (whereas Frege's notion of a *Gedanke* may be). The crucial point here is that the entities which are the subject matter of the proposition are, on Russell's conception, paradigmatically, *contained* in the proposition. Thus the proposition expressed by the sentence 'Socrates is mortal' *contains* the actual person, Socrates. More to the point of the example used above, a proposition about some particular moment of time will contain that moment of time. Thus Russellian propositions are hybrid entities. On the one hand, they are, like Fregean *Gedanke*, abstract entities representing or embodying the content of a declarative sentence. On the other hand, unlike their Fregean analogues, these abstract entities can contain concrete entities, such as people and moments of time.

It is not explicit in what Russell says that he adopts this conception of a proposition, as an abstract entity which may contain concrete entities, in order to counter Bradley's argument.[6] It is, however, quite plausible that Russell designed his notion of a proposition to meet the threat of Bradley's argument. And a closely connected, more general, anti-idealist point is explicit. On a Fregean conception, which has become widely accepted, propositions or their analogues contain entities (*Sinne*, for Frege) other than the objects they are about; they are about those objects in virtue of some relation which their constituents stand in to them. We might generically call this relation *designation*.[7] On Russell's conception, however, propositions paradigmatically do not contain ideas or senses which in some way designate the reality that the proposition is about; the proposition itself contains that reality, and does not merely designate it. It is clear that Russell is deeply distrustful of the idea of designation. Thus he holds that in grasping a proposition the mind is in direct contact with the entities that it thinks or speaks about. Intermediate entities, such as Fregean *Sinne*, would be a denial of this direct contact; for Russell, however, it is only our being in direct contact with entities outside the mind that makes it possible to speak or think of them at all.[8]

---

[6] In G. E. Moore's early work it is clear that his analogue of the notion of a proposition, which was an important influence on Russell, evolves out of disagreement with Bradley. It is, however, not explicit that the disagreement is at the point relevant to my discussion here. See Moore's 'The Nature of Judgment', *Mind*, 1898.

[7] Frege uses the word *bedeuten*; there are, however, great difficulties in Frege's philosophy with the view that there is some *one* relation here.

[8] See the exchange of letters with Frege, Frege to Russell, 13 November, 1904, Russell to Frege, 12 December. Published in Frege, *Nachgelassene*

According to *The Principles of Mathematics*, then, propositions paradigmatically have two fundamental features. First, a proposition will, in general, have the same structure as the sentence expressing it. We noted one problem here, arising from the possibility that two sentences of different structures may express the same proposition. A further issue concerns the qualification 'in general'. Russell holds back from saying that the normal case is universal; what sorts of factors could justify departing from the norm? The answer to this question is by no means clear. The second fundamental feature is, to put it negatively, the denial of designation: that propositions, at least paradigmatically, do not contain entities (such as Fregean *Sinne*) which *designate* the things they are about; propositions, rather, *contain* those things. The paradigm of a proposition is that expressed by 'Socrates is mortal'. This proposition has exactly the structure of the sentence. Also it contains Socrates, and the property of mortality. A crucial consequence of the denial of designation is that for Russell at this point there is no independent notion of a *fact*: since the proposition that Socrates is mortal contains Socrates and the property of mortality, it simply *is* the fact that Socrates is mortal. Facts, for Russell, are true propositions. It follows immediately from this that we cannot explain what it is for a proposition to be true by appealing to the holding of a corresponding fact, or indeed in any other way. Truth and falsehood are for Russell (as for Moore and for Frege) 'incapable of analysis' (Russell, 1904, p. 76); this point, as we shall

Schriften und wissenschafliche Briefwechsel, vol. 2 (Hamburg, Felix Meiner, 1976); and translated in Frege, *Philosophical and Mathematical Correspondence* (Oxford, Blackwell, 1980). See also Russell's 'Knowledge By Acquaintance and Knowledge By Description', in *Mysticism and Logic* (New York, Longmans, Green and Co., 1918), pp. 221–2.

see, comes to play an important role in Russell's finally abandoning the doctrine of propositions (see below pp. 210–11).

This kind of paradigm seems to make the notion of a proposition quite straightforward and attractive. Even at the time of writing *Principles*, however, Russell could see that it would not work in general. It is a paradigm that exerts great influence, but it cannot be universally applied. What works well for sentences such as 'Socrates is mortal' does not seem to work at all for the sentence 'I met a man', as Russell himself points out. Suppose the sentence is true; I did meet a man – Quine, let us say. Still 'I met a man' does not seem to say the same as 'I met Quine', so it ought not to express the same proposition. Worse, suppose the sentence is false, that I did not meet a man. False sentences too ought to express propositions, but clearly if I did not meet a man there is no one who even seems to be a good candidate for being the constituent of the proposition corresponding to the words 'a man'. In short, the sentence 'I met a man' seems absolutely to resist assimilation to the paradigm mentioned above. How then can Russell treat such sentences? The answer is in Russell's notion of *denoting*, and the theory of denoting concepts, a theory articulated in *Principles* and subsequently rejected in 'On Denoting'. A *denoting concept* is an entity with the following useful and agreeable property: when it occurs in a proposition, the proposition is not about it (the denoting concept), but rather about some other entity, that denoted by the denoting concept. Thus in the case of the sentence 'I met a man', the words 'a man' correspond to a constituent of the proposition, but that constituent is not Quine or any other man. It is, rather, the denoting concept *a man*, which denotes a curious sort of disjunctive combination of all men. This entity is stipulated to have exactly the properties needed to yield the required result, that the proposition is true if I met at least one man, and false if I met no men.

In general Russell holds that the presence in a sentence of any description, ie. any phrase formed with 'a' or 'the' or 'all' or 'any' or 'some' or 'every', indicates the presence, in the corresponding proposition, of a denoting concept. It is perhaps an advantage of this theory that it enables us, in general, to preserve the idea of the isomorphism of structure between sentence and proposition: a phrase such as 'a man' or 'every man' corresponds to a constituent of the proposition, namely the relevant denoting concept. There are also, however, drawbacks to the theory. One is its formidable complexity, and the vexing philosophical difficulties which it seems to throw up at every turn. In some cases these difficulties result in an undermining of the isomorphism of structure between sentence and proposition: thus Russell distinguishes two propositions which may be expressed by 'Socrates is a man', namely that more accurately expressed by 'Socrates is a-man', and that more accurately expressed by 'Socrates is-a man' (see *Principles of Mathematics*, p. 54, second footnote).

A second, more obvious, drawback to Russell's theory of denoting concepts is of course that the theory of denoting concepts relies on the idea of designation which Russell's paradigmatic conception of the proposition avoided; indeed we might almost say that 'denotation' is just another word for designation. It is this, I think, that lies behind many of the philosophical problems that Russell has with denoting; in particular it is at work in his arguments against the notion in 'On Denoting'.

Russell introduces the theory of denoting concepts to extend his conception of propositions so that it covers cases which do not seem to fit his paradigm. He also uses it in response to another issue, which plays little role in his thought at first, but later comes to dominate it. This issue we might broadly call epistemological. The primary focus here is not so much on how we can *know* this or that proposition, but rather on how we can *understand* propositions. I call the issue epistemo-logical, even though it is not directly concerned with knowledge, because it is concerned not with what propositions there are, or what they are like, but with our relation to them.

Russell's fundamental epistemic relation – the means by which, on his view, the mind can escape from its own boundaries – is *acquaintance*, a relation of direct and presuppositionless contact between the mind and objects outside it. Clearly to say we are acquainted with things does not explain how the mind escapes its own bound-aries, it simply asserts that it does. But that's the point. For Russell there can be no complexity to our contact with outside things, no story to be told: we simply are in contact with them, and that's that. It is not a defect but a virtue of acquaintance that there is nothing more to be said about it beyond the little I have indicated. Now in *The Principles of Mathematics* Russell pays very little attention to issues of knowledge and under-standing. He seems, however, to presuppose that to understand a proposition is to be acquainted with it, and thus with its constituents.

This view of understanding is in tension with the conception of propositions that we have discussed. It seems to be true that I understand the proposition expressed by 'Socrates is mortal', and on Russell's account this proposition contains Socrates. According to his inchoate view of understanding, it would follow that I am acquainted with Socrates. As soon as one considers such a claim carefully it is likely to seem quite implausible, so that there must be something wrong with the theory that implies it. In *The Principles of Mathematics*, however, Russell's attention is elsewhere, and this sort of fact does not seem to worry him. At that time he seems to accept that we are acquainted with Socrates, and with the King of France, and with anything else that one can mention (later, as we shall see, he focuses more on such issues, and takes a narrower view of the objects of acquaintance). In one instance, however, Russell does give careful consideration to the question of our ability to understand. This instance is the case of propositions about infinitely many objects, eg. the false proposition expressed by 'All prime numbers are odd'. If we were to construe this proposition according to the Russellian paradigm, it would contain all the prime numbers, ie. it would be a proposition of infinite complexity. Russell is agnostic about the question whether there *are* such propositions, but he does say that, in any case, we are not acquainted with any: 'all the propositions known to us', he says, 'are of finite complexity' (*Principles of Mathematics*, p. 145). How, then, does Russell account for our ability to understand the proposition that all prime numbers are odd? The answer is that he invokes the theory of denoting concepts. Our false proposition about the primes does not contain all of the prime numbers, and does not need to. What it contains in their place, so to speak, is the denoting concept *all prime numbers*. In virtue of containing this denoting concept, the proposition is about all the primes. And this idea can be used to explain how we can understand the proposition. It may be implausible to suppose that I am acquainted with each of the prime numbers, but it is open to Russell to claim that I *am* acquainted with the denoting concept,

all prime numbers (indeed one of the advantages of
denoting concepts is that it is open to Russell to claim
almost anything about them).

In the period immediately after *The Principles of
Mathematics* issues of understanding come to be increasingly prominent in Russell's writings. This can be seen
most clearly in a number of works which he left unpublished – perhaps because he found no theory of such
matters which satisfied him even for a short period. In
the manuscript 'On Meaning and Denotation', written
when Arthur Balfour was Prime Minister of England,
Russell says that the two phrases 'Arthur Balfour' and
'the present Prime Minister of England' in some ways
function the same: each can be used to talk about a
certain man. In other ways, however, he says there is a
significant difference between the two phrases:

> When we make a statement about Arthur Balfour, he
> himself forms part of the object before our minds, ie.
> of the proposition stated ... no one who does not
> know what is the designation of the name 'Arthur
> Balfour' can understand what we *mean*: the object of
> our thought cannot, by our statement, be conveyed to
> him. But when we say 'the present Prime Minister of
> England believes in retaliation', it is possible for a
> person to understand us completely without his
> knowing that Mr. Arthur Balfour is Prime Minister,
> and indeed without his even having heard of Mr
> Arthur Balfour. (fn. 3)

Perhaps even more striking in this regard is the earlier
manuscript, 'Points About Denoting'. Here Russell
distinguishes the meaning of a proposition from its
denotation: the meaning of the proposition that the
Prime Minister of England in 1904 advocates retaliation would contain a denoting concept which denotes

Balfour; the denotation of the proposition would contain Balfour himself. Using this distinction, Russell very clearly articulates what I shall call *the principle of acquaintance*: 'It is necessary, for the understanding of a prop[osition], to have *acquaintance* with the *meaning* of every constituent of the meaning, and of the whole; it is not necessary to have acquaintance with such constituents of the denotation as are not constituents of the meaning' (fn. 6).

The manuscripts from which the above passages are drawn cannot be dated precisely, but internal evidence shows that they were written after *The Principles of Mathematics* and before 'On Denoting', ie. while Russell held the theory of denoting concepts. What they clearly indicate is that during this period Russell increasingly subjected the analysis of propositions to epistemological constraints: roughly, it became an explicit and self-conscious criterion of an acceptable analysis that it show that the proposition is made up of constituents with which we are acquainted. Putting it this way may be misleading, because it makes it sound as if the notion of *acquaintance* which we are invoking is itself fixed and clear-cut, whereas in fact this notion is no firmer than is the notion of the analysis of propositions. The principle of acquaintance is articulated – for the first time in Russell's work, as far as I know – in the manuscript 'Points About Denoting'. It is not, however, a fixed and definite principle which Russell denied until that time, and then began to accept for some reason. There is probably no time, during the period we are concerned with, at which Russell would have *denied* the principle. What changes is that Russell becomes increasingly interested in epistemological questions. He articulates the principle, and begins to use it to determine how propositions are to be analysed (or, more accurately, what proposition we may take a given sentence to express). Whereas in *Principles* Russell had been willing to accept that we are acquainted with almost anything, he later takes an increasingly stringent view of the objects of acquaintance. This is not a sudden change, but takes place gradually over the ten or more years following the completion of *Principles*.

What is crucial about this from our point of view is that the epistemological constraint which the principle of acquaintance embodies, and especially the notion of acquaintance itself, cannot be the *result* of analysis. They are, rather, requirements imposed from the outside on that notion. Once imposed they drastically affect what counts as a satisfactory analysis, and hence also what propositions are like, ie. they function as constraints upon the notions of a proposition and of analysis. At any given moment Russell tends to take a given group of constraints for granted, and speak as if analysis were a neutral process; but the way the constraints shift makes it clear that this is not so.

Russell only briefly explores his increasing epistemological concerns in the context of the theory of denoting concepts. 'On Denoting', written in 1905, rejects that theory in favour of a quite different view. Before we discuss that development, however, it is worth noting that the shift to the view of 'On Denoting' is neither necessary nor sufficient for this increasing concern with epistemology. If Russell had not made that shift, his new concerns would have led, rather, to an increasing application of the theory of denoting concepts. A sentence such as Russell's 'Arthur Balfour advocates retaliation' is in fact understood by those who are not (in Russell's sense) acquainted with Balfour; so surely Russell would have come to the view that most proper names stand not for their bearers but for denoting concepts (indeed

Russell does explicitly take this step in the case of proper names which fail to name anything).[9] This kind of development – the increasing epistemic constraints imposed on the analysis of propositions – would presumably have continued. If so it would have led him to see denoting no longer as the exception, introduced to account for a relatively small number of particularly troubling sentences, but as the usual case. The paradigm of a proposition containing the object which it is about, a paradigm which exercised great influence on Russell in *Principles* was being undermined by epistemic considerations in the period before 'On Denoting'. Russell's increasing epistemic concerns led him to rely more heavily on the theory of denoting concepts. The reliance on the theory of denoting concepts, however, is also, as we pointed out, a reliance on designation: the denoting concept denotes (or designates) its object. This by itself provides Russell with a reason to be suspicious of the theory of denoting concepts, and this suspicion is a crucial part of the background to the rejection of that theory in 'On Denoting'.

There are, of course, other factors at work in 'On Denoting'. One is simply the internal difficulties of the theory of denoting concepts as Russell attempted to articulate and develop it. These difficulties may be traced out in unpublished manuscripts in the period leading up to 'On Denoting', and issue in a notoriously complex and difficult argument in that essay. Another factor is the need to come up with an analysis of propositions which meshes in the right way with the logic

---

[9]   See 'The Existential Import of Propositions', *Mind*, vol. 14 ns (July 1905), pp. 398–401; reprinted in Bertrand Russell, *Essays in Analysis*, ed. Lackey (New York, George Braziller, 1973), pp. 98–102. See especially p. 100 in Lackey.

that Russell had developed. It ought, one might think, to follow *by logic* from the proposition that John is the man who broke the bank at Monte Carlo that someone broke the bank at Monte Carlo, that if James is distinct from John then James did *not* break the bank at Monte Carlo, and so on. If we analyse propositions using the theory of denoting concepts, however, these inferences are obscure, and do not appear to be a matter of logic at all. The analysis put forward in 'On Denoting', by contrast, makes them straightforward inferences in (what we would call) first-order logic with identity. So here, then, is another constraint on analysis: that it ought, as far as possible, to assimilate obviously correct inferences to valid inference patterns of logic.

Clearly there is a great deal more that could be said about Russell's reasons for making the change from the theory of denoting concepts to the view put forward in 'On Denoting'. I shall not, however, discuss this matter any more here.[10] More relevant to our concerns is the fact that according to the method of analysis put forward in 'On Denoting' most propositions have a structure which is very unlike the grammatical structure of the sentences which are usually used to express those propositions. Russell now completely rejects the isomorphism between sentence and proposition which *Principles* had assumed as the usual case, if not the invariable rule. Thus take the sentence which in our earlier discussion functioned as a paradigm of such isomorphism: 'Socrates is mortal'. When Russell comes to apply the method of analysis implicit in 'On Denoting' to (ordinary) proper names, he draws the conclusion that this sentence does *not* express a subject-

---

[10] For some discussion on this matter, see the present author's *Russell, Idealism, and the Emergence of Analytic Philosophy* (Oxford, Oxford University Press, 1990), chapter 6, especially pp. 249–54.

predicate proposition. It expresses, rather, a proposition whose large-scale structure is that of an existential quantification. This is a striking result. The structure of a sentence is no longer to be taken as a guide to the structure of the underlying proposition. On the contrary: Russell's work from this point on is full of warnings that the superficial structure of language is misleading, and does *not* reflect the underlying structure. There is thus a sort of dialectic. The idea of a proposition having a structure is clearly drawn from the fact that sentences have structure; a proposition is initially conceived of as having a structure isomorphic with that of the sentence which expresses it, the ontological composition of the proposition mirroring the semantic composition of the sentence. But then it is claimed that most or all of our actual sentences do not in fact succeed in reflecting the real structure of the proposition; this real structure becomes something hidden, which we try to find.

This development highlights one presupposition of the idea of philosophical analysis, as we find it in Russell (and in Moore, and in many others). That idea requires not merely that propositions be articulated, that they have a certain structure, but also that this structure may be reflected, more or less accurately, by sentences which express that proposition. It makes clear sense to say of a sentence that it contains an existential quantifier, say. It is, however, far less clear what could be meant by saying that a proposition, an abstract entity, contains a quantifier. Yet Russell must be able to say such things. The claim of Russell's theory of descriptions – 'that paradigm of philosophy' in the words of Ramsey, in a description endorsed by Moore (Ramsey, 1931, p. 263) – is not merely that for certain purposes it may be *convenient* to rewrite definite descriptions according to a certain protocol, say, to make sure that within a given formal language we are never left with names that fail to refer. The claim is, rather, that propositions expressed by sentences containing definite descriptions *actually have* a structure which is accurately, or more accurately, expressed by the rewritten version. This rewritten version is itself, of course, a sentence, and a sentence which draws on the resources of (what we would call) first-order logic with identity. And of course the claim is that such propositions always *did* have that structure, even before the discovery of first-order logic. This no doubt accounts in part for the confidence, even arrogance, that one sometimes finds in Russell's writings: only now, after centuries of confusion, do we have the tools which enable us to discover the real structures underlying our discourse.

The aim of philosophical analysis, seen in this light, is to find that sentence which most accurately reflects the real structure of the proposition that we are interested in. We can illustrate this conception of analysis by talking briefly about Moore's so-called paradox of analysis. The paradox is roughly this: in analysing a sentence, we simply pass from one sentence expressing a proposition to another sentence expressing the same proposition. If the first sentence really did express the proposition, surely this transition cannot represent philosophical progress. Yet – and this is where the paradox comes – there *does* seem to be philosophical progress, at least in some cases of analysis. Now the answer which our framework suggests is that we are not, in general, aware of the structure of the proposition that we grasp; and that one sentence which expresses a proposition may correspond more closely to the structure of the proposition than another sentence which expresses the same proposition. Then philosophical progress consists in passing from a sentence which does not reflect the structure of the underlying proposition, or does so only very loosely, to a sentence which comes closer to reflecting that structure, or even to one that is completely isomorphic to it. It may be a discovery to find the structure of the proposition which a given sentence expresses. What is actually discovered, or produced, however, is a new sentence, which is claimed to reflect the structure of the underlying proposition. The point to emphasize is thus that all of this depends upon the idea that a proposition has a structure, and that a *sentence* can reflect that structure more or less closely. Yet if propositions really are abstract entities, they are completely unlike sentences; so a crucial assumption is made when we assume that a sentence may reflect the structure of a proposition.

This idea of underlying structure, of the deep structure that backs up and makes possible the sentences we utter, has had a formative influence on philosophy – and, indeed, on linguistics – since Russell. Certainly this idea can be found, at least in a limited context, in Frege. In Russell, however, we see the idea full blown and quite generally applied. As Wittgenstein says in the *Tractatus*, in a passage that seems to allude to the theory of descriptions: 'Russells Verdienst ist es, gezeigt zu haben, dass die schienbare logische Form des Satzes nicht seine wirchliche muss' (*Tractatus* 4.0031: It is Russell's service to have shown that the apparent logical form of a proposition does not have to be its real one).

Although of fundamental importance, this idea of philosophical analysis is also very problematic. The obvious problem is that what we actually have to deal with are not propositions but utterances of sentences. If we cannot assume that the proposition expressed by a sentence has the same structure as the sentence itself, then we need some other guide to the structure of the proposition. If two philosophers consider a given sentence, and one says that its analysis is so-and-so, and the other says it is such-and-such, how can this dispute be settled? Saying that analysis is a process of finding a sentence which accurately reflects the structure of the underlying proposition is of no help, for each philosopher can claim to have done that. Russell, at least at certain points, would have claimed to be able to perceive the proposition, in some non-sensuous sense of perception (for this reason he would perhaps have disagreed with the statement that what we actually have to deal with are not propositions but utterances of sentences). But reliance on non-sensuous perception hardly recommends itself as a method of settling disputes, for each party can simply claim to 'perceive' the given proposition as having the structure that he or she attributes to it. Clearly this will not help to settle any dispute about the real structure of the proposition.

I talk in this way of the dispute being unsettleable not from some dogma that every real question must be settleable, but rather because it emphasizes a crucial point. The idea of philosophical analysis – the process of trying to find the structure of the proposition that underlies a given sentence – is empty until some constraints are imposed upon it. We must have some idea of what constitutes a satisfactory analysis, some criterion of success, before the idea has any content at all. Thus for Russell, as we saw, one criterion of success came to be that a final analysis of a sentence should enable us to assimilate its behaviour in inference to established procedures of logic. A second criterion is that embodied in the principle of acquaintance: the analysis must show that a given proposition is made up only of constituents with which we are acquainted. As

Russell says at the end of 'On Denoting': 'in every proposition that we can apprehend (ie. not only those whose truth or falsehood we can judge of, but in all that we can think about) all the constituents are really entities with which we have immediate acquaintance' (Russell, 1905, p. 119). Russell there speaks of this as a *result* of the theory of descriptions, but this seems to me quite misleading; it is something more like the aim of the theory – the result being that the aim is indeed achieved, or anyway a step towards its achievement taken, at least to Russell's satisfaction. (In speaking of this as a criterion of the success of the analysis it is important also to bear in mind that it is not at all obvious or uncontroversial which entities we are in fact acquainted with, or even whether the idea of acquaintance is a sensible one at all. As we have seen, Russell changed his mind significantly and frequently on the question of just which entities we are acquainted with.)

The increasing weight given to the epistemic factor creates further difficulties for Russell. One is simply that as Russell interprets the notion of acquaintance after 1905, the principle of acquaintance embodies a demand that he cannot meet. It requires that any sentence I understand can be shown to express a proposition composed only of elements with which I am acquainted; as Russell becomes increasingly stringent in his account of the things we are acquainted with, this demand seems less and less plausible. A second point is perhaps even more troubling, for it threatens the motivation behind the idea of a proposition. I said that according to 'On Denoting' the sentence 'Socrates is mortal' expresses a proposition of existential form. But this is not quite accurate. According to Russell's view, when the Greek equivalent of the sentence was uttered by Socrates himself it presumably expressed a proposition of *subject-*

predicate form, a proposition of which Socrates himself is a constituent. For those of us not acquainted with Socrates, however, the sentence, as we have mentioned, expresses an existentially quantified proposition. More significantly, even for those of us now living, however, there is no one proposition that is expressed by the sentence. Which proposition it expresses will vary from person to person. For any given person, his or her utterance of the sentence will express a proposition containing constituents, in some way related to Socrates, with which the utterer is acquainted. Since different people are acquainted with different entities, it may be that no two of us express the same proposition when we utter the sentence.

This is a very remarkable conclusion. The notion of a proposition, as we saw at the outset, was to be an abstract entity which summed up the content of a sentence in a wholly impersonal and context-independent way. Part of the motivation for the notion comes from the idea that, as Frege puts it, there is not your Pythagorean Theorem and my Pythagorean Theorem, but simply *the* Pythagorean Theorem (Frege, 1984, p. 362). This still holds, on Russell's new view, for the theorems of mathematics, but it does not hold for much else. In the case of 'Socrates is mortal', for example, it *does* seem as if there is your proposition and my proposition. Russell has some work to do to explain how it can be that if you say 'Socrates is mortal' and I say 'Socrates is not mortal' we have in fact contradicted one another; and it is by no means obvious that he succeeds in giving a satisfactory explanation of this fact – yet it is this sort of fact which in some sense underlies the whole idea of the content of a declarative sentence which Russell's talk of propositions aims to articulate. Thus the epistemic constraints which give content to the notion of analysis, as Russell employs it, also threaten to undermine the intuitive foundation of the idea of a proposition.

Russell becomes increasingly sceptical about the existence of propositions, and finally concludes that there are no such things. The chief reasons for this, however, do not have to do with the issue just discussed but with points touched on earlier. We saw above that Russell's paradigmatic conception of a proposition, as containing the entities it is about, allows no room for a distinction between facts and true propositions: facts simply *are* true propositions on this conception. But propositions, of course, can be false as well as true; if facts are simply true propositions then we cannot explain the distinction between truth and falsehood in what might seem to be the most natural way, ie. by saying that true propositions express facts, and false ones do not. As we saw, indeed, Russell in 1904 thinks that we cannot *explain* the distinction between truth and falsehood at all: it must simply be taken for granted, as the starting point of explanations.

Even in 1904, the way that Russell expresses the indefinability of truth and falsehood, and the conclusions that he draws from it, suggest that it is a view about which he is deeply uneasy. Thus, as if hankering after an explanatory notion of a fact, he says: 'it *seems* to remain that, when a proposition is false, *something* does not subsist which would subsist if the proposition were true' (Russell, 1904, p. 75). And most strikingly, he says: 'this theory [ie. the view that truth and falsehood are undefinable] *seems* to leave our preference for truth a mere unaccountable prejudice.' And he concludes the essay by saying: 'as for the preference which most people ... feel in favour of true propositions, this must be based, apparently, upon an ultimate ethical proposition: "It is good to believe true propositions, and bad to believe false ones"' (*op. cit.*, p. 76). He adds a joke whose cleverness is unlikely to allay the unease he clearly feels about this position, saying of his ultimate ethical proposition: 'This proposition, it is to be hoped, its true; but if not, there is no reason to think that we do ill in believing it' (*loc. cit.*).

Even though Russell is here *advocating* the view that truth and falsehood are indefinable, one senses that he is not fully convinced; the consequences that he draws from it are, as he states them, simply too implausible, and he cannot get rid of the feeling that the truth of a true proposition is due to the existence (or subsistence) of something which would not exist if that proposition were false – ie. he cannot get rid of the feeling that there are (proposition-independent) facts, or entities which will play the same role.[11] He later expresses this worry in a way that connects with another theme we have mentioned: his increasing stringency about just what entities we are acquainted with. He begins, that is to say, to have doubts about whether we are in fact acquainted with propositions – in particular, with false propositions. Writing in 1913, for example, he says 'It seems plain that a false proposition is not itself an actual entity' (Russell, 1992, p. 109). What this indicates is a shift from a view which takes *proposition* as the fundamental notion of metaphysics to takes *fact* as fundamental. While the notion of a proposition was funda-

---

[11] It seems likely that Russell's inclination to think that there are *facts* which are independent of propositions – and, indeed, to take the notion of a fact as fundamental – was strengthened by his reading of the pragmatists. In particular, he used the notion of a fact to express his opposition to the pragmatist view of truth. See 'James's Conception of Truth', first published in the *Albany Review* for January 1908, and reprinted in Russell's *Philosophical Essays* (London, George Allen and Unwin, 1910; revised edition, 1966).

mental, it was merely a curiosity that some propositions, the true ones, are also called facts, while others are
not. But when the notion of a fact becomes fundamental, true propositions can be retained by equating
them with facts, but false propositions become
problematic, at best.

At some time between 1906 and 1910, then, Russell
abandons the idea that there are propositions in the
sense which he had previously advocated.[12] *Principia
Mathematica* makes free use of the notions of proposition and propositional function, and presupposes that
we can quantify over such entities; yet according to the
doctrine of that work there simply are no propositions.
Instead of the theory of propositions, Russell attempts
to develop the multiple relation theory of judgement,
according to which a belief is not a relation between a
mind and a proposition, but rather a relation between
a mind and various objects – exactly those objects
which, according to the old view, are the constituents of
the proposition. Here too he is confronted by
insuperable obstacles, which result in his abandoning
the book in which he had intended to set out the new
theory.[13]

I began this essay by claiming that the notion of a

---

[12] Russell's 'The Nature of Truth' (*Proceedings of the Aristotelian Society*,
1906–1907) puts forward an early version of the multiple relation theory
of judgment as a possible alternative to his earlier conception of propositions; Russell is there agnostic as to which view is the correct one. In 1910,
when Russell reprinted the essay in his *Philosophical Essays*, the first two
sections are published under the title 'the Monistic Theory of Truth'; the
third section, where the multiple relation theory had been expounded, is
replaced by a new essay 'On the Nature of Truth and Falsehood', in
which the earlier agnosticism is replaced by an advocacy of the multiple
relation theory. That theory is also advanced in the first volume of
Principia Mathematica (Cambridge, Cambridge University Press, 1910);
see especially pp. 43ff.

[13] *Theory of Knowledge.*

proposition, and the concomitant notion of analysis, should not be taken as uncontroversial or commonsensical notions, to be presupposed at the beginning of philosophical discussion. My attempt to sketch the development of Russell's notion of a proposition has been in service of this thesis. The idea that there are propositions, and that they can be analysed, already makes crucial philosophical assumptions. And the idea of analysis itself gets us nowhere until we put constraints upon the process. Even those who would agree with Russell about the importance of philosophical analysis might put different constraints on the process, and so come up with quite different results. Both the vindication of the process, and the constraints to be put on it, must be the result of philosophical thought. They are presuppositions of the process of philosophical analysis, and cannot themselves be justified by appeal to it. Whatever else philosophical analysis may be, it cannot be a *starting point* for philosophy.

These comments on philosophical analysis can be put in a broader context by contrasting Russell's views on the subject with those of his most distinguished living successor: Quine. Quine speaks of the definition of ordered pair, either by the method of Wiener or by that of Kuratowski, as a 'philosophical paradigm' (surely a conscious echo of Ramsey's comment on Russell's theory of descriptions). Right away we see a difference between Quine and Russell. Wiener's method is not the same as Kuratowski's. (According to the former, for example, the empty set is a member of a member of any ordered pair; not so according to the latter.) But then which method is correct? Which most closely reflects the underlying structure of propositions in which reference is made to ordered pairs? For Quine, unlike

Russell, these are misleading questions, better rejected than answered. The definition of ordered pair, he says,

> ... is paradigmatic of what we are most typically up to when in a philosophical spirit we offer an 'analysis' or an 'explication' of some hitherto inadequately formulated 'idea' or expression. We do not claim synonymy. We do not claim to make clear and explicit what the users of the unclear expression had in mind all along. We do not expose hidden meanings .... We fix on the particular functions of the unclear expression that make it worth troubling about, and then devise a substitute, clear and couched in terms to our liking, that fills these functions. Beyond those conditions of partial agreement, dictated by our interests and purposes, any traits of the explicans come under the head of 'don't-cares'. (Quine, 1960 pp. 258–9)

Quine's appeal to the definitions of Wiener and Kuratowski clearly represent a continuation of a trend that Russell, along with Frege, began: the use of technical methods in philosophy. What is striking, however, from the present point of view, is how the technical methods stand aloof from the philosophical disagreement. Quine uses Russell's analysis of definite descriptions. The technical method is the same, yet the philosophical purpose, the philosophical gloss, is about as different as it could be. From Quine's point of view, his version of, or substitute for, philosophical analysis is a way of preserving the insights of Russell and others without their excess metaphysical baggage. From the point of view of Russell, and indeed of many current authors, Quine has thrown out the baby with the bathwater. Who is correct is obviously not an issue that can be settled here. Indeed, one aim of this paper is to call into question the very idea of correctness as applied to such questions, or the idea that they can be settled. The methods that one might suppose could be employed to decide such questions, such as Russell's method of philosophical analysis, turn out to have philosophical presuppositions, and internal difficulties, which makes them far from neutral. It thus seems to me an evident truth that sound philosophy cannot hope to *begin* with an analysis of propositions.[14]

[14] I am indebted to Stewart Candlish, Thomas Ricketts and, especially, Burton Dreben for their comments on earlier versions of this essay.

BIBLIOGRAPHY OF WORKS CITED

Frege, G., 1984. *Collected Papers*, ed. by Brian McGuiness (Oxford, Blackwell), p. 362 ('Der Gedanke', translated as 'Thoughts').

Hart, W. D., 1990. 'Clarity', *The Analytic Tradition*, ed. by David Bell and Neil Cooper (Oxford, Basil Blackwell).

Quine, W. V. O., 1960. *Word and Object* (Cambridge, Mass., MIT Press).

Ramsey, F., 1931. *The Foundations of Mathematics and other Logical Essays* (London, Kegan Paul).

Russell, B., 1904. 'Meinong's Theory of Complexes and Assumptions', *Mind*, reprinted in D. Lackey, (ed.), *Essays in Analysis* (New York, George Brazillier, Inc., 1973).

—— 1905. 'On Denoting', *Mind*, reprinted in D. Lackey (ed.), *Essays and Analysis* (New York, George Brazillier, Inc.).

—— 1937a. *A Critical Exposition of the Philosophy of Leibniz* (London, George, Allen and Unwin, 1900; new edn., 1937), p. 8.

—— 1937b. *The Principles of Mathematics* (London, Allen and Unwin; 1st edn., 1903).

—— 1992. *Theory of Knowledge* (London, Routledge).

RUSSELL'S PERILOUS JOURNEY FROM ATOMISM TO HOLISM 1919–1951[1]

Francisco A. Rodríguez-Consuegra
Universtity of Valencia

'On propositions: what they are and how they mean' (Russell, 1919) opened a new period in Russell's philosophy, which was characterized by: the rejection of the distinction between subject and object; the subsequent monism (no matter how 'neutral' it might have been); a behaviouristic theory of meaning; and a new epistemology avoiding the dualism implicit in the notion of *acquaintance*. All of these features had important consequences for the increasing holistic tendency, which was already implicit in the theory of logical constructions and the physical character of sensations in 1914. Thus, the philosophical subject is constructed out of sensations, the same material used to construct physical objects, no matter how many different names Russell was going to use in the period.[2] This is very important for sensations no longer involve the same dualism which was implicit in acquaintance. On the other hand, the

---

[1] This paper is a preliminary version of the last chapter of a book which is now near completion. Hopefully, the book will soon appear with the title *Rational Ontology and Analytic Philosophy Bertrand Russell and Bradley's Ghost*, and shall include a full edition of the Russell-Bradley correspondence. This final version was prepared under the benefits of the Spanish grant DGYCIT PS93–0220.

[2] *Sensation* was replaced by *noticing* in 1948 because of the admission of qualities as defining *events* from 1927.

already admitted behaviourism contributed, to some extent, to the previous holistic tendency, for meaning is now considered only in a causal way, and language is seen only as a fact, which, has nothing to do with any possible referentialism, whose remnants were definitely abandoned. As a whole, we can say that this new (and last) period of Russell's philosophy was characterized by the drawing of the ultimate consequences already implicit in previous stages.

The 1919 paper contained another important point: the official rejection of the multiple relation theory. Curiously enough, the theory is not rejected because of Wittgenstein's criticism (which coincided in essence with Bradley's) but *only* because there is now no longer a subject which can provide the 'mind' we need to be one of the constituents of the judging complex: 'The theory of belief which I formerly advocated, namely, that it consisted in a multiple relation of the subject to the objects constituting the 'objective', ie. the fact that makes the belief true or false, is rendered impossible by the rejection of the subject' (Russell, 1919, pp. 306–307). However, the new theory introduced here is similar in structure, for Russell limits himself to replacing the constituents of the former judging complex by 'images', which are also related by a multiple relation. In addition he defines truth and falsehood in terms of a similar correspondence to the one defended before. Thus, we have an 'objective' complex related in the same way as the complex of images.

> The objective of a proposition consists of the meanings of its constituent images related (or not related, as the case may be) by the same relation as that which holds between the constituent images in the proposition. When the objective is that the same relation

holds, the proposition is true; when the objective is that the same relation does not hold, the proposition is false. (Russell, 1919, p. 316)

Therefore, the solution to the former problems consisted chiefly in psychologizing the proposition, and in the same way as the official multiple relation theory already did, ie. by regarding the proposition as a complex whose unity proceeded from the fact that the mind was its main constituent. Now there is no need to be concerned about the theory of types, or about Bradley's objection against relations ('Bradley's paradox' in what follows), because Russell has abandoned any hope of maintaining the old epistemological realism, and, through the abandonment of the subject, even the old dualism. Whether or not we can describe his new position as idealism is not important; what is important is to be able to follow the main consequences of these changes in Russell's actual philosophical practice. And when we do so, we see that the sort of analyses he introduced in the new period were again and again more holistic, giving pre-eminence to relations over terms, which practically disappeared in favour of structures, forms and qualities, so leading to a new view of knowledge as being something merely 'structural'. However, as we shall see in the last section of this paper, the new methodological novelties did not give rise to similar changes in Russell's philosophically explicit accounts of forms and relations, as he continued to maintain exactly the same theory as in former stages. In the following, I will briefly consider Russell's four last major works in order to point out these tendencies, although I will avoid any study of the details of the constructive method of replacing (ie. of constructively defining) 'inferences' by 'logical construc-tions'. Finally, I shall say something about the things

Russell wrote on relations and forms during the same period (1919–51), which can be regarded as the relevant background.

1. *Mind, Behaviour and Language*

The Analysis of Mind (Russell, 1921) was devoted to systematically constructing all psychological entities out of sensations and images, but in this work there are many places in which increasingly idealistic ideas and some holistic connotations already appear. As for idealism, this was a consequence of a monistic and behaviouristic view, which made it impossible to maintain the old conception of knowledge as a fully external relation. Now knowledge is only a complex of complex relations depending on causal laws, which govern the accuracy of the responses to the stimuli. Truth is now defined in in a way similar to that of 1919 as a property of beliefs as they are expressed in propositions; thus a proposition is true when it points to its objective, which is a fact, and false when it points away from it (Russell, 1921, p. 273).

Yet it is unclear how Russell can maintain this view against some of his own criticisms of other alternative views. For instance, he says that any theory about the verification of our beliefs through a criterion collapses: 'If we believe we have found a criterion, this belief itself may be mistaken; we should be begging the question if we tried to test the criterion by applying the criterion to itself' (Russell, 1921, p. 269). First, it is obvious that this argument is a clear anticipation of the classical argument against the neo-positivistic criterion of meaning, and also that it is constructed by applying once more Bradley's paradox. But, second, it can also be used against Russell's definition of truth as a proposition pointing to its objective, for the fact of stating the pointing itself must have, again, another objective, and so on.

Besides, the old problem of relations, as constituents of the complexes in which they occur is avoided, perhaps by supposing that present complexes are formed only by images (or words). But it is interesting to see Russell trying to handle the annoying 'relating relation' as a new constituent of the proposition, which takes place when he tries to set up the 'objective' of a relational atomic proposition: '[it] is obtained by replacing each word by what it means, the word meaning a relation being replaced by this relation among the meanings of the other words' (Russell, 1921, p. 278). And this is interesting especially when he says, a few pages before, that the same example ('Socrates precedes Plato') points out the fact that we have no parallelism between relational propositions and the corresponding objectives (or facts), precisely because 'the objective which makes our proposition true consists of *two* terms with a relation between them, whereas our proposition consists of *three* terms with a relation of order between them' (Russell, 1921, p. 275). Thus, the problem of the ontological status of relations remains.

Regarding the holistic traits, they take place mainly in contexts where language is considered. One of the most important is related to the consequences of the behaviouristic account of language, where we can even find some anticipations of the second Wittgenstein, although this fact may depend on Wittgenstein's own debt to behaviourism. Russell writes that understanding a word does not involve what this word means.

Understanding words does not consist in knowing their dictionary definitions, or in being able to specify the objects to which they are appropriate. Such understanding as this may belong to lexicographers and students, but not to ordinary mortals in ordinary life. Understanding language is more like understanding cricket: it is a matter of habits, acquired in oneself and rightly presumed in others. To say that a word has a meaning is not to say that those who use the word correctly have ever thought out what the meaning is: the use of the word comes first, and the meaning is to be distilled out of it by observation and analysis. (Russell, 1921, p. 197)

Therefore, the old mechanical correspondence between word and objects must be completely forgotten, and replaced by an alternative one where the particular words are only 'nodes', which are located in complex systems or structures. Being these structures is what gives words their meanings. This can be, then, interpreted as saying that particular words are only 'implicitly defined' by the systems where they are located in particular places, and that the relations which are internal to those systems are to replace terms.

Another impressive anticipation of the holistic view of knowledge takes place in Russell's account of *data*. Now they are no longer something given to us directly by means of the relation of acquaintance, for this relation has been replaced by sensation, which dispenses with the distinction between subject and object. Instead, as the new physics suggests to Russell, data are also subjective, for 'the physical world itself, as known, is infected through and through with subjectivity' (Russell, 1921, p. 230). Besides, 'there can be no datum apart from a belief' (Russell, 1921, p. 297), for sensations involve memory, perception involves judgement, and even mere consciousness already involves belief. Thus, data can no longer be regarded as the things with which science begins, for observation is not independent from theory itself: a datum 'is just as sophisticated and elaborate as the theories which he [a trained observer] bases upon it, since only trained habits and much practice enable a man to make the kind of observation that will be scientifically illuminating' (Russell, 1921, p. 298).

As a whole, the interpretation points out the fact that the structural approach to language, knowledge and science was already present in this work of 1921, for in fact it began with the explicit acceptance of the very principle of replacing inferences by logical constructions. And as we shall see in the following, logical constructions were bit by bit transformed into mere structural accounts of the entities to be defined, which could no longer be constructed through classes of simples. In the end, there were no simples at all, and even simples were to be constructed out of complexes of relations.

2. *Physics and Structures*

We can now say that *The Analysis of Matter* (Russell, 1927) is the up-to-date version of the logical constructions of 1914, by taking into consideration quantum and relativity theories. From the logical point of view, Russell considered here a more general kind of scientific laws, which were seen as axiomatic systems which we can 'interpret' by replacing the undefined terms of the axioms by names of entities taken from the perceptual world. From the epistemological point of view, the main effect of the new physics was to replace the old approach, which admitted the consideration of momentary stages as the starting point, by another where these stages are impossible because of quantum theory, where only a much more abstract notion of matter was needed, and where the old 'bridge' between physics and sensation was hardly intuitive. Therefore, although Russell tried from time to time to insert his old ontological atomism into this framework, the truth is that the increasing holism had a clear pre-eminence, despite the fact that the whole construction is presented as the usual chain of reductive definitions, according to the usual linear, foundational epistemology.

Thus, although in some publications of the period Russell continues to speak of terms and external relations, the holistic consequences of neutral monism impregnate the whole construction, and provide us with a structural epistemology where we can only propose interpretations more or less coincident with the mathematical laws of physics, and where there are no longer epistemological 'simples'. Instead, we have a complete non-distinction between data and inferences,[3] together with the assertion that the abstract laws in themselves somehow 'define' the objects which are actual objects.

In this general context, Russell anticipates the present day more or less standard view of scientific theory, according to which the meanings of scientific terms somehow change according to the changes in the scientific theory, which is very similar to the view that terms are nothing in themselves apart from the set of relations which provide them with a significance. Thus, Russell writes that when we have certain physical postulates which are not verified by certain measurements, 'we invent physical laws to save the postulates', and he adds: 'With each fresh law it becomes more and more difficult to say exactly what we do mean' (Russell, 1927, p. 93). This presumably, means that the relevant terms are

---

[3] Even arriving at a system of methodological postulates of scientific knowledge, which is very similar to the one appearing in 1948.

involved in so great a number of different relations (the mathematical form of the scientific laws) that to try to extract a particular intuitive meaning for those terms, apart from these pure mathematical relations, becomes almost impossible.

Also, we find here the same rejection of the distinction between datum and theory that we found in 1921, but now in the context of a more general framework where even facts depend upon theories. We read, 'What is recorded as the result of an experiment or observation is never the bare fact perceived, but this fact as interpreted by the help of a certain amount of theory' (Russell, 1927, p. 187). And so, the interpretative element can only be eliminated by means of a more complex theory, where the former 'sensation' is no longer a datum, but an inference. This made it impossible to maintain particulars,[4] for they should be regarded a simples, and the new epistemology no longer contains simples. But we can also regard the need for a new theory to explain the relation between the former one and its data as a further application of Bradley's paradox, so that the present complications are very similar to the old difficulties of trying to maintain a theory of truth as correspondence.

Yet I think that the best sign of Russell's holism is present in his new 'implicit definition' of matter by means of the general 'axioms' which set up the physical laws. The claim that matter is only what is involved in the physical laws is developed into two steps. Firstly, we have the 'epistemological' basis asserting that our knowledge is only structural: 'whatever we infer from perception, it is only structure that we can validly infer; and structure is what can be expressed by mathematical

---

[4]   Russell admits that in denying that particulars can be regarded as absolute metaphysical terms (Russell, 1927, p. 278).

logic, which includes mathematics' (Russell, 1927, p. 254). Secondly, we have the 'logical' (we would rather say semantical) definition asserting that material entities are only those which can serve as an interpretation of physical laws: matter stands 'for the existents satisfying the equations of physics' (Russell, 1927, p. 207).[5]

Through this approach to the problem of the philosophical nature of matter Russell falls precisely into what he emphatically rejected in *Principles of Mathematics*, for example regarding Peano's definition of number 'by postulates' according to which numbers are merely the entities which satisfy the five celebrated axioms. Thus Russell seems to renounce the need for providing nominal, explicit definitions, in spite of all his previous attempts to maintain that his usual constructive definitions offered a genuine 'analysis' of the constructed entities. I think that this was a consequence of the impossibility of inserting 'forms' into the atomistic scheme of analysis, and then of the implicit recognition that forms can only be captured in an 'internal' way (as I think Wittgenstein tried to say in the *Tractatus*). As a whole, we can also say that this was the ultimate consequence of admitting logical constructions where what is 'simple' was constructed by means of what is 'complex'.

There is another way of interpreting Russell's difficulties with structures (or forms) as being the only thing we are supposed to know about the world, and this way is very interesteing for according to it I think we can find a further link with Bradley's paradox. As Demopoulos and Friedman have pointed out (Demopoulos and Friedman, 1985), the mathematician M. H. A. Newman, in his almost unknown article

---

[5]   With this approach Russell was obviously following Eddington.

(Newman, 1928), already criticized Russell's approach. Newman's argument was that since structures depend only on cardinal numbers (for they are ultimately defined as relation-numbers), to say that the physical world has a particular structure is only to talk about a cardinal number, which is quite trivial and of course hardly empirical, unless we admit some additional knowledge about certain 'important' structures, which means precisely to violate the main requirement, ie. that we 'only' know structural (mathematical) properties.

As Demopoulos and Friedman also point out, Russell's reply (in a letter to Newman) involved an important change in the original claim, for he admitted that in fact we know something beyond pure structure, for instance spatio-temporal continuity among percepts, which, we can add, is another sort of relational knowledge too. The link with Bradley's paradox might be this: if to say that our knowledge is only structural (ie. relational) is only meaningful when we *add* some other knowledge (which is also relational) to try to set up some relation between the former structure and original perceptions, then we fall into endless regress, for the additional knowledge should be correctly stated only by means of a further relational knowledge which relates it to the previous complex, and so on. I think that is why Newman pointed out that the admission of some 'perceptual' criterion to choose between the different possible mathematical structures which are available violates the main requirement that knowledge is to be only structural. Russell used to say that he maintained his old realism even in spite of all these problems, but there are also passages which show an open acceptance of the increasing idealism involved in this stage. The following is one of these passages, and it was written in 1931, that is precisely four years after writing *The Analysis of Matter.*

> As regards, metaphysics, when, under the influence of Moore, I first threw off the belief in German idealism, I experienced the delight of believing that the sensible world is real. Bit by bit, chiefly under the influence of physics, this delight faded, and I have been driven to a position not unlike that of Berkeley, without his God and his Anglican complacency. (Russell, 1967, p. 160)

As we shall see, this kind of holistic idealism, which was characterized by the constant and unsolved problem of the relation between relations and terms, is also present in the rest of Russell's important works.

3. *Truth and Qualities*

It is difficult to classify the materials contained in *An Inquiry into Meaning and Truth*, for this work faced a wide variety of very different topics, but I think we can say that in it Russell continued to develop the holistic tendencies we have pointed out above. This was done first by reacting to the new influence from the logical positivists, some of whom had defended a theory of truth as mere coherence, and second by discussing Dewey's pragmatism, which rejected truth as correspondence as well. But Russell's own analysis of truth in terms of correspondence had to face exactly the same problems already present at former stages. In addition, the work contains new interesting constructive definitions, but the most important idea is the introduction of qualities (universals) as raw material for defining (ie. for eliminating) spatio-temporal names and egocentric particulars (that is, indexical terms), so that the former tendency towards the vanishing of any epistemological 'simples' was being more and more consolidated.

With the elimination of particulars, it seems to me that the idea underlying the theory of descriptions, ie. the elimination of proper names, was finally accepted. Thus, we can say that in this work such names are replaced by sets of empirical qualities, so they can no longer be regarded as naming genuine, simple objects. Russell recognizes the point when he writes that 'every proper name is the name of a structure, not of something destitute of parts' (Russell, 1940, p. 31). He also denies that this supposes a real elimination of proper names, but only 'an unusual extension for the word "name"', for the words for qualities can also be regarded as names, at least 'in the syntactical sense' (Russell, 1940, pp. 89–90). Yet this seems to me to be nothing but a way to avoid the holistic consequences of the elimination.

Also, Russell's way to defend a correspondence theory of truth, within a holistic context, led him, in the last analysis, to the old problems with Bradley's paradox. The starting point in stating that theory was the traditional view that truth depends upon some relation between propositions and occurrences, ie. facts. But when Russell tried to make precise the idea of experience involved here, he had to reject momentary empiricism (for it admits only present percepts and memory), and then had to admit that habits are also involved (Russell, 1940, p. 279). However, to do that supposed the implicit admission of a transition from perceptual space to physical space, then of causal links between events, and finally of further events belonging to other people and even of the entire science of physics (Russell, 1940, pp. 286–7). Summing up: the rejection of a narrow and unacceptable empiricism led Russell to admit events which no one experiences, as well as propositions whose truth we cannot prove, so that 'if we are to retain beliefs that we all regard as valid, we must allow principles of inference which are neither demonstrative nor derivable from experience' (Russell, 1940, p. 288).

This is really a very strange theory of correspondence, for it accurately avoids the explanation of the correspondence itself between propositions and facts, only by saying that 'the difficulty is to define the relation which constitutes truth' from a realistic viewpoint (Russell, 1940, p. 232). With that, Russell must have been thinking of Moore's (and Bradley's) old objection which prohibited any explicit explanation of the correspondence (on pain of requiring further and further 'true' explanations), as well as of Wittgenstein's view that we *cannot* refer to the relation between proposition and fact, for this relation is a *form*, and we cannot capture forms at all. That is why Russell openly admits the need for resorting to principles of non-demonstrative inference, which come to play the role of the impossible account of the relation between experience and fact. And this, if true, is very important, for the status of these postulates can be interpreted to be a sign that Russell was explicitly thinking of Bradley's paradox as well. Thus, the postulates cannot be empirical and cannot be inferred, so they cannot be admitted as epistemological premises nor can they even be 'known' at all. This leads Russell to admit that they cannot be easily reconciled with empiricism, and it seems to me that the argument he uses is plainly Bradleian.

> Empiricism, as a theory of knowledge, is self-refuting. for, however, it may be formulated, it must involve *some* general proposition about the dependence of knowledge upon experience; and any such proposition, if true, must have a consequence that itself cannot be known. While therefore, empiricism may be

true, it cannot, if true, be known to be so. (Russell, 1940, pp. 156–7)

Russell did not explicitly offer a list of postulates in this work; rather, some of them are more or less scattered here and there. Also, the full treatment of the problem is delayed until his next, and last, major work, but I think with that it can be enough to see that the realist and empiricist alternative was not really consistent with Russell's deepest thoughts at the time.

4. *Holistic Knowledge*

Human Knowledge: its Scope and Limits (Russell, 1948) supposed the consolidation of the general tendency towards holism we are pointing out. The technical novelties in the constructions taking place in that work were two: the abandonment of coordinates to eliminate spatio-temporal proper names (for they require an absolute original, ie. at least a proper name), and the elimination of particulars, not by means of isolated qualities (as in the previous work), but through 'complexes' of qualities and the relation of 'compresence', in a very similar way to the one he had used before to define points and instants. Thus, each particular can be constructed as a 'complete complex of compresence', and so proper names are definitely abandoned.

The philosophical implications of this procedure are mainly holistic, for they suppose the admission of structures, ie. sets of relations, to replace particular things, and these structures cannot be reduced to their constituents. Thus, a complex of compresence, 'though defined when all its constituent qualities are given, is not to be conceived, like a class, as a mere logical construction but as something which can be known and named without our having to know all its constituent qualities' (Russell, 1948, p. 325). But Russell's attempt to make a distinction between logical constructions (classes) and these kinds of complexes is misleading, for obviously we also can know and name classes without knowing all their members, at least in a certain sense of the word 'know'. This problem is also alluded to when Russell adds that when we have a purely logical structure, 'a statement about the structure can be reduced to one about its components, but in the case of the time-order this is not possible on the theory of "particulars" adopted in this Chapter' (Russell, 1948). With that I think Russell was trying to give a solid status to their complexes, but so he seems to forget that logical structures, ie. forms, can by no means be reduced to their constituents, as Russell himself said again and again.

Anyway, the most interesting point is that Russell is clearly defending the view that particulars can be 'reduced' to sets of relations among qualities. That is why the complexes involved cannot, again, be reduced to their components, ie. to particulars. Thus, particulars are now regarded as 'complexes', at least in the sense that they can be 'analysed' although the raw materials were, in some 'pre-systematic' way, even more complex than the particulars themselves. Therefore, Russell's procedure can be regarded as the converse of the one followed in 1903, where it was supposed that all complexes can be reconstructed out of 'simple' terms and relations, being terms named by proper names. On the contrary, here proper names are finally abandoned in favour of qualities and relations, although the status of relations as entities is by no means clear. Russell says that a complex is definitely regarded as an irreducible entity, for although it is formed out of qualities, and 'is of the same logical type as a single quality', it is 'something new, over and above the qualities' (Russell, 1948, p. 325). However, this seems to be a violation of the theory of types, for it proposes to consider classes and relations on the same level as terms.

On the other hand, the reduction involved seems to suppose a decomposition of substance precisely by maintaining the subject-predicate form, which was heavily criticized by Moore and Russell in abandoning Bradley's idealism. Now, the rather Leibnizian relation between the complexes of compresence and our way of seeing the world seems to lead to 'monadism', rather than to the original pluralism. But even for Russell monadism involved monism, because it depended upon a view of knowledge as being to some extent an 'internal' relation. That is why the increasing holistic tendency ended in the open recognition that our knowledge of the world is only structural, which unavoidably supposes at least a renunciation of empiricism, as we saw above.

The new vision of data and epistemological premises comes to coincide with the former holistic line, where we no longer find primitive ideas and propositions, in the atomistic sense of the expression. Russell tries to preserve his old linear, foundationalist epistemology by writing that 'an epistemological premise may be defined as a proposition which has some degree of rational credibility on its own account independently of its relations to other propositions'. However, he also says that 'while there are beliefs which are only conclusions of arguments, there are none which, in a rational artic-ulation of knowledge, are only premises' (Russell, 1948, p. 401). We even find the open recognition that any attempt to distinguish between intrinsic and derivative credibility leads to unmanageable complications, and then to 'a certain approximation to the theory of Hegel and Dewey', which is lucidly described in the following passage. (The emphasis is mine.)

> Given a number of propositions, each having a fairly high degree of intrinsic credibility, and given a system of inference by virtue of which these various propositions increase each other's credibility, it *may be possible* in the end to arrive at a body of interconnected propositions having *as a whole* a very high degree of credibility. Within this body, some are only inferred, but *none are only premises* for those which are premises are also conclusions. (Russell, 1948, p. 413)

Thus, although Russell immediately adds the famous analogy of a bridge whose piers are the propositions with intrinsic credibility, and whose upper portions represent what is inferred, it is obvious that the analogy makes no sense without a clear distinction between intrinsic and inferred credibility, and when one admits no clear first link in the chain, then one is dangerously near idealism and its doctrine of degrees of truth.

Now the attempt to offer a list of postulates justifying scientific knowledge can be better understood. They are destined to be the only primitive knowledge, which makes possible the whole building of science. But, as we already pointed out above, the postulates can by no means break the circularity involved in any attempt to justify knowledge. For they cannot be really 'known', on pain of falling into the usual paradoxes, so they cannot constitute the piers of the bridge of knowledge, and so the bridge has no piers at all. Ultimately, that means, once and for all, that Bradley's arguments are fully admitted, and that we cannot overcome the paradoxes infecting the nature of relations and forms. The postulates of scientific knowledge cannot be known, because they are that what make it possible that we know the rest of things, so they should rather be regarded as 'forms' which we 'impose' on reality. Thus, if they were explicitly known, we would require other forms to justify our knowledge, and so on, with the subsequent endless regress. Therefore, Bradley's paradoxes of relations and truth are one and the same, as soon as we realize that the justification of knowledge involves some attempt to define truth, and this can be made also by means of a relational approach, if we do not want to accept a coherence view.

5. *The Always Elusive Forms*

I shall finish the paper by taking briefly into consideration Russell's three last philosophical attempts to give an explicit account of forms in the period 1919–51. They all are an additional sign that Russell was never able to philosophically justify his actual analytic and constructive practice, and they are also an additional proof that Bradley's paradox was also present in the purely 'logical' approaches of the period.

The first is 'Logical Atomism' (Russell, 1924) a rather chaotic attempt to give a global account of Russell's ontology, but with the advantage that it was the last place where he explicitly considered Bradley's arguments. Russell begins by describing his usual theory of external relations, but now he replaces the terminology of 'unities' and 'complexes' by one of 'facts', which of course changes nothing. As for the explicit presentation of external relations, Russell chooses here the version according to which subject-predicate propositions cannot in general give an account of relational propositions, then he adds that this is the very kernel of the doctrine of external relations, and that these should be rejected by Bradley. But first, Bradley explicitly rejected the view that relations can be reduced to properties (predicates), and second, Russell is ignoring here his former presentations according to which 'external relations' means, first of all, that the distinction between relating relations and relations in themselves does make sense.

I think that in ignoring the old presentations Russell was motivated by the need to avoid the problems he was unable to solve in the abandoned manuscript *Theory of Knowledge* (1913). However, the present discussion has the important advantage that Russell does not evade, as he did in 1913, the important links between Bradley's paradox, Wittgenstein's objections and the theory of types. That is why Russell suggests that in the question of internal or external relations, the usual formulations on both sides 'are inconsistent with the theory of types' (Russell, 1924, p. 334). With that he must have meant that we cannot really consider relations at the same level as terms, ie. as being independent entities at all, for this procedure sins against types, which force us to state different ontological categories for them.

Yet he is also forced to admit that for Bradley relations are as unintelligible as terms, precisely when they are regarded as being independent realities. I think this is implicit in the following lines: 'The doctrine of types profoundly affects logic, and I think shows what, exactly, is the valid element in the arguments of those who oppose "external" relations' (Russell, 1924, p. 333). But this is equivalent to a recognition that there was a strong link between Bradley's rejection of relations and Wittgenstein's objection against the possibility of making the form a constituent in complexes. However, it is a pity that Russell did not recognize that the only possible way out for the problem was, for Wittgenstein, the admission of internal relations, ie. the admission that complexity can by no means be expressed in terms of constituents.

Russell quotes the passage from Bradley where the old master accused him of inconsistency in admitting first only terms and external relations, but, second, unities and complexes which cannot be analysed into terms and relations. But the subsequent defence of his view deeply differs from the one he developed in 1913, where he maintained a multiple relation theory of judgement in which forms (ie. complex relations or structures) *can be* inserted into complexes together with relations and terms, with no reference to the obvious problem concerning the theory of types. Now Russell says that he already had abandoned his view of 1903, where complexes were admitted in the same sense as simples, then he adds 'I regard simples and complexes as always of different types' (Russell, 1924, p. 336). However, the main difference now is that he is beginning to think that there are no simples at all, for we can eliminate them in terms of complexes: 'It is quite possible that, by greater logical skill, the need for assuming them could be avoided' (Russell, 1924, p. 337). Thus, the old theory that complexes are composed of simples, although still maintained, no longer makes sense, except from a merely relativistic point of view.

In the final outline (which was developed in technical works from 1927 to 1948) Russell continues to handle qualities and relations, together with entities or 'events'), as being the ultimate constituents of the world. However, he already recognizes that, ultimately, attributes and relations can by no means be regarded as entities at all, which is stated *precisely with Bradleian arguments.*

> Attributes and relations, though they may be not
> susceptible of analysis, differ from substances by the
> fact that they suggest a structure, and that there can
> be no significant symbol which symbolizes them in
> isolation. All propositions in which an attribute or a
> relation *seems* to be the subject are only significant if
> they can be brought into a form in which the attribute
> attributes or the relation relates. If this were not the
> case, there would be significant propositions in which
> an attribute or a relation would occupy a position
> appropriate to a substance, which would be contrary
> to the doctrine of types, and would produce contra-
> dictions. (Russell, 1924, p. 337)

I think that the 'contradictions' alluded to here are the
ones involved in Bradley's paradox, and the doctrine of
types is involved precisely in the sense of Wittgenstein's
objections against forms as constituents. Thus, Russell
is explicitly renouncing, at last, the difference between
relating-relations and relations-in-themselves. And that
makes it very difficult to accept his parallel view
according to which relations and qualities (attributes)
are parts of the ultimate stuff of the world, for if this
stuff cannot be regarded as genuine 'substance' (as
relations and qualities cannot), another ultimate
category should be provided, and Russell never spoke
about that.

The second place where the problem of relations,
forms and structures appears is in the 1937 Introduction
to the second edition of *The Principles of Mathematics*,
which can be regarded as a further step towards a
syntactical approach (regarding the topic of forms).
The problem was the same as always: to know whether
or not there are logical constants (logical forms), and

whether or not they can be explicitly characterized. But the difficulties were also the same as always, for the first thing to know would be the exact meaning of the expression 'occurring in a proposition', ie. to know how we can divide propositions into constituents. And this is really difficult for 'logical constants ... must be treated as part of the language not as part of what the language speaks about'.

Thus, when Russell, already under the influence of Carnap, tries to define, once again, what is logic, he says that to do that we first need to be able to find a set of premises which are true only in virtue of their form, but 'it is hard to say what makes a proposition true in virtue of its form'. Curiously enough, Russell openly admits the relativity of logico-mathematical propositions as regards demonstrability, for a given proposition can be an axiom in a system and a theorem in another system. However, he by no means admits that the whole problem of identifying his logical premises can be treated in the same way, because he was convinced that Carnap's approach was too linguistic, and that a given axiom must have or have not the property of being formally true in itself. But then, although 'there must be some way of defining logic otherwise than in relation to a particular logical language', however, 'I confess ... that I am unable to give any clear account of what is meant by saying that a proposition is "true in virtue of its form"'.

The third, and last, relevant place in the writings of this period was an (unpublished) continuation of the syntactical approach: 'Is Mathematics Purely Linguistic?' (Russell, 1951). The paper has the advantage that it relates the new approach to a further attempt to discuss the nature of logic and mathematics, and this, again, to Bradley's paradox. To be brief, I can say that the essay tries to define mathematics and logical propositions as those containing, apart from variables, only syntactical words. Then Russell adds that these propositions are true because of the meaning of these syntactical words, which is said to be the same as the traditional expression 'in virtue of their form' (Russell, 1951, p. 305). So it seems clear that Russell is giving us his last ideas about the possibility of capturing forms.

However, when he tries to analyse simple propositions, he immediately admits that we can by no means make the relations among the different words explicit, for when we try to do that, we obtain only another string of words where the new relations among them are again essential. This is, of course, a form of Bradley's paradox, as it is shown in the following lines.

> Whatever we do, we can never free ourselves from the necessity to take account of non-verbalised relations between words. When any such relation is verbalised, new non-verbalised relations take its place. (Russell, 1951, p. 305)

Russell concludes by saying that these non-verbalized relations are precisely what 'constitute syntax' (Russell, 1951), so presumably the object of syntax would be the study of these relations, which I think is the same thing as Russell expressed in previous writings through the claim that logic is the study and classification of logical forms.

The application of this conclusion to mathematics and logic is immediate. As mathematics and logic are characterized precisely by these syntactical words, 'the propositions of logic and mathematics are purely linguistic', and then 'they are concerned with syntax' (Russell, 1951, p. 306). Russell also recognizes that this conclusion can be regarded as 'an epitaph on

Pythagoras', for in this way mathematics and logic are no longer dealing with transcendent objects, but only with assertions about 'the correct use of a certain small number of words' (Russell, 1951). It must have been a conclusion hard to accept by an old realist, but for us it is a good conclusion to Russell's journey from atomistic realism to holistic idealism. And this journey, as we have seen, was always made by thinking of Bradley.

BIBLIOGRAPHY OF WORKS CITED

Russell, B., 1903. *The Principles of Mathematics* (Cambridge, Cambridge University Press; 2nd edn. with a new preface, London, Allen and Unwin, 1937).

—— 1913. *Theory of Knowledge*, see 1984.

—— 1914. *Our Knowledge of the External World* (London, Allen and Unwin).

—— 1921. *The Analysis of Mind* (London, Allen and Unwin).

—— 1927. *The Analysis of Matter* (London, Allen and Unwin).

—— 1937. 'Introduction to the second edition', *The Principles of Mathematics* (1st edn., 1903), pp. v–xiv.

—— 1940. *An Inquiry into Meaning and Truth* (London, Allen and Unwin; reprinted, London, Pelican Books, 1962).

—— 1948. *Human Knowledge: its Scope and Limits* (London, Allen and Unwin).

—— 1951. 'Is Mathematics Purely Linguistic?', 1973.

—— 1956. *Logic and Knowledge*, ed. R. C. Marsh (London, Allen and Unwin).

—— 1956. 'On Propositions: What they are and How they Mean', *Proceedings of the Artistotelian Society* supplement, vol. 2, pp. 1–43.

—— 1956. 'Logical atomism', *Contemporary British Philosophy*, 1st series (London, Allen and Unwin).

—— 1973. *Essays in Analysis*, ed. by D. Lackey (London, Allen and Unwin).

—— 1984. *Theory of Knowledge: the 1913 Manuscript*, ed. by E. R. Eames and K. Blackwell (vol.

7 of *CP*) (London, Allen and Unwin).

Demopoulos, W., and M. Friedman, 1985. 'The concept of structure in the *Analysis of Matter*', in Wade Savage and Anthony Anderson (eds.), *Rereading Russell: Essays in Bertrand Russell's Metaphysics and Epistemology, Minnesota Studies in the Philosophy of Science*, vol. 12 (Minneapolis, University of Minnesota Press, 1989).

Newman, M. H. A., 1928. 'Mr Russell Causal Theory of Perception', *Mind*, vol. 37.

Rodríguez-Consuegra, F., 199–. *Relational Ontology and Analytic Philosophy. Bertrand Russell and Bradley's Ghost* [in preparation].

RUSSELL'S TRANSCENDENTAL ARGUMENT IN *AN ESSAY ON THE FOUNDATIONS OF GEOMETRY*

A. C. Grayling
Birkbeck College

Russell was generous in attributing the sources of his inspiration to others, and never more so than in explaining what he described as the 'revolution' in his philosophical thought which occurred in the closing years of the nineteenth century. At Cambridge he had been made to feel the influence of Kant and Hegel, and especially of the latter, with whom he sided whenever he encountered disagreement between them. His great plan for two series of books effecting a synthesis of philosophy and science was Hegelian in inspiration, and his Fellowship dissertation, *An Essay on the Foundations of Geometry*, was Kantian not just in inspiration but in aim and, to a significant degree, content.

Russell gave the credit for the revolution in his thought to Moore: 'Moore led the way but I followed in his footsteps' (Russell, *My Philosophical Development*, hereafter *MPD*, p. 42). Several times he cites Moore's paper 'The Nature of Judgment' as the key document in this change. Commenting on its influence, he says that its most important doctrine is its realist commitment to the independence of fact from experience. But each of them pursued differently-emphasized routes from this

245

agreement: Moore was concerned to refute idealism, while Russell was more interested in refuting monism. Nevertheless Russell took these two -isms to be connected through the doctrine of relations. In his view monism arises from commitment to the view that all relations are grounded in their terms; the application to idealism is that relations between thought or experience and their objects are asserted to be internal likewise, rendering them interdependent in ways that make what we pre-theoretically take to be *objective* relata in some sense mental or grounded in the mental.

So much is familiar enough. But there is reason to think that another paper Moore published in 1899 had as big an effect on Russell from the viewpoint of its reach into Russell's later philosophical work. This is Moore's Critical Notice of Russell's *Essay on the Foundations of Geometry* (hereafter *EFG*). One is tempted to compare it in character and effect to Frege's celebrated conversion of Husserl from psychologism by his review of Husserl's *Philosophie der Aritmetic*. This would not be gathered from *MPD*, where Russell dismisses the argument of *EFG* on the grounds that the General Theory of Relativity made it obsolete. (Note however that Russell says in a letter to Moore of 18 July 1899: 'I had not written to you about your review, because on all important points I agreed with it.') But when one considers what Russell says in *Human Knowledge, Its Scope and Limits* about Kant and about the postulates of scientific inference, one sees that the revolution in his philosophical views is as profoundly rooted in the temptations of transcendental philosophy as it is rooted in monism, but, it might be argued, hardly with so positive an effect, because Russell ended by believing that there can be no *ultimate* appeal to a priori knowledge in the constitution of knowledge in general:

hence the tottering version of fallibilism in *Human Knowledge*, with its reliance, at the base of the argument, on supposed contingencies about evolution and animal habits. The flight from sophisticated psychologism had, so to say, crash-landed in crude biologism. Thereafter Russell made no more use of Kantian strategies and took to calling him by Cantor's disagreeable label for him, 'Yon sophistical Philistine'.

Yet in *EFG* Russell not only employs a transcendental argument of great interest, but gives a characterization of the nature of transcendental arguments which is of even greater interest. On the first head: it is noteworthy that espousing or rejecting some version of the transcendentalist strategy in *something* like Kant's sense (one need not accept much else of the Kantian luggage; compare Strawson's selectivity in *The Bounds of Sense*) is a matter quite independent of espousal or rejection of either or both of pluralism and realism, two of the commitments which mark Russells philosophy after *EFG*. If Russell had not lumped together everything Kantian for wholesale rejection, but had made use of transcendental arguments as he subtly understood them in *EFG*, he might have spared himself many of his later epistemological insecurities. On the second head: as is characteristic of Russell, his account of the nature of transcendental arguments in *EFG* anticipates later revived interest in the strategy, not only as Strawson and some others of us have deployed them, but in variant forms; as for example in the generalized notion of presuppositions, whose role in the solution of certain semantic problems was later to return to haunt him.

Russell's insights into the transcendental strategy is well brought out by Moore's interesting failure to understand them, which is why I enter Russell's account by way of Moore's devastating-seeming attack on *EFG* in his Critical Notice. In recent studies of Russell both Nick Griffin and Peter Hylton[1] give Moore's argument attention, the former as part of his detailed account of Russell on geometry and the latter more briefly as constituting an attack on psychologism, which in important part it was indeed intended to be; but Hylton leaves aside questions as to the merits of Moore's attack, and therefore does not consider whether Russell should have capitulated to it, bearing in mind that, as Russell saw and indeed insisted, the philosophical consequences of theories of geometry are not confined to choice of geometry for physical theory, but impinge significantly on our theories of perceptual experience, representation and indexical thought.[2] On this question Griffin takes the view that the jury remains out on whether Russell's way with the Kantian strategy in particular, his reworking of a transcendental argument to the necessity for experience of a form of externality is in any degree successful.[3] I am inclined to think that Russell's argument indeed has something to offer: but in proceeding by way of a discussion of the merits of Moore's attack on *EFG* I shall, except in relation to one matter, only obliquely indicate part of why that is so here.

It is useful to have a reminder of what Russell was attempting to do in *EFG*. His aim was to survey the

---

[1] Nicholas Griffin, *Russell's Idealist Apprenticeship* (Oxford, 1991); Peter Hilton, *Russell, Idealism, and the Emergence of Analytic Philosophy* (Oxford, 1990).

[2] ie. we need to know – granting that perceived space is not purely Euclidean – something about what is philosophically at stake for our thinking about perceptual space in theories of geometry in relation to (a) its role in indexical modes of thought (b) its relation to the space or space-time of our best current theories about the structure and properties of the physical world, etc.

[3] Griffin, p. 132.

foundations of geometry in the light of the revolutionary advances that had occurred in that science since Kant's time. Kant had claimed that space is the form of outer sensibility, and that Euclidean geometry describes it; but nineteenth-century mathematicians called into question both the belief that space is Euclidean and the claim that a Euclidean form of space is necessary to outer experience. Moreover, they showed that Euclidean (space has zero curvature), Lobatchevskyan (with Gauss and Bolyai: hyperbolic geometry, space has negative curvature), Riemannian (spherical or double elliptic, space has positive curvature) and Kleinian (single elliptic) geometries can be derived as special cases of projective geometry, which deals with the qualitative (descriptive) properties of space, whereas Euclidean and the other non-Euclidean basic geometries deal with its quantitative (metric) properties. So a set of properties not recognized in Euclidean geometry, namely, the qualitative ones, had been shown to be logically prior to Euclidean properties. The question of what if anything constitutes the a priori foundation of geometrical knowledge therefore needed to be considered afresh, and this task Russell undertook in *EFG*.

Russell accepted the Kantian view that there must be such a thing as a 'form of externality' as a condition of possibility for spatial experience. In an interesting modification of Kant's thesis he argued that the possibility of such experience rests not just on the constitution of sensibility but on the world's receptiveness to the adjectives we impose on it. But he locates the properties of the form of externality not in Euclidean but in projective geometry, its transcendental status – carefully disentangled from the question of the *subjectivity* of a priori elements in experience consisting in its applying to all spaces independently of experience of any of them.

The chief argument is that qualitative relations must be prior to quantitative ones. There are four fundamental qualitative principles: (1) all parts of space are homogeneous, that is, are qualitatively similar, and all are relative, that is, lie outside one another; (2) space is continuous and infinitely divisible, with the point as the limit of infinite divisibility; (3) two points determine a straight line, three points not on a line determine a plane, and so on for higher figures; and (4) the dimension of space must be finite.

Certain refinements of these constitute further a priori principles required for metrical geometry, required because measurement presupposes them. Homogeneity of space becomes free mobility (analytically equivalent to the constant curvature of space); and the 'two points-straight line' principle becomes an axiom about distance. (These principles are presupposed by measurement, and turn out to lie in the domain of meta-geometry, and therefore to apply to physical space.) Russell concluded that because these geometries are the only mathematically possible ones whose spaces are homogeneous, they are the only ones that can apply to physical space. Therefore physical space must be one of Euclidean, Lobatchevskyan, Riemannian or Kleinian. On empirical grounds Russell said that it is Euclidean.

Two developments subsequent to the writing of *EFG* rendered its views, as Russell says, obsolete. One, the development of topology, which generalizes on projective as projective had generalized on Euclidean geometry, imposes an obligation on any Kantians staying the course to review afresh the question of what, if any, geometrical principles are a priori. But much more seriously, every feature of the four dimensional, non-Euclidean, nonhomogeneous (not having a constant curvature) space of the General Theory of Relativity had been effectively or explicitly denied by Russell, who had not registered Riemann's point that a belief in the constant curvature of space depends upon ignoring the existence of matter. When matter is taken into account, homogeneity disappears, as the General Theory states (matter is absorbed into the geometry of space-time which therefore varies regionally according to the matter in it).[4]

The fourth and final chapter of *EFG* contains the discussion of the philosophical aspects of these views which interest us here, because it is these that Moore attacks. Here Russell argues that the a priori axioms of geometry can be deduced from the form of externality as a transcendental ground of experience, that is, the condition of the possibility of experience (see esp. section 189 *EFG*). Russell's view differs in significant ways from Kant's, especially in the interesting respect that it requires the mutual externality of things presented in sense-perception rather than (to begin with anyway) the externality of things to the self. This and other points in Russell's account are independently interesting and perhaps important for theories of perceptual representation, which makes them worth pursuing on their own account.

Russell defined the a priori as that which is logically presupposed in experience, where (as Hylton reminds us)[5] the force of 'logically' is the Kantian transcendental one in which questions about the conditions of the possibility of experience are at stake. But whereas for Kant these are *synthetic* judgements only, for him,

---

[4] There is a useful survey in Morris Kline's Introduction to the addition of *EFG* published by Dover in 1956

[5] Hylton, pp. 73–6.

analytic ones follow from the principle of contradiction alone, for Russell this division will not do, and along with other post-Kantians he rejected it.[6] But he also objected to the conflation of the a priori with subjectivity, on the grounds that it places a priori truth at the mercy of empirical psychology,[7] and so a second import of Russell's use of 'logically' is its marking a refusal to accept that the validity of Euclid waits upon empirical facts about human spatial intuition.[8]

Russell's argument goes as follows. Knowledge starts from sense experience, the objects of sense experience are complex, whatever is complex has parts, parts have to be mutually external to one another, and therefore a form of externality is logically prior to experience. This form of externality cannot be purely temporal, for the reason, among others, that things given in experience must be 'various' or 'diverse' to allow for complexity, and one crucial way in which they are so is by occupying different positions in space, hence space as the form of externality required. The notion of a form of externality is an essentially relative one; nothing can be external to itself, and so for any one thing there must be another thing to which it is external; the externality is of course mutual, and there have to be yet other positions from which the positions they occupy in turn differ. (The second main contention of *EFG* is that geometry contains contradictions: this is the Hegelian aspect of the thesis. I leave this aside; see Hylton.)[9]

Moore took himself to have two fatal objections to Russell's project. One is that the most that could be

[6] Hylton, pp. 75–6.

[7] *EFG*, p. 3; Hylton, p. 76.

[8] *EFG*, p. 93; Hylton, p. 77.

[9] Hylton, p. 84 et. seq.

established by an argument of this kind is something about what is presupposed by the kind of experience we in fact have, and that therefore the argument is philosophically valueless because it tells us only about certain psychological contingencies.

His other objection is less easy to state briefly. Russell said that an a priori judgement is one whose truth-value is insensitive to empirical considerations, and can only be rendered false 'by a change which should render some branch of experience formally impossible, ie. inaccessible to our methods of cognition' (*EFG*, p. 60). Moore seems to have taken Russell to be saying that there is something, a subject matter of some sort, to which cognitive access can be had only if a certain a priori judgement is true; and that the judgement's being rendered false would be the effect of the necessary falsehood of judgements about that subject matter; to which Moore responded, 'that which is "inaccessible to our methods of cognition" would seem only to mean that which we cannot know; it cannot imply that the judgments in question cannot be true' (Moore, p. 398). Moore labels the conflation of questions about what is true with what can be known the 'Kantian fallacy' (compare Frege's insistence on holding apart questions about the truth of a proposition and questions about the grounds we have for holding it true).[10] In his view it is for psychology to answer questions about what and how we know, so such questions are philosophically irrelevant (compare Frege's anti-psychologism).[11] The crucial commitment in this view is to the independence

---

[10] Compare Frege on exactly the same point. All this anti-psychologism was in the air after Kant's and post-Kantian attacks on psychologism: Kant himself attacked the empiricists for psychologism in basing truth on experience in the way they did.

[11] cf. Wittgenstein in the *Tractatus*.

of judgements from thought: hence the reason for Russell's citing Moore's other 1899 paper, 'The Nature of Judgment' (hereafter *NJ*), as the engine in their break with the Kantian and Hegelian traditions (in 'The Nature of Judgment' Moore specifically addressed himself to Bradley's views).

There is much to contest here. The two points Moore addresses are intimately connected in Russell's strategy, in a way that Moore fails to see. He misunderstands the second of them, the one about the presuppositional relationship, and opposes to it a familiar realist claim the argument for which, offered in *NJ*, is inadequate (there might be better arguments for it, but Moore does not give them). He does however see that the first part of Russell's argument requires a particular supplementation, the satisfaction of an ancillary requirement, one which involves a break with Kant on an important matter and which, on the face of it, seems impossibly difficult to give. (I give it below.) Russell evidently took Moore's argument on this point to be conclusive in view of his complete abandonment of the Kantian enterprise.

I take the second point first, concerning the relation of a priori judgements to the branches of experience which presuppose them. Moore seems to be confused about what Russell is claiming here. He seems to take Russell's claim to be that unless such judgements are true, judgements about the subject-matter in question must be false (taking the modalities seriously). Moore thus reads 'inaccessible to cognition' as implying that *there is* something about which we are not in a position to make judgements. His realist commitment to the independence of judgements from knowledge of their truth or falsity accordingly portrays this as a straightforward mistake. But Russell is not saying this; his claim is the familiar Kantian one that there could be no such branch of experience as the one in question unless we know a priori the judgements that make it possible. He put the point by saying that the only thing that could make such a priori judgements false is if the branch of experience in question were impossible; again taking the incorporated modalities seriously, his talk of the 'inaccessibility to cognition' of a branch of experience is not to be read as implying or (as Moore sees it) conceding that there is something to be known if only we could get at it; this is Moore's mistake; rather it says that if nothing constitutes the a priori condition of possibilty for there being such cognition, there could be no such subject-matter.

Russell's point here in fact concerns the very nature of transcendental arguments. He offers a novel and interesting way of capturing what is essential to such arguments, which, contrary to what is often thought, are not in the least logically peculiar or special, but are distinguished from other argumentative strategies by a certain distinctive aim, which is to establish conceptual title to a principle or claim which, accepted as true, licenses our activity in some region of judgement (and I intend that to be a terminological variant for 'makes a certain kind of experience possible'). Kant is somewhat to blame for leading some commentators, in this connection I have Griffin in mind, who in his discussion of Moore on Russell's *EFG* expects more from transcendental arguments without quite saying what, to think that transcendental arguments have to take us beyond their premises, which concern the nature of a certain kind of experience (or thought), and thereby to establish something not already implicit in its character and conditions. But the attempt to show that we have a title to some principle or claim proceeds exactly by showing that we could not do something we in fact do, enjoy spatial sense-perception for example, unless a condition for doing so were satisfied; from which it follows that the principle is satisfied. For Kant as for Russell in *EFG* the spotlight of attention is on the conditions, because once the deduction of title (the legal metaphor was consciously intended by Kant) has been achieved, the next step is to note that the judgement whose acceptance as true is a condition for the experience in question is a priori, since it could not itself have been derived from that experience but, instead, is logically anterior to it.   Part of their transcendental task was to identify what has to be known a priori as a ground for that experience.

Put in the most schematic way, transcendental arguments state that there would not be A unless there were B, and that since there is A, there is B. Familiarly and prosaically, the underlying move is a statement of necessary conditions: B is a necessary condition for A, and since A is the case, so therefore is B. (If one said: therefore B has to be the case too, the 'has to' has to be understood purely conditionally.)   Arguments of this form are very common; they only cause a stir when applied in ambitious Kant-type contexts. Russell in *EFG* succeeded in capturing their character by casting them as portrayals of presuppositionality in terms of truth-value, partly (but only partly: see below) anticipating later variants of the move. We see this by noting Moore's mistake in taking Russell to have asserted that there is a presuppositional relation between A and B such that if judgements as to B are false, those as to A must be necessarily false. This makes the relation very peculiar, for it issues in the necessary falsehood of A-judgements when B-judgements are contingently false, a view it is not clear how one might motivate. But the mistake takes us close to what Russell intended.   In later debate, presupposition is more familiarly (if no less problematically) taken as a relation obtaining between judgements such that a given presupposing judgement has a truth-value only if a given presupposed judgement is true. (I am adhering here to the Russell-Moore terminology of the day: mutatis mutandis, the same points can be made in more careful ways, thus bringing out the fact that it is as a semantic relation that the notion is now standardly understood, rather than an epistemic one between, on the one hand, an asserter or judger seeking to assert or judge a content p and, on the other, another content q required for p's being assertable or judgeable as true or false). This is only part of what Russell intends, for the good reason that it is only part of what is implied in a transcendental argument, in which a stronger claim is at stake, namely, that the falsity of a given judgement – a B-judgement, say – renders impossible even the circumstances for making or entertaining a would-be A-judgement, a matter far antecedent to the determination of the would-be A-judgement's truth-value. So on the Kantian view B's being true makes A either true or false; but B's being false makes it impossible to make or even entertain A-type judgements: they are empty. Moore took it that Russell meant that B's being false makes A-judgements necessarily false. But the two claims are entirely different, and it is unclear whether what Moore imputes to Russell is even coherent. Russell, however, gives us a deep insight into the style of argument at stake.

In the foregoing there is no suggestion that either Moore or Russell had anticipated exactly what has come to be meant by talk of 'presupposition' since Pears and Strawson; rather, their debate illustrates the sense in which that later debate itself captures something close to but weaker than the relation which a transcendental argument asserts to hold between a given kind of experience (or conceptual practice) and what makes it possible. But in the uncertain oscillation between talk of experience and talk of judgements as we find it in Russell and Moore, it is easy to see that, in one mode, the appropriate locution is 'ground of possibility' and, in the other, talk about the condition for possession by a judgement of truth-value as lying in the truth-value of another judgement. The two jargons do not mean the same, but once that is recognized there are no irreducible difficulties in straying between them as our protagonists do.

It is worth remarking at this juncture that this account of Moore's attack does not agree with the accounts given by Hylton and Griffin. On the reading each of the three of us give of Moore there might be a little latitude for interpretation because of the unclarities in Moore's presentation, but not that much; and Griffin, as noted, mis-identifies the character of the transcendental strategy in general and Russell's in particular, chiefly by asking too much of it. I defer an itemized comparison here. But the crucial respect in which I hope that this supplements their discussions is in recognizing that the more significant argument of Moore's is the one directed not against the style of argument Russell uses, but against the argument itself: this occurs as the first point criticized by Moore above, together with its all-important ancillary requirement.

It is also worth noting at this juncture the argument Moore gives in *NJ* for the realist commitment he opposes to what he takes to be Russell's point here. It is remarkably weak. Writing of 'the nature of a proposition or judgment', Moore says, 'A proposition is composed not of words, nor yet of thoughts, but of concepts. Concepts are possible objects of thought; but that is no definition of them. It merely states that they may come into relation with a thinker; and in order that they *may* do anything, they must already *be* something. It is indifferent to their nature whether anybody thinks them or not' (*NJ*, p. 179). 'Concepts form a *genus per se*, irreducible to anything else' (*NJ*, pp. 178–9). This Platonism about concepts itself seems to be enthymematically premissed, among other things, on the view that relations of acts of judging to their contents are external. But nothing is offered in support of that claim, and no other reason, of the better kinds needed, is offered for hypostasizing concepts and judgements. Since Moore goes on to assert that the world is made of concepts, thus realistically conceived, some such argument is surely called for. (In Frege one at least has a strong motivation for assigning Thoughts to a Platonistically-conceived Third Realm, namely that the publicity constraints on sense require that it have a greater degree of objectivity than mappings across the psychological states of language-users can yield. I argue elsewhere that Frege's requirement, backed as it is in this coherent way, is overstrong.)[12]

Russell's transcendental argument has it, as we saw, that a form of externality is necessary for the possibility of experience, because the givens of experience are complexes, that is, have parts which must be external to each other. Moore's first point is directed at this proposition. He quotes Russell's claim that necessity always involves a ground, and says

> But this ground must itself either be simply categorical, or else it must itself be necessary and require a further ground. In the former case we are actually trying to

deduce an a priori proposition from one that, as categorical, is merely empirical; in the latter, which Mr Russell seems in the end inclined to accept, we must either allow an infinite regress of necessary propositions, and thus never reach the absolutely a priori, or else we must accept the view that knowledge is circular, and shall in the end return to the proposition from which we started as empirical, as being itself the ground of necessity of the a priori, and therefore itself as much a priori as the latter. Mr Russell seems actually to accept this latter view [pp. 57–60] – a view which renders his logical criterion nugatory, since it asserts that that which is presupposed in the empirical equally and in the same sense presupposes the empirical.

Moore is here arguing in effect that, leaving aside a regress of conditions which never terminates in an absolute a priori, however one otherwise tries to state the case the *starting point* is the nature of experience and the *conclusion* concerns what is required for it to be thus and so; and therefore 'to show that a "form of externality" is necessary for the possibility of experience, can only mean to show that it is presupposed in our actual experience' (*CN*, p. 399). And Moore immediately sees that 'this can never prove that no experience would be possible without such a form, unless we assume that our actual experience is necessary, ie. that no other experience is possible' (*ibid.*).

It no more occurred to Moore to consider whether this ancillary requirement can be met than, evidently, it occurred to Russell, who like most Kantians might have simply accepted that Kant was right to allow the possibility of other forms of experience, for example he allowed that animals might have forms of spatial experience quite different from ours. For this reason

Moore read Russell as having to find another way out for the argument, and therefore attributes to him what he calls the 'subterfuge' (*ibid.*) of the presuppositional argument. Moore thus views Russell's point about presuppositions as an ad hoc step taken to avoid a difficulty, not as a characterization of the argument to the necessity of a form of externality itself. As we saw, in this he is wrong. For it is of the essence of a transcendental argument that, in identifying what is necessarily presupposed to something which is the case, it tells us something else about what is the case as its condition. Instead of being a criticism of Russell's strategy, Moore's anatomization describes it.

But it does show that the condition identified as necessary for spatial experience is relative unless the ancillary requirement be met that no alternative experience is possible. At first sight this seems to pose too tall an order. But subsequent debate in philosophy has provided an interesting if controversial means of showing that there might indeed be a way to satisfy the requirement. (A polite form of execratory howl usually greets this assertion, chiefly because of now orthodox assumptions about possibility. When possibility is understood as an epistemic notion, as conceivability, in effect, the task is recognisably much more manageable. But the argument I'm about to borrow does not require a demonstration that most philosophers until the time of Kant were right to construe the modalities, all of them, as epistemic notions.) The argument, furnished by Davidson, is his celebrated case for saying that the idea of alternative conceptual schemes is incoherent. It has more texture than I am going to bring out here,[13] but in any case I only need its bones for present purposes.

---

[13] I give it an extended discussion and proposed modification elsewhere – see my *Refutation of Scepticism*, 1985.

The argument goes as follows.

The idea of 'other ways of having experience' can be generalized into the idea of alternative conceptual schemes, alternative, that is, to our own, for arbitrarily constrained 'us' (it does not matter how restrictive one is about who 'we' are in talk of 'our' conceptual scheme, for the argument goes through whatever one says about this), – and conceptual schemes can be provided with criteria of identity by identifying them with languages or sets of intertranslatable languages. Then, in turn, questions about the possibility of the existence of conceptual schemes other than our own, perhaps existing undetectably from the point of view of our own, can be framed in terms of translatability. In this idiom, the question of whether there can be *other* or *alternative* schemes comes down to the question of whether there can be languages that we cannot translate. But since we can have no grounds for treating as a language anything that cannot be translated into our own language, since, in effect, the criterion of language-hood is 'translatability into a familiar idiom', and since intertranslatability defines membership of the same scheme, the conception of distinct schemes, in particular, of mutually inaccessible schemes, is incoherent. But to say that there can be no such thing as an alternative scheme is, transposing back into the idiom of ways of experiencing, to say that ours can be, still taking our modalities seriously, the only such way. The argument is a strongly anti-relativist one; which is appropriate, because Moore's rebuttal of Russell's project takes precisely the form of a sceptical counter-claim to the effect that forms of experience are relative. As is usual, no argument is offered for the claim: its sole ground seems to be the now orthodox view of possibility mentioned.

One characteristic reaction to this application of the Davidson argument, here cavalierly seeming to keep the 'Ptolemaic counter-revolution' going, is to say that no contradiction infects the idea of something which is recognizably an untranslatable language. The usual example offered is the uncracked Minoan script. A response to this example is to point out that the inaccessibility here at issue is not to a language but to a script embodying a fragment of what we suppose to be a language, and moreover one not in use, which places a contingent barrier to translation which by itself is not relevant to the question of its languagehood. But another, more general, response is to contrast the notion of an untranslatABLE language with that of an untranslatED language. Contingent barriers to translation of one established language into another (such as the current but, I surmise, reducible inability of most English speakers to translate Magyar into their own tongue) do not, obviously, put them beyond the pale of languagehood; which tells us much, on reflection, about what would. Rather, the accessibility point rests, as Davidson convincingly argues, on these general thoughts: that the concept of differences between languages, or schemes, or ways of having experience, essentially trades upon there being enough access between supposed alternatives for the differences to be apparent. There has to be a background of shared assumptions and beliefs giving rise to the degree of mutual comprehensibility which alone makes differences recognizable. And this is not a point about mere cultural relativities, about what might be called anthropological divergences, differences of opinion and high-level social practices, but about the most basic levels of cognitive activity turning on individuation, reference, property-attribution and assent. In the fuller treatment of these points referred to above, I argue (diverging from Davidson) that this shared basis has to be rather rich and fine-grained, to the extent that it rules out indeterminacy of reference.[14] As applied to the question of language, one can connect points about shared background beliefs and holdings-true as a condition of getting translation started, with points about the recognizability of devices in the language for reference, predication and assent and dissent: so a much more articulated grasp of an alien tongue is required even by Quine's philosophical anthropologist before he can fairly get going. Alternatively put, the requirement for starting a translation manual is that there should already be one available.

Another response to these claims is that there are certain identifiable possessors of conceptual schemes which are not possessors of language, for example cats and cows, so the identification of schemes and languages fails, and with it the putative access required and therefore afforded by translation. One can leave aside the short answer from the inescapability of 'reading-in' in such cases, which might be (so say those who do not belong to a cat) what our attribution of concept-possession to languageless creatures consists in. We can leave this aside because it is obvious that one can give a strongly motivated and cogent argument for attributing concept-possession and attitudes, at least to a certain level of complexity (remembering the strictures of Frege and Wittgenstein on this subject), to at least the higher mammals, among other things on the grounds of the successful pragmatics attached to doing so: as witness Fodor's famous feline. The point might be put by saying that much of what can be attributed concerning the beliefs and intentions of such mammals

---

[14] cf. *ibid.*, chap. 3, passim.

is representable in one's own language in statements having as good a chance of being true on the evidence as those about creatures capable of making their own avowals. On this head, there is nothing second-class about third-party attribution.

These points are made, remember, in response to questions about the intrinsic merits of Moore's attack on *EFG*, and whether Russell was without recourse in defending the philosphical strategy there adopted. These points at least show that both Moore and Russell were too swift here. And this can be substantiated by noting that there is of course a similar but much weaker response, or set of responses, that can be made to this aspect of Moore's criticism. As Strawson has argued (in *Scepticism and Naturalism* and elsewhere) there is much to be gained from an investigation of what our kind of experience requires, even if it is not the only kind there can be. This either allows philosophical interest to what Moore dismisses as merely parochial, or it refuses to interpose so impermeable a membrane between psychological and philosophical considerations as was all the rage at the turn of the century. But in the presence of a stronger argument for the cogency of the general enterprise, I do not say Kant's or Russell's in particular, it is worth contesting Moore's rejection of their style of argument.

It might be asked what difference would have been made, outside his philosophy of mathematics, if Russell had retained some part of his early convictions about a priori knowledge. With the exception granted, one answer is: less than one might suppose, since it would not have interfered with his pluralism, his atomism or with his adoption of certain sustainable versions of non-Platonic realism; and another answer is that it might have offered resources to his epistemology from the lack of which they badly suffer. This is well illustrated by one salient consequence of dispensing with a priori constituents in knowledge, namely, Russell's reliance on the notion of acquaintance. His response to Moore's Platonism about concepts and judgements, which remained when the objects of acquaintance had become simultaneously far more various and refined, was to treat our relation to them as direct, theory-free, unmediated and conditionless. The relation is curiously thin and undefined; it comes without constraints, as if it were primitive; and in so far as it admits of being described as a mental operation, it is distinctively passive, the very opposite, one might say, of a relation in thought or experience in which some act, of perceiving or judging, plays a constitutive or partly constitutive role with respect to its objects. Now one need not be interested in specifically Kantian strategies for understanding how this works to feel the deficiency in the theory of acquaintance. One thing one can safely say is that if he had not abandoned the approach in *EFG* so entirely, Russell would have written differently later about knowledge and perception.

One of the really interesting features of *EFG* is that in it Russell is not an idealist; he as an anti-realist (so is Kant in fact, on a certain best reading). The differences are considerable. Idealism is a metaphysical thesis which asserts that reality is fundamentally mental; it says that reality is Mind (eg. Bradley) or that it consists of minds and their ideas (eg. Berkeley). Anti-realism is an epistemological thesis, which asserts that the relations between thought and things, perception and its objects, experience and its accusatives, language and the world, or whichever of these (different) pairings one takes as primary, is not external, as realists claim. To say that the relations in question are internal is far from saying that thought or experience *creates* the world or is in some other way ontologically responsible for them: that is metaphysics, and specifically idealist metaphysics. Talk of the nature of the relations between mind and world is purely epistemological; it is not of course independent of considerations about what there is, but it does not by itself involve constitutive ontological claims.[15]

Now, Russell did not see the difference, so his unpreparedness to defend against Moore's attacks on *idealism* led him to abandon his *anti-realism*, a much more moderate position which he replaced, at first, with a most immoderate realism. It is precisely the anti-realist features of Russell's thought in *EFG* which would have served his later epistemology well.

---

[15] See my 'Epistomology and Realism', *Proceedings of the Aristotelian Society*, 1990–91.

A CERTAIN KNOWLEDGE?
RUSSELL'S MATHEMATICS AND LOGICAL ANALYSIS

C. W. Kilmister

I

When the National Gallery in London was refurbished after the Second World War, the top of the main staircase was decorated by mosaics of leading Britons. Russell is seen there as a figure seeking to draw truth out of a deep well.[1] This artistic perception captures the common view of that time and, as usual, there is something in the common view. Some might argue that the well was not all that deep. Others might talk of the young Russell as an idealist, of Russell the neutral monist and so on. It is certainly useful to pigeon hole the development of his ideas in this way. But I want to proceed in the opposite direction, to seek the common strand in his developing thought. That Russell was content to have changed his mind over many matters does not alter the fact that there is one person to be discovered behind the changing views. More specifically, I want to draw out the connexions between various well-known features: the need he felt for certainty, his view of truth, his unorthodox view of

---

[1] See front cover illustration to this book.

logical calculi and his notion of analysis. These four topics occupy one section each of what follows.

II

Russell felt very early on an acute need for certainty of knowledge, originally about the truth of religion but then more generally, till this need crystallized into the more practical possibility of finding a reason to believe in the truth of mathematics. Already at the age of eleven, in a well-known passage:

> I began Euclid with my brother as tutor. This was one of the great events of my life, as dazzling as first love …. Like all happiness, however, it was not unalloyed. I had been told that Euclid proved things, and was much disappointed that he started with axioms.

After his death, the *Times* obituary stated, without qualification, that the reason that Russell was only seventh wrangler was because his interest was in mathematics as certain knowledge, not for its own sake. Ironically, this is the same person who, as a graduate, spent some time in the Cavendish to see how experiments were carried out and to see if he would be good at it. Perhaps his disappointment here was not from any failure in experimental flair, but a realization of the extreme fallibility of knowledge in physics.

There is no surprise, then, to see Russell turn to the foundations of geometry as a theme for his fellowship dissertation in 1895. He had by now taken Part 2 of the Moral Sciences tripos and come under the influences of Ward, Stout and McTaggart:

> I was at this time a full-fledged Hegelian, and I aimed at constructing a complete dialectic of the sciences … I accepted the Hegelian view that none of the sciences

is quite true, since all depend on some abstraction, and every abstraction leads, sooner or later, to contradiction. Whenever Kant and Hegel were in conflict, I sided with Hegel. (Russell, 1959, p. 42)

None the less, the book is very Kantian and, in particular, Russell accepts Kant's criticism of empiricism, although as a Hegelian he accepts that there is no such thing as space. The fact that it is an abstraction does not, however, prevent him from believing a theory of it is possible. It will inevitably contain contradiction but this only means that the truths are only relative truths. This has led some to write this book off as part of Russell's misspent idealist youth and later Russell thought the book much too Kantian. He thought this because Kant would not have mathematics as unconditionally true but as resting on space and time. So Russell would in due course turn from such a foundation to rest it on logic.

This is all to take the book too much out of context. Russell came to write it very much from a Cambridge position. Already in the early part of the nineteenth century there was a tradition of seeing philosophy of science as fundamental to metaphysics. The idealist Whewell saw man as having true knowledge in his mind in its capacity to recognize such an idea as space. The empiricist Herschel saw minds having a structure that, in interaction with experience, leads to true knowledge, and both saw geometry as a clear example of this. Just as Kant had seen it as a clear example of the a priori. Now it is important to recognize that this geometry was no abstract formal system; it became that only much later in the century, and at this time was just the ordered development of the notion of space. Thus Whewell is quite clear that 'the certainty of mathematical reasoning arises from it depending on definitions' and that the definitions in question 'are not arbitrary or hypothetical but necessary definitions'. So it is not surprising to see Russell echoing this in his *Foundations of Geometry*: 'mathematics is about the actual world and consistency proofs are of little value.'

While the dissertation does have some somewhat negative Hegelian aspects, there are positive features which are more relevant to Russell's search for certainty. Russell argues for a sharp philosophical distinction between metrical geometry (whether Euclidean or non Euclidean) and non-metrical projective geometry. Kant's failure to attend to this distinction (however forgivable historically) is an error which led to his untenable attribution of synthetic a priori status to Euclidean geometry. It is necessary to go into this argument a little more fully to assess its effect on Russell's development. There are really two disconnected parts to be considered. Euclidean geometry deals with points and lines together with a relation between points called the distance between them. If three points lie on a line, the distance between the outside ones is the sum of the other two distances. There is also a relation between lines (the angle between them) but this can be defined in terms of the length relation and then, when three points form a right-angled triangle, the theorem of Pythagoras relates the three lengths. This, and all the consequent properties of Euclidean geometry, then remain true when the figures are transformed by translation or rotation, that is, under the transformations of the Euclidean group.

For reasons that do not concern us here (the discontent, from at least Proclus in the fifth century AD, over Euclid's parallel postulate) two different versions of non-Euclidean geometry arose in the nineteenth century.

These were still considering points, lines and a distance relation with the additive property still holding but for right-angled triangles the theorem of Pythagoras did not hold. One example had been familiar to mariners for many years: that of the geometry of the surface of a sphere with great circles playing the part of straight lines. The corresponding group of transformations was a different one but not any larger than the Euclidean one. Now unless one held fast to the view that Euclidean geometry was in some way the evidently true one, and these others were consistent but wholly fictional, Kant's 'geometry is a science which determines the properties of space synthetically and yet a priori' is in great difficulty. And yet it is hard to keep to that view. For one thing there is no sharp distinction between Euclidean and non-Euclidean geometry. In the mariner's example, if the radius of the sphere is very large compared with the region considered, the geometry is almost Euclidean. To summarize this first part, then, we may say that, although the discovery of non-Euclidean geometry was disastrous for Kant's doctrine, yet the changes from the Euclidean situation were not otherwise philosophically interesting.

The second part of the argument is much more interesting for Russell's development. It concerns the philosophical position of 'projective geometry', which deals with the properties of figures unchanged not only by rotations but under projection from a point. Thus this geometry can be viewed as arising from a deliberate widening of the group of transformations envisaged. The length relation is now evidently not unchanged, since it is clear in the figure that BC ≠ FG, and even ratios of lengths are changed (AB/BC ≠ EF/FG).

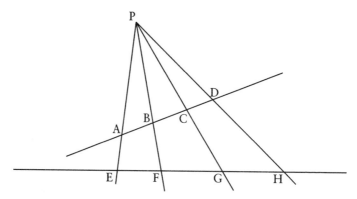

But Desargues discovered early in the seventeenth century that the ratio of ratios, (AB/BC)/(AD/DC), called the cross-ratio, was unchanged. Thus this geometry is concerned with points, lines and with a four-term relation between points. There is, however, one obvious defect from a foundational point of view, in the explanation I have just given. The greater generality of this projective geometry is only an appearance, because the definition of the four-term relation is given in terms of the Euclidean distance. It was in 1847 that the surprising technical achievement of Von Staudt was to show how to define the cross-ratio without appeal to Euclidean distance.

In Russell's *Foundations of Geometry*, projective geometry is deduced, it is claimed, by a transcendental argument from three principles. By a transcendental argument is meant, in a somewhat Kantian sense, a metaphysical discussion, rather than one inside the geometrical system. The three principles are, firstly, that different parts of space can be distinguished, although all parts are qualitatively similar, by the immediate fact that they lie outside one another. Secondly, space is continuous and infinitely divisible and the result of infinite division is a point. The third principle limits the number of dimensions of space to being finite. This deduction then leads Russell to a modified Kantian position in which projective geometry plays the role that Euclidean geometry played for Kant, and to that extent the quest for certainty is crowned with success. This seems to be the first time in Russell's thinking that a philosophical argument is completed (in this case, corrected) by two purely technical investigations. The investigations are, firstly, Desargues' invention of projective geometry, then von Staudt's purging of all assumptions of Euclidean metric. I do not see Russell's transcendental argument as such a technical investigation, though some might wish to do so. The belief in the efficacy of technical investigations in solving philosophical problems seems to me to be one of the hallmarks of analytical philosophy. This early success must have conditioned Russell's later thinking and remained with him as a way forward to the desired certainty.

III

I began this paper by setting on one side the usual characterizations of Russell's development in favour of a search for a more unified view. But there is one piece of the usual characterization which cannot be over-estimated: his rejection of idealism, under the influence of Moore. From that moment onwards truth becomes an absolute concept for him. There are things that are either true or false, with no qualifications or hedging and these are the real subject matter of philosophy. This is a philosophical claim and one which is easy enough to make by itself. But as a bed-fellow of the acute need for certain knowledge, it becomes rather uncomfortable. This discomfort did not prevent the new realization remaining supreme in Russell's later life and thought. In his differences from Frege, for example, Russell ultimately failed to be the sort of reader Frege relied on 'who does not begrudge me a pinch of salt'. And seeing the importance of this view of truth helps one to make sense of the notorious 'bicycle ride' incident over Alys:

> ... suddenly, as I was riding along a country road, I realised that I no longer loved Alys ... I had no wish to be unkind, but I believed in those days (what experience has taught to think open to doubt) that in intimate relations one should speak the truth. (Russell, 1967, p. 147)

Continuing at the personal level, one might enquire how one could believe that such an over-ambitious black-and-white view of truth could be humanly sustained. I do not want to be diverted into amateur psychology. It would in any case be impossible for me to understand fully the outlook of a patrician Whig whose grandfather had been Prime Minister of the United Kingdom. Indeed Russell himself saw the general danger of intellectual arrogance: disillusioned in St Petersburg in 1920 he noted that 'the governing classes had a self-confidence quite as great as that produced by Eton and Oxford'. I wonder, however, if one can see historical influence at work here. We are talking of around the turn of the century, the very time at which physics, in which Russell maintained a friendly interest, turned from a continuous picture of the world with infinite gradations of measurement to the major task (still not wholly completed) of incorporating the discrete true/false observables of quantum mechanics. As Russells says:

My philosophical development, since the early years of the present century, may be broadly described as a gradual retreat from Pythagoras. Science had not then arrived at the 'all or nothing principle' of which the importance was only discovered during the present century. I thought, when I was young, that two divergent attractions would lead to a Whig compromise, whereas it has appeared since that very often one of them prevails completely. This has justified Dr Johnson in the opinion that the Devil, not the Almighty, was the first Whig .... (Russell, 1959)

I turn to the effects of Russell's blinding realization on his current efforts on the foundations of mathematics. Absolute truth left no room for Hegelian contradictions, so any remaining contradictions in geometry would have to be simply due to mistakes. Indeed the same must be true of the whole of mathematics and the need was for a technical instrument to show it to be so. As we know, from 1900 onwards, after the meeting with Peano, logic was awarded the task, with increasing confidence. There is a puzzle here. A need for certainty about the absolute truth of mathematics is a radical platform which brings to mind at once the austere doctrines of L. E. J. Brouwer. His thesis dates from 1907, it is true, but from then onwards he sought the very same aim. Brouwer began from a position of disgust at the way in which, as he saw it, society used language as a means of enslaving the individual. He moved on to seeing mathematics as a 'language-less activity of the human mind', with an emphasis on its possibilities of free creation and as 'synonymous with the exact part of our thinking'. One might have expected Russell to have given a sympathetic reception to such views but this never became the case. For example, as late as 1930 Russell, asked to comment on some written work of Wittgenstein (roughly, what was later to become part of *Philosophical Investigations*), says:

> He discusses 'infinity' at considerable length and links it with the conception of possibility that he has developed in connexion with his various 'spaces'... What he says about infinity tends, obviously against his will, to have a certain resemblance to what has been said by Brouwer.... (Russell, 1968, p. 199)

Russell then hastens to assure the committee that the resemblance is only superficial and of no importance. Earlier on, both he and Wittgenstein, in correspondence, had seen Brouwer's ideas as a dangerous trap to be avoided. I think that a major part is played here by the fact that Brouwer's approach to the foundations of mathematics was one that made much of current mathematics false and so in need of replacement. Such a view was anathema to the Cambridge mathematicians who were still able then to hold pretty closely to their traditional view that mathematics was defined as that which was taught in the mathematics tripos. This view certainly rubbed off on Russell and through him, perhaps, on Wittgenstein.

Whatever the reason, Russell turned a blind eye to such a Brouwerian approach. The quest for certainty was still on, the unequivocal view of truth necessitated some true and sure foundation and logic was the candidate for this.

IV

The contribution of Peano to this turning to logic was not a small one. The notion of the subject-predicate logic of the syllogism had already been noticed as inadequate by Russell, for example, in discussing Leibniz's doctrines on space. But Russell, under the direct influence of Whitehead and the indirect one of Boole, had already realized that Aristotle's was not the last word on logic and Peano opened a door that was already ajar. Now in discussing the *Foundations of Geometry* I distinguished Russell's view of geometric axioms from the modern one of a formal system. For Russell, mathematics is seen as about the actual world and its axioms have to be true. The same happens over logic but the background is a little different. In holding 'Logical propositions are such as can be known a priori, without study of the actual world' and in seeing logic as made up of truths, Russell is taking a position very different from our current thinking about logic. The question of the completeness of a set of (logical) axioms, for example, just does not arise, because of its reliance on some independent view of what the logic ought to do. But in taking this position, he is simply standing put at the end of two thousand years of tradition. Noone had earlier seen logic as anything less than a codification of correct reason: indeed, some had even taken it as a codification of thinking. It is this favoured position of logic which gives it exactly the required independence and certainty to serve to assure the correctness of mathematics. I do not want to digress today about the triumphs of logicism; it certainly gives considerable insight into the nature of mathematics and helps the mathematicians over concepts which they had failed to understand themselves. This was another success for the programme of solving philosophical troubles (which is a correct description of the difficulties in mathematics) by technical means. Neither do I want to spend too much time over its failure; the need for something like the theory of types to avoid the paradoxes and the consequent need for the axiom of reducibility. When Russell says:

> One point in regard to which improvement is obviously desirable is the axiom of reducibility... This axiom has a purely pragmatic justification: it leads to the desired results and not others. But clearly it is not the sort of axiom which we can rest content. (Russell, 1925)

he is stating no more than the truth. We were supposed to be achieving the certainty of mathematics from the a priori knowledge of the absolute truth of logic and such an axiom clearly had no place.

Two points are worth making, however. Firstly, the Gödel surprise of 1930, notwithstanding its title involving *Principia Mathematica* by name, was no attack on logicism as Russell understood it. Gödel simply proved some incompleteness results, which have no more relevance than the completeness proofs discussed above. The direction of attack was on Hilbert instead. Against that positive point must be set a negative one about the slightly blinkered view that the early success of logicism gave Russell. Wittgenstein in 1919 had cause to point out:

> Now I'm afraid you haven't really got hold of my main contention, to which the whole business of logical props is only a corollary. The main point is the theory of what can be expressed (gesagt) by props – ie. by language – (and, which comes to the same, what can be thought) and what cannot be expressed by props, but only shown (gezeigt). (Russell, 1968, p. 118)

I conclude by drawing together three ways in which

Russell's thinking in *Principia Mathematica* and in the work that led up to it was important in the genesis of both Russell's philosophy of logical analysis and of the analytical tradition. It is not very easy to say just what this tradition is but at least we have a clear statement of how Russell saw it in its infancy:

> a philosophy grew up which is often described as 'realism', but is really characterised by analysis as a method and pluralism as a metaphysic. It is not necessarily realistic....
>
> The first characteristic of the new philosophy is that it abandons the claim to a special philosophical method .... It regards philosophy as essentially one with science, differing... merely by the generality of its problems, and by the fact that it is concerned with the formation of hypotheses where empirical evidence is still lacking....
>
> The new philosophy maintained ... that knowledge, as a rule, makes no difference to what is known ... Consequently theory of knowledge ceases to be a magic key to open the door to the mysteries of the universe and so we are thrown back upon the plodding investigations of science.
>
> The new philosophy... is constructive, but as science is constructive, bit by bit and tentatively. It has a special technical method of construction, namely mathematica logic...
>
> A good deal of modern pluralist philosophy has been inspired by the logical analysis of propositions. (Russell, 1928)

Russell's retrospective view of the genesis of logical analysis, then marks a substantial step back in the search for certain knowledge – it is to be no more certain than the fallible truths of science. I return to the three particular points I want to make about Russell's thinking.

The first is the confidence that technical advances can 'solve' philosophical problems. This started over the foundations of geometry and it developed into the notion that mathematics and logic (for Russell, identical) could solve such problems as the paradoxes of the infinite, the nature of time and, as in *Foundations of Geometry*, of space. If *Principia Mathematica* had been successful, it would have been a wonderful example of this. But it was not successful, so why has symbolic logic remained as one of the characteristic features of analytical tradition? Unlike the position in *Principia*, the technical tricks of logic are not often essential and symbolic arguments are prone to conceal rather than illuminate. Who is the beneficiary, for example, of the clarification of the way in which Peano's axioms in first order form fail to be categorical, that is, fail to charac- terize their subject matter up to isomorphism, when first year mathematics undergraduates are routinely taught an 'easy' proof that they are? Perhaps since *Principia Mathematica* only the 1930 paper of Gödel has been a really convincing example of the power of symbolic reasoning.

One might imagine – as I did myself – that the real function of symbolic logic was to embed in the heart of the tradition the absolute unqualified nature of truth and falsehood which was adopted so enthusiastically and which still survives. Yet this it fails to do. For what would be the situation if it did? It would surely mean that some formulation of the propositional calculus – and it seems only appropriate here to take the first three and the fifth primitive propositions of *Principia Mathematica* (since Bernays showed the fourth was derivable) – was such as to be consistent *only* with a two-valued truth table. But a little trial and error shows this is far from being the case. There are plenty of other truth-table interpretations. For example, one such is to take three truth values, 0 (false), ½, 1 (true) with the usual tables for negation and disjunction when 0, 1 are concerned, and with -p having the value 1 if that of p is ½, p ∨ q having the value ½ if both p and q have value ½ and other values of p ∨ q being filled in by 'common sense' if ½ is regarded as some sort of intermediate value between true and false. The table for p ⊃ q as defined in *Principia Mathematica* is then

	⊃	0	½	1	q
	0	1	1	1	
P	½	1	1	1	
	1	0	½	1	

so that *modus ponens* is preserved as a rule of inference. It is only a few minutes work to verify that the primitive propositions are tautologies. So I must confess that I see, on the one hand, the continuing respect for symbolic logic as a legacy from Russell, but, on the other I doubt its value.

I have no such doubts the second way. This predates *Principia Mathematica*, is related to the first and is based on Russell's realization of the importance of definitions. The point is really this: the use of definitions is commonplace in mathematics, in much of philosophy and even in everyday life. But they acquire a renewed force when set beside the notion of absolute truth. Russell makes some confusing remarks about definitions. He contrasts those in mathematics with those in philosophy. These he sees as 'the analysis of an idea into its constituents' in contrast with the mathematical ones where we give necessary and sufficient conditions. It is true that the definitions at the beginning of most parts of pure mathematics fit in with this description. But definitions can, as it were, be read in two ways. An early clue to Russell's understanding of the importance of definitions comes in his description of his state of mind when he went up to Cambridge:

> I was influenced by Darwin, and then by John Stuart Mill, but more than either by the study of dynamics; my outlook, in fact, was more appropriate to a seventeenth- or eighteenth-century Cartesian than to a post-Darwinian. (Russell, 1938)

Moreover, he notes in his undergraduate journal his satisfaction at finishing a page of exercises in rigid dynamics. Now the elegant structure of rigid dynamics, as taught at Cambridge at the end of the nineteenth century, was a very striking example of the power of definition. Very curious phenomena like the top and the gyroscope, which respond to applied forces in ways unexpected to the uninitiated, are all deduced from the elementary mechanics of particles together with a single further definition; a rigid body is defined as a set of particles, any two of which are constrained by internal forces to remain a constant distance apart. This definition has a form fitting much better with Russell's philosophical version. So it is not fanciful to detect its probable effect on the young Russell, perhaps for the first time, a positive value in the Cambridge teaching of rigid dynamics.

The third way is related to both of the others. It is the success that Russell had, at least till the paradoxes intervened, in rectifying, by purely technical means, Peano's defective definition by abstraction. Talking of a one-to-one relation, Russell notes that 'these properties of a relation are held by Peano and common sense to indicate that when the relation holds between two terms, these two terms have a certain property ... this common property we call their number'. Russell's objection to this is conclusive: neither the existence or the uniqueness of what is supposed to be defined is assured. But not entirely unlike the rigid dynamics example, Russell puts matters right in terms of a set of entities, or as he would put it, in terms of classes. The number of a class is simply defined as the class of all classes similar to it.

These three interlocking aspects of Russell's early thought seem to me his main contribution to the analytic tradition, but the latter two seem to be the most important.

BIBLIOGRAPHY OF WORKS CITED

Russell, B., 1959. *My Philosophical Development* (London, Allen and Unwin).

—— 1967. *The Autobiography of Bertrand Russell*, vol. 1 (London, Allen and Unwin).

—— 1925. *Principia Mathematica*, vol. 1, Introduction to the 2nd edn. (Cambridge).

—— 1928. *Sceptical Essays* (London, Allen and Unwin).

—— *The Rationalist Annual* (C. A. Watts and Co).

WILL THE REAL
PRINCIPIA MATHEMATICA
PLEASE STAND UP?
REFLECTIONS ON THE FORMAL LOGIC
OF THE *PRINCIPIA*

Gregory Landini
University of Iowa

Introduction
There are many different renditions of the formal system of *Principia Mathematica* (*PM*). To name just a few, there are Schütte (1934), Church (1956), Hatcher (1968), Copi (1971), and Chiahara (1973). The contention between them lies in the degree of significance each attributes to certain features of the philosophical explanations set out in the Introduction of the work. All regard the explanations as inconsistent and concur that pruning is necessary for coherence. This presentation offers a new rendition of the formal system – a rendition which at last shows that the real *Principia* comports with its Introduction.

1. *The Formal System of 'Principia' (Cum *10)*
Let us use 'A', 'B', 'C' as meta-linguistic letters for wffs. The primitive signs of the formal language are '–' and 'v', brackets and parentheses. (We no longer have braces for nominalizing a wff; in *Principia* there are no propositions and so no singular terms for them.) The signs '–' and 'v' of *PM* are now to be *statement* connectives.

The individual and predicate variables now come with order/type superscripts. The variables are x, y, z with any positive numeral subscript and any order/type superscript. (For convenience we shall often omit the subscript and use further lower-case letters of the English alphabet.) To get at the notion of an order/type symbols we let us render a definition.

A order/type symbol is any expression which satisfies the following recursive definition: (i) 'o' is an order/type symbol. (ii) If $t_1,...,t_n$ are order/type symbols, then the expression $(t_1,...,t_n)$ is also an order/type symbol. (iii) These are the only order/type symbols.

Examples of our variables are then x^o, $x^{(o)}$, $x^{((o),o)}$, and so on. The intent is that the variable x^o is an individual variable (ie. a variable of type o). The variable $x^{(o)}$ is a predicate variable whose type is such that its admissible arguments will be individual variables; $x^{((o),o)}$ is a dyadic predicate variable whose first argument is a predicate variable of type (o) and an individual variable. The aspect of *order* of the order/type symbol is to be understood by means of our next definition:

The *order* of an order/type symbol is given by the following recursive definition: (i) the order/type symbol 'o' has order 0. (ii) An order/type symbol $(t_1,...,t_n)$ has order $n+1$, if the highest order of the order/type symbols $t_1,...,t_n$ is n.

One can give a parenthesis-counting algorithm for determining the order of an order/type symbol. Count parentheses from left to right, adding +1 for each left parenthesis and -1 for each right. The order of the order/type symbol is the highest positive integer obtained in the counting process.

Now our order/type symbols are formally convenient but it is useful to adopt an alternative notation which is handy when it comes to the demonstration of certain important points about *Principia's* order/types. We can put superscripts on the right for the order/type of the arguments to a variable and superscripts on the left of the variable for the order of the whole order/type symbol. The individual variables then look like: ${}^{0}x^{0}, {}^{0}y^{0}, {}^{0}z^{0}$, and so forth. The predicate variables of the form $x^{(0)}$, can be written as ${}^{1}\emptyset^{(0\backslash 0)}$; the predicate variables of the form $x^{((0))}$ can be written as ${}^{2}\emptyset^{(1\backslash(0\backslash 0))}$; variables such as $x^{((0),0)}$ can be written as ${}^{2}\theta^{1\backslash(0\backslash 0),0\backslash 0)}$, and so on. In this way we can more easily see what will come to be a rule governing wffs of the system – viz., that arguments to a predicate variable must match in order/type.

The terms of the language are as follows: (i) All variables are terms; (ii) There are no other terms. The 'atomic wffs' of the language are of the form,

$$x^{(t1,...,tj)}(y^{t1}{}_{1},...,y^{tj}{}_{j}).$$

The wffs of the language are determined inductively as the smallest set K containing all atomic wffs of the language and such that $-A$, $(A \text{ v } B)$, and $(\forall x^{t})C$ are in K if A, B and C are in K and C contains the variable x^{t} free. We use $\lceil A(y^{t}|x^{t})\rceil$ for the wff exactly like $A(x^{t})$ except for having free occurrences of the term y^{t} for every free occurrence of x^{t} in A.

Set within this background grammar, the deductive system of *Principia* with *10 comes to the following:

*1.2   Pp   AvA .>. A
*1.3   Pp   B .>. AvB
*1.4   Pp   AvB .>. BvA
*1.5   Pp   A v (BvC) :>: B v (AvC)

*1.6   Pp   B>C :>: AvB .>. AvC

*1.1   Modus Ponens

From A and A > B, infer B

*1.01 A > B =df –A v B
*3.01   A & B   =df –(–A v –B)
*4.01   A≡B   =df A>B .&. B>A

We have here used our meta-linguistic 'A', 'B' and 'C' since on the method of *Principia's* *10 these apply to any wffs, elementary or otherwise. For the identity sign, we have the following definition:

*13.01 $x^t = y^t$ =df $(\forall z^{(t)})(z^{(t)}(x^t) \equiv z^{(t)}(y^t))$

This definition is tied to the reducibility schema discussed below.

The quantification theory developed in *Principia's* *10 is next given (with minor modifications). We have the schemata:

*10.01 $(\exists x^t)A$ =df $-(\forall x^t)-A$

*10.1   Pp $(\forall x^t) A(x^t)$.>. $A[y^t | x^t]$,

where the variable y^t is free for x^t in A.

*10.11 From A infer $(\forall x^t)A$,

where the variable x^t occurs free in A.

*10.12 Pp $(\forall x^t)(B > A(x^t))$.>. $B > (\forall x^t) A(x^t)$,

where x^t does not occur free in B. To complete the system, we need a general formulation of *Principia's* (schemata) of reducibility.[1]

*1910(Reduc)

---

[1]   *Principia* gave only two reducibility axioms, one for monadic functions and one for dyadic functions. The intent, however, that further axioms for any finite number of variables would be introduced where needed.

$$(\exists x^{(t1,...,tj)})(\forall y^{t1}),...,(\forall y^{tj})$$
$$(x^{(t1,...,tj)}(y^{t1},...,y^{tj}) \equiv A),$$

where $x^{(t1,...,tj)}$ does not occur free in A.

Compared with most of the literature surrounding *Principia*, the system *PM* above must appear shocking. It is time then that we offer arguments for its historical accuracy.

2. *Meta-language* versus *Object-language*

Principia is infamously poor in distinguishing its statements about its formal language from statements made within that language. Of course there are those who argue that the very idea of a meta-language within which we set out the formal system is out of sorts with Russell's conception of Logic. Entrenched though this opinion is, it is far from true. We do well then to pause long enough for a eulogy.

For Russell, Logic is a synthetic a priori science and has a subject matter – viz., structure (or 'logical form'). Russell's logicism is the thesis that all of non-applied mathematics is none other than the pure logic of relations (the foundation of structure and 'order'). Now our intuition of logical form informs our generation of a calculus for Logic. But Logic is not itself a formal calculus nor the study of formal calculi in general. The study of formal calculi is properly a branch of mathematics – a branch which (we now know) employs a good deal of mathematics to perform. An effort to demonstrate Logicism, then, cannot employ mathematical principles (such as mathematical induction) which have been taken to be paradigmatic of principles based on uniquely *mathematical* intuitions. Logicism must show that these intuitions are really logical intuitions, and any such demonstration cannot employ them with out quite obviously begging questions.

Well, it might be said, now the point is proved that Russell is forced to the view that Logic 'embraces its meta-theory' (Grattan-Guinness, 1977, p. 113). Not so. The fact that an articulation of any calculus will employ methods such as a recursive characterization of wffs does not imply that logicism cannot embrace a calculus for logic. This only shows that one must use some Logic to set forth a calculus for Logic. To be sure, one must not use mathematical induction – something taken to be paradigmatic of a distinctively mathematical intuition.[2] But Logicism is not harmed by admitting that *Logic* must be used in the statement of a calculus for logic.

Yes, yes, but it will be claimed that for Russell Logic is universal and 'all encompassing' so that any reasoning will fall within its domain. A calculus, on the other hand, cannot be all encompassing. The Tarski result, for instance, shows that for any formal calculus, its truth predicate is not representable within it. What of it? Russell's conception of logic can embrace the result that for any given calculus for Logic there will be patterns of reasoning and notions (pertaining to the relationship between expressions of the calculus and their referents) necessarily outside of it. Indeed, in two separate articles published prior to *Principia* Russell embraced just this idea to solve the Richard and King/Dixon and Berry paradoxes. The notion of 'nameable in L' is necessarily not a notion of L, for 'nameable' has meaning only with respect to some fixed and finite set of symbols (*INS*, p. 209 & *ML*). The essential point is not to conflate Logic with a calculus for Logic.

---

[2] In *Principia*, Whitehead and Russell explicitly reject the use of mathematical induction in setting out their calculus for logic.

What then of Russell's infamous doctrine of the unrestricted variable? Any pure calculus will admit of different interpretations over restricted domains. Russell, it is often said, sought to exclude such interpretations with the doctrine (Hylton, 1990, p. 203). This is but another oft repeated misunderstanding. In *Principles* the doctrine is simply that since Logic treats all entities alike, any calculus for Logic must adopt only one style of genuine variable – the 'individual' ('being', 'entity', 'logical subject') variable. All other 'variables', eg. those for natural numbers, classes, concepts, propositions, and so on, are 'variables with structure' – ie. defined signs. We shall see that by the time of *Principia* this has changed a bit. While some of the 'variables with structure' (such as those for classes and relations-in-extension) are introduced via definition, the structure of others (in particular, order/type indices on predicate variables) get their explanation via a semantic gloss. Nonetheless, the point is the same: the doctrine of the unrestricted variable in no way excludes a calculus for Logic.

Russell's conception of logic is consistent with his adoption of a calculus for Logic. Evidence that *Principia* adopts inference rules and statements of a formal grammar pertaining to a calculus are everywhere – once the blinders have been removed.[3] Consider the following which introduces the notion of an 'individual'. We find (*PM*, p. 132):

> Primitive idea: *Individual*. We say x is 'individual' when it is neither a proposition nor a function.

An individual, we are told, is 'something which exists on its own account; it is then obviously not a proposition,

---

[3] The matter is taken up again in chapter 13.

since propositions, as explained in chapter 2 of the Introduction (*PM*, p. 43) are incomplete symbols ...' (*PM*, p. 162). And further (*PM*, p. 51):

> ... we shall use such letters as a, b, c, x, y, z, w, to denote objects which are neither propositions nor functions. Such objects we call *individuals*. Such objects will be constituents of propositions or functions, and will be *genuine* constituents, in the sense that they do not disappear on analysis, as (for example) classes do, or phrases of the form 'the so and so'.

Well if these passages are not about grammar then they are incoherent. In *Principia* there are no propositions in the ontological sense. So how can, eg. *a* denote a proposition and how can an individual (qua entity in the world) be its constituent? Moreover, if 'x is an individual' is a primitive of the object-language, then one may as well have 'x exists' which is explicitly excluded from the symbolism (*PM*, p. 175).

Russell is just sloppy. The word 'individual' has two uses. First, it means 'individual variable' (ie. one among the lower case Latin letters 'a', 'b', 'x', 'y', etc.) But, of course, on the intended interpretation, individual variables are assigned entities. This is its second use.

There are many more examples of *Principia*'s sloppiness. But we should not let them lead us to generate pseudo-problems by a mule-headed adherence to the view that Russell's conception of Logic makes his statements ontological ones about entities in the world and not meta-linguistic statements about the object-language of a formal calculus. Consider this. Russell tells us that '... any symbol whose meaning is not determinate is called a *variable*, and the various determinations of which its meaning is susceptible are called the *values* of the variable' (*PM*, p. 4). But then goes on to say 'variables will be denoted by single letters' (*ibid.*, p. 5). Dismissing the first, many explain the second by assuming that *Principia*'s 'propositional functions' are Platonic entities with variables (albeit in an admittedly obscure way) their ontological constituents.[4] The proper interpretation of Russell's words is simply that certain letters *are* variables; a variable is just a symbol. But, of course, we can talk about (denote) these symbols too, and this happens in setting forth the formal deductive system. For example, we find (*PM*, p. 140):

> *10.11 If øy is true whatever possible argument y may be, then *(x)* .øx is true.

This is just *universal generalization*; and here the italicized 'y' is used to denote variables.

Care must be taken with *Principia*'s use of the word 'individual'. But even more care is need in interpreting its use of the words 'function' and 'propositional function' and 'n-order matrix'. In a number of instances, these are simply alternates of the modern expression 'predicate variable'. Consider the following (*PM*, p. 165):

> We shall use the small Latin letters (other than *p, q, r, s*) for variables of the lowest type concerned in any context. For functions, we shall use the letters ø, , X, θ, f, g, F ...

This just sets out the predicate variables of the formal system. Paralleling 'individual' as a primitive idea, we find (*PM*, p. 164):

> 'Matrix' or 'predicative function' is a primitive idea.

----

4 Most recently, Hylton (1990) takes this view.

And further, (*ibid.*):

> A function is said to be *predicative* when it is a matrix
> .... The variables in occurring in the present work,
> from this point onward, will all be either individuals
> or matrices of some order in the above hierarchy.

A matrix is a symbol; it is a variable. As we shall see,
there are different sorts of variables for (although they
are suppressed) variables come with order/type indices.
The point of the above passage is just that function
terms are predicative when they are matrices, ie.
variables; and, moreover, that all variables are to be
either individual variables or predicate variables.

3. *Free Variables* versus *Schematic Letters*

With the distinction of meta and object language as an
ally, we can finally clear away the fog that has
surrounded interpretations of *Principia*. In setting out
the formal calculus of the work, Whitehead and Russell
rely upon what they call 'typical ambiguity' – ie. the
convenient avoidance order/type indices. Their use of
the convenience is deplorable and has generated upteen
misinterpretations. Here is some sorting out.

'Typical ambiguity' is only intelligible as a convention
of *suppressing* order/type symbols; the formal language
and deductive system must be stated with them, and
then (with rules for restoration) they can be suppressed.
Unfortunately, Whitehead and Russell attempt to set
out the language and rules of their calculus without
indices. This leads them to speak as if schematic letters
are predicate variables and to proceed as though
'apparent' (bound) variables could be fixed in order/type
while some 'real' (free) variables *occurring in theses* can
be ('ambiguous') as to order (*PM*, p. 128). (This is the
heart of Whitehead and Russell's distinction between

'all' and 'any'.)[5] This won't do. Whitehead and Russell cannot have indices on bound variables but drop them from free variables in theses, else the ramified type regimented rules of *Universal Generalization* and principles like *Universal Instantiation* become a jumble. Free and bound object-language variables must come with order/type indices and they must be notionally distinguished from schematic letters for wffs.

A woeful use of 'typical ambiguity' is also behind the presence of quite a few 'principles' of *Principia*. Consider principles such as the following:[7]

*10.121   If 'øx' is significant, then if a is of the same type as x, then 'øa' is significant, and vice versa.

*10.122   If, for some a, there is a proposition øa, then there is a function øx̂ and vice versa.

All too commonly it is objected that such principles violate type theory. As Hylton recently put it, '... a single propositional function (ø̂ is *predicative*) is applicable (truly or falsely) to entities of different type; this contravenes type restrictions. Another example concerns the notion of type itself. Proposition *9.131 is a definition of "being the same type as" ... The relation is one which itself violates type restrictions' (Hylton, 1990, p. 317). The objection is unfounded. The fact is, the notion '... is predicative', principle *9.131 governing '... is same type as ...', and principles such as the above are meta-linguistic. They concern the formal grammar of *Principia* and the conditions for well- formedness of symbols. Observe how the above

---

[5] It also arises in expressing the Reducibility principles.

[6] Goldfarb (1989, fn. 22) takes these as introducing circumflexion as a predicate term forming operator. This is not so as we shall see.

principles are used. If øa is a proposition, Whitehead and Russell tell us, then (by *10.122) øx̂ is a function; and since 'øx̂ always' is a primitive, there is a proposition (x)øx. (See the proof of *9.62.) The intent here is just to say that if there is a wff Aµ, we shall have a wff (µ)Aµ. Take another example:

> If øx̂ and θx̂ are functions of the same type, then (by *10.121) there is an *a* for which 'øa' and 'θa' are significant. So 'øa v θa' is significant. So (by *10.122) there is a function øx̂ v θx̂. Hence '(x)(øx̂ v θx̂)' is significant.

Since the µ of Aµ is typically ambiguous, it does not follow that (µ)(Aµ v Bµ) is a wff simply because Aµ and Bµ are wffs. So Russell introduced principles to assure that we can generate wffs we want in appropriate cases. These principles are necessitated only by the fact that order/type indices are absent. Moreover they do not really govern 'functions' in an ontological sense; they govern predicate terms. The same holds for principles (such as *9.131) which govern 'sameness of type'. They are not really about functions in an ontological sense; they are about *symbols* – they are used to characterize the wffs in a system which has avoided having order and order/type indices on its variables.[7]

Curiously, Whitehead was actually on to the point that the above 'principles' are really about well-formedness of expressions of the symbolism. During the the printing of volume 1, he wrote to Russell in May 1910:[8]

---

[7] This is wholly independent of the question as to whether *Principia* was committed to propositional functions in an ontological sense.

[8] See letter RA: 210.057451. Compare also RA: 710.057442.

I don't feel sure that *3.03 is right as it stands – or at least as it is explained. It appears to me as if two ideas are muddled up together – namely, a true logical premise and a test which supplements the incompleteness of our symbolism.

A true logical premiss must [be] such as would still be required, if our symbolism were complete and adequate. Now in such a case the type is always in evidence. For example, let every letter representing an individual have i as subscript, then we have $\vdash.\varnothing x_i$ and $\vdash.\theta x_i$, we do not need any axiom to assure that x_i and y_i are of the same type, and that any possible value of x_i is a possible value of y_i and vice versa ....

The analog of *3.03 for quantification is,

*10.13   If $\varnothing\hat{x}$ and $\theta\hat{x}$ take arguments of the same type, and we have '$\vdash.\varnothing x$' and '$\vdash.\theta x$', we shall have "$\vdash.\varnothing x$" θx .'

Whitehead is quite correct. That the type (order/type) of the variable 'x' in the first is the same as in the second would be given if the language had indices. There would be no need for this theorem or the principles (such as *9.131) from which it is derived.

4. *Comprehension Principles in 'Principia'*

Having prepared ourselves for understanding the hackneyed locutions produced by Whitehead and Russell's abuse of typical ambiguity, we can finally arrive at points about *Principia*'s calculus that have been lost for some eighty years.

In *Principia* the symbol '$\varnothing!x$' as opposed to 'fx' is used to indicate predicativity. Misusing typical ambiguity, Whitehead and Russell speak of letters such as '$\varnothing$', and 'f', without the shriek, as special 'variables' not restricted in order. They write (*PM*, p. 165):

> ... it is unnecessary to introduce a special notation
> for non-predicative functions of a given order and
> taking arguments of a given order ... We require,
> however, a means of symbolizing a function whose
> order is not assigned. We shall use 'øx' or 'f(X!ẑ)' or
> etc. to express a function (ø or f) whose order, relative
> to its argument is not given. Such a function cannot
> be made into an apparent variable unless we suppose
> its order previously fixed. As the only purpose of the
> notation is to avoid the necessity of fixing the order,
> such a function will not be used as an apparent
> variable; the only functions which will be so used will
> be predicative functions ... .

The point of this passage is this:

(*) ALL VARIABLES ARE PREDICATIVE.

Properly put, it is $\lceil A(x^0) \rceil$ not 'ø(x)' and $\lceil B(X^t) \rceil$ not
'f(X!ẑ)' that is used; and not for a 'function' whose
order is not assigned relative to its argument, but for a
wff containing a variable of a given order/type.

Shocking? Well, an even stronger point can be demonstrated concerning the 1910 *Principia*:

(**) ALL AND ONLY VARIABLES ARE
      PREDICATIVE

(This means, on a Platonistic semantics for predicate
variables, that there are only predicative attributes
according to *Principia*.) How can this be? How can it
comport with the following (*PM*, p. 53):

> We will define a function of one variable as *predicative*
> when it is of the next order above that of its argument,
> ie. of the lowest order compatible with its having that

argument. If a function has several variables, and the highest order of function occurring among the arguments is the *n*th, we call the function predicative if it is of the *n+1* th order, ie. again of the lowest order compatible with its having the arguments it has.

This makes it seem as though there are functions (attributes) which are not predicative – and such has been the interpretation of *Principia*. But this is just another error produced by Whitehead and Russell's abuse of typical ambiguity. Recall that 'function' is often used to mean predicate variable. Because free variables are sometimes used as schematic letters, Russell has to speak as if only some among them are predicative. Once schematic letter are distinguished from predicate variables, we see that this concurs with our (**). Moreover, we can see as well that the account of predicativity of *Principia*'s *12 also concurs (*PM*, p. 167):

A predicative function is one which contains no apparent variables, ie. a matrix.

A predicate variable obviously contains no quantifier symbols; it is a matrix. The obviousness, however, only comes out when schematic letters are sharply distinguished from predicate variables. Whitehead and Russell try to explain this. They write (*PM*, p. 52):

Thus, 'ø!x' is a function which contains no apparent variables, but contains the two real variables ø!ẑ and *x*. (It should be observed that when ø is assigned, we may obtain a function whose values do involve individuals as apparent variables, for example if ø!x is (y).θ(xy). But so long as ø is variable, ø!x contains no apparent variables.)

So '$\emptyset!x$ is used to indicate a variable such as '$1_\emptyset(o\backslash o)$' and similarly '$f!(\hat{X}!\hat{z})$' is used to indicate the variable $2_f(1\backslash(o\backslash o))$', and so on. We see at once that Church's oft repeated claim that there are two distinct accounts of predicativity in the first edition of *Principia* (one at the Introduction and another more austere notion at *12) is entirely unfounded.

Of course, central to this reunification of *12 with the Introduction is that circumflexion not be taken as a predicate term forming operator. If one can form the term

$$(\forall^o x^o)1_\emptyset(o\backslash o,o\backslash o)(o_x o,o\hat{z}o)'$$

then there are predicative terms that are not predicate variables (matrices). Accepting circumflexion, Church could not escape from his conclusion. And now comes our third shocker:

(***) CIRCUMFLEXION IS NOT A PREDICATE
    TERM FORMING OPERATOR IN *PRINCIPIA*

Contrary to a long standing tradition of interpretation, the fact is that there are no predicative circumflex predicate terms for the simple reason that there are no such terms. This, some will say, is more than they can bear. It is high time we demonstrated (**).

To see that (**) must be correct, and consequently to arrive at (***) we need only reflect on three points about *Principia*'s grammar:

(i)   Arguments to a predicate variable must agree in order/type;
(ii) All variables are predicative;
(iii) (Predicative) predicate variables must take predicative arguments.

Central among these is (i). Given (i) Russell, has an important motivation for (ii) and (iii). With (i) in place, clauses (ii) and (iii) are required when Russell's treatment of class and relation-in-extension symbols is regimented by ramification. Suppose (i) is true and (ii) and (iii) false. Then there are predicate variables such as '$2_{\emptyset}(o\backslash o)$', and '$3\sum(2\backslash(o\backslash o))$', and the second would be allowed to be predicative. Next consider the following contextual definition,

$$o\hat{z}^{o}A \in 3\hat{\alpha}(2\backslash(o\backslash o))B =df$$
$$(\exists 3\sum(2\backslash(o\backslash o)))(\forall 2_{\emptyset}(o\backslash o))(3\sum(2\backslash(o\backslash o))(2_{\emptyset}(o\backslash o)) \equiv$$
$$B(2_{\emptyset}o\backslash o)) \& (\exists 1_{\emptyset}(o\backslash o)((\forall_{o}x_{o})(1_{\emptyset}(o\backslash o)(^{o}x^{o}) \equiv A^{o}x^{o})$$
$$.\&. 3\sum(2\backslash(o\backslash o))(1_{\emptyset}(o\backslash o))$$

As we can see, the last clause is not well-formed given constraint (i). The result is that *Principia* has no non-predicate variables such as '$2_{\emptyset}(o\backslash o)$'. The text is explicit. The reason is that their presence would wreak havoc for the contextual definition of classes – given constraint (i). The needs of the theory of classes and relations-in-extension are clear.[9] Reducibility must afford a notion of predicativity according to which a monadic predicate variable is 'predicative' only when the arguments it can take are themselves predicative. If not for this, Reducibility would not be able to afford a means of facilitating the contextual definition of classes.

Now once we see points (i)–(iii), it is clear that circumflexion could not have been a predicate term forming operator. Suppose (for reductio) it was. It follows from (ii) that since circumflexion always involves capping a variable, there can be no predicate terms which take a

---

[9] Boer has seen this, but draws the wrong conclusion. He argues that *Principia*'s contextual definitions of class symbols cannot work because of the problem of the presence of non-predicative functions.

non-predicative term as an argument. Circumflexion would then allow non-predicative terms and no variables appropriate to them. So UG and UI are not possible with respect to such terms. Moreover, *Principia*'s definition of the identity sign cannot apply to such purported terms. *Principia* has:

*13.01 $x=y =df (\emptyset)(\emptyset!x \equiv \emptyset!y)$.

By clause (i) no predicate term can take arguments differing in order/type. If we can formulate terms by circumflexion then *Principia* would include terms in its language which are not admissible substituents for quantified variables, which cannot flank the identity sign, and which cannot be argument to any predicate terms!

This is obviously intolerable.

How could this have been missed for so long? The answer is that the matter has been suppressed[10] because interpreters, seeking to 'improve' *Principia* have commonly ignored its grammatical constraint (i) that arguments to a function term must have the same fixed order/type. Accordingly, (ii) and (iii) are ignored as well, and non-predicative variables are allowed. But (i) cannot be dropped if the system of the historical *Principia* is to be respected. Indeed, we shall see in subsequent sections that (i) plays a central role in Russell's explanation and justification of the order/type indices of the system.

Circumflexion is not a term forming operator in *Principia*. Aside from its use to mark subject positions of predicate variables,[11] circumflexion is used only as a heuristic device in introducing and explaining the

---

[10] Hatcher (1982) is aware of it.

[11] This role is quite minor and is easily omitted as we have in section 1.

system. Whitehead and Russell themselves say as much, writing (*PM*, p. 19):

> ... we have found it convenient and possible – except in the explanatory portions – to keep the explicit use of symbols of the type 'ø$\hat{z}$,' either as constants [eg. $\hat{x}$=a] or as real variables, almost entirely out of this work.

Wait, wait! It will be objected that *Principia* has no comprehension principles and so circumflex must have been a predicate term forming operator. Common as this interpretation is, it is quite misguided. *Principia* has comprehension principles – the schemata (*PM*, p. 167):

*12.1 $(\exists f): øx .\equiv x. f!x$ Pp

*12.11 $(\exists f):ø(x,y) .\equiv x,y. f!(x,y)$ Pp

(And similar principles for any finite number of variables.) The comprehension principles of *Principia* are precisely its reducibility schema.

5. *Orders Within Types or Types Within Orders*

And now, as of with a great fog lifted, we can end the dispute over whether orders are 'within' types or types 'within' orders – a dispute that has generated so many different interpretations of *Principia*'s ramified hierarchy.

Copi's (1971) rendition of *Principia*'s ramified-type theory claims that types came first and were split, in an effort to avoid new 'semantic' paradoxes, into orders. In contrast, Chiahara (1973) claims that *Principia* was ramified from the onset. Orders come first and are split into 'types'. Now the historical development of ramified types shows that types came first and later were split into orders. This follows because we must include the substitutional theory as itself embodying a theory of types.[12] So Copi is partly right. Nonetheless, both the Copi and Chiahara accounts are unhistorical.

Copi does not have order/type indices. He has separate order indices and type indices. Arguments to a predicate variable need only match in their type index. (Presumably, Copi would maintain that the order index of the argument cannot exceed that of the predicate variable to which it is argument.) Moreover Copi goes astray in allowing an order 1 predicate variable whose arguments are order 1 variables which take individual variables as arguments. This, however, is understandable. Copi allows instantiation of variables to circumflex terms. Consider the predicate term,

$$(\forall x^0)1\,\hat{\phi}^{(0)}(x^0)\,.$$

Copi is right to insist that it have order index '1'. Surely, circumflexing a variable to construct a term from a wff should not raise the order. Only the presence of a quantifier binding a predicate variable raises order. Suppose the order index were '2'. Then the principle of *concretion* for circumflex terms, the second-order wff would be equivalent to a first-order wff. This just seems wrong. So Copi is quite correct; there is no reason the presence of circumflexion should raise the order index. He admits that in *Principia* one can find the claim that a first-order function is one whose arguments must be individual variables and that (in general) the order must

---

[12] Linsky disagrees, writing that 'type theory was effectively ramified from its earliest formulations around 1906–1907' (Linsky, 1991, p. 129). Linsky has 'Mathematical Logic' in mind and dismisses the substitutional theory as not properly a type theory since there are not types of entities.
   But as we have seen, 'Mathematical Logic' has no types of entities and advocates the technique of substitutional. Now *Principia* was originally formulated with ramified type stratification in mind. Even here, however, Russell may well have intended a nominalistic semantics for predicate variables so that there are no types of entities.

be next higher than its type (*PM*, p. 167). But he dismisses them.

Chiahara, like Copi, labours under the error of thinking there are circumflex predicate terms in *Principia*. Hoping to find a closer fit to the text, Chiahara decides to make the order index of the circumflex '2'. He writes that 'the order of a propositional function is the least integer greater than the order of all its bound variables (quantified or circumflex)' (Chiahara, 1973, p. 20). Chiahara maintains that the hierarchy begins from orders, and splits into types. (Let us use the expression 'types*' to distinguish Chiahara's use of the term.) The type* of a monadic function, Chiahara explains, depends on more than simply whether it is a function of individuals, a function of functions of individuals, etc. The order of the arguments it can take is also relevant. All first-order functions are functions of individuals. But second-order functions are split into two types*: those that can take individuals and those that can take as arguments only first order functions (of individuals). Accordingly, third-order functions are split into four types*: those that take individuals, those that take first-order functions of individuals, those that take second-order functions of individuals, and those that take second-order functions of first-order functions of individuals (Chiahara, 1973, p. 20). Where individuals are type* T0, the following chart presents the possible type* indices (ie. order and order/type indices) for monadic propositional functions (*ibid.*, p. 21):

T4.0 T4.1.0 T4.2.0 T4.2.1.0   T4.3.0   T4.3.1.0   T4.3.2.0   T4.3.2.1.0

T3.0 T3.1.0 T3.2.0 T3.2.1.0

T2.0 T2.1.0

T1.0

T0

Chiahara decides that the predicative propositional functions are those whose indices descend numerically from left to right, eg. T1.0 T2.1.0 T3.2.1.0 T4.3.2.1.0 etc.

Chiahara's types* reflect the fact that *Principia* does not have independent order and type indices but has order/type indices. That is, arguments to a predicate variable must match in both order and type. Unfortunately, he fails to fully appreciate the consequences of having order/types for the notion of 'predicativity' and for *Principia*'s treatment of class and relation-in-extension symbols. Allowing predicate terms formed by circumflexion, he seems unaware that their identity conditions will not be supported by reducibility. The system, and the Reducibility schema in particular, would have to count not only T3.2.1.0 as predicative but also T3.2.0. Since arguments to a predicate term must match in order/type, there would be no other way for reducibility to apply to a non-predicative propositional function of with an order/type such as T4.2.0.

Hatcher is more careful. But his view of *Principia* is quite unhistorical. Hatcher finds no grammatical requirement in *Principia* that arguments to a term must match in order/type. Arguments to a predicate variable can have any order less than or equal to the order of the variable (Hatcher, 1982, p. 124). He takes *Principia* to allow all manner of non-predicative predicate variables whose order index have nothing to do with their type index (Hatcher, 1982, p. 112).

Alas, Chiahara, Hatcher and Copi all leave the historical *Principia* incoherent. It is not surprising then to find them remarking that they cannot understand the philosophical justifications offered for the system. Chiahara goes so far as to say that '... many of the distinctive features of his [Russell's] system receive no real justification at all. Why cannot a single variable range over the propositional functions of, say T4.0, T3.0, T2.0 and T1.0?' (Chiahara, 1973, p. 43). The fault in not finding a philosophical justification, however, does not lie with Russell (and Whitehead). The fault lies with the misguided accounts of the formal language of ramified type-theory. *Principia's* philosophical justifications do match its formal theory, once one has hold of the formal theory.

6. *The Philosophical Justification of the Type Part of an Order/Type Index*

Having set out and defended a new characterization of the formal system of *Principa*, we are in a position to examine the philosophical justification of the system set forth by Whitehead and Russell. The philosophical justification is given through an informal semantics – an intended interpretation which formed the guiding ideas for the development of the formal grammar of the calculus of *Principia*. Whitehead and Russell separate the matter of justifying the grammar of the formal calculus into two parts: the justification of the type part of an order/type index; and the justification of the order part of the order/type index. The type part is rendered in the section of *Principia's* Introduction entitled 'Why a Given Function Requires Arguments of a Certain Type' and shall be the concern of this section. Orders will be examined in the next.

The philosophical justification of the type part of the order/type indices on predicate variables lies is the so-called 'direct inspection' argument of *Principia*. We are to glean the need for the type part of the order/type index by inspection of the nature of 'propositional functions' themselves.

According to the argument, 'propositional functions'

are said to by 'ambiguities awaiting determination'. Now we have seen that Whitehead and Russell often use the phrase 'propositional function' equivocally. Sometimes they intend to speak of an open wff of the object-language, other times a predicate variable of that language. But we are now concerned with semantics – the intended interpretation of the predicate variables. What, then, is intended in saying a propositional function is an 'ambiguity'?

The 'direct inspection' argument offers a philosophical justification of type indices on lines similar to Frege's hierarchy of 'levels' of functions. For Frege, a function is unsaturated. Second-level functions *mutually saturate* with first-level functions. First-level function do not *fall under* second-level functions; they *fall within* them in such a way that the first-level function always preserves (as it were a predicate position. For this reason, Frege's formal grammar did not permit function expressions from occurring in subject positions. The direct inspection argument is akin to Frege's view that *falling within* must be distinguished from *falling under*. But it diverges from Frege in allowing predicative variables in 'subject positions' insofar as the variables are fixed with type indices that represent (in Frege's words) *falling within*.

The passages in *Principia* concerning the 'ambiguity of a function' can be interpreted so as to support this reading. Whitehead and Russell write (*PM*, p. 47):

> ...a direct consideration of the kinds of functions which have functions as arguments and the kinds of functions which have arguments other that functions will show, if we are not mistaken, that not only is it impossible for a function $\phi\hat{z}$ to have itself or anything derived from it as argument, but that if $\theta\hat{z}$ is another

function such that there are arguments *a* with which both 'øa' and 'θa' are significant, then θẑ and anything derived from it cannot significantly be arguments to øẑ. This arises from the fact that a function is essentially an ambiguity, and that, if it is to occur in a definite proposition, it must occur in such a way that the ambiguity has disappeared, and a wholly unambiguous statement has resulted.

The idea is that a 'function' (ie. a predicate variable) can occur in a subject position (argument position) of another predicate variable only if this position represents a predicate position in the semantics. Whitehead and Russell go on to generalize (*PM*, p. 48):

> ... when a function can occur significantly as argument, something which is not a function cannot occur significantly as argument. but conversely, when something which is not a function can occur significantly as an argument, a function cannot occur significantly.

If the semantics is nominalistic (with predicate variables interpreted as dummy schematic letters for formulae) this idea is validated.

To see this, let us take the illustration that Whitehead and Russell used to make the direct inspection argument. They write (*PM*, p. 48):

> Take, eg. 'x is a man,' and consider 'øẑ is a man'. Here there is nothing definite which is said to be a man. A function, in fact, is not a definite object which could be or not be a man; it is a mere ambiguity awaiting determination, and in order that it may occur significantly it must receive the necessary determination....

Taking a nominalistic semantics for predicate variables, consider '$\emptyset(\theta)$'. If the semantics assigns '$\emptyset$' to the formula '... is a man', and assigns 'θ' to '... is mortal' the semantic interpretation of '$\emptyset(\theta)$' would be the ungrammatical '... is mortal is a man'. However, if '$\emptyset$' is to be assigned 'Every thing is such that ... it ...', then the result is 'Everything is such that it is mortal'. Putting '$\emptyset^{((o))}$' and '$\theta^{(o)}$' to track the semantics requirement that the formula assigned to '$\theta^{(o)}$' must occupy a predicate position in the formula assigned to '$\emptyset^{((o))}$'. Type indices on the predicate variables of the formal grammar are thereby philosophically justified.[13]

7. The Philosophical Justification of the Order Part of an Order/Type Index

As is well known, *Principia* offers two renditions of quantification theory. In our first section we set out the system they call *10. This system is regarded by Whitehead and Russell as something of a formal convenience. The system of quantification theory which reflects the philosophical foundations of the system of order/types is *Principia*'s *9.

Let us give an updated rendition of *9. The individual variables and predicate variables are just those of *10. The set of *elementary* wffs of the language is next determined inductively as the smallest set K containing all the atomic wffs and such that –A (A v B) are in K if A and B are in K. The set of *Q-formulae* wffs of the language is then determined inductively as the smallest set K'

---

[13] This interpretation has the merit of being testable. For disconfirmation, we have only to find an occasion where Russell allows a predicate variable to occur in a context which cannot represent a *falling within*. Interestingly, the Grelling Paradox requires the two place predicate 'Denotes' and it would not be possible to have 'Denotes$^{(o,(o))}$' for the type index '(o)' would not represent a *falling within* in this case. The Grelling appeared in 1908. Curiously, Russell did not mention it. Perhaps we see why.

containing $(\forall^mV^t)A$ and $(\exists^mV^t)A$ where A is an elementary wff containing $^mV^t$ free and such that $(\forall^mV^t)C$ and $(\exists^mV^t)C$ are in K' whenever C is in K' and contains $^mV^t$ free. The wffs of the language are then the elementary and Q-Formulae.

Using the letters 'p', 'q', 'r', etc., as schematic letters for *elementary* wffs, the deductive system for elementary wffs is then

*1.2 Pp pvp .>. p
*1.3 Pp q .>. pvq
*1.4 Pp pvq .>. qvp
*1.5 Pp q>r :>: pvq .>. pvr
*1.6 Pp p v (qvr) :>: q v (pvr)

*1.1 Modus Ponens₁

From p and p>q, infer q

*1.01 p>q =df −p v q
*3.01 p&q =df −(−p v −q)
*4.01 p q =df p>q .&. q>p

This is then extended to quantified wffs in virtue of the following definitions (which have been modernized below):

*9.01 $-(\forall_mV_t)A$ =df $(\exists^mV^t)-A$

*9.02 $(\exists^mV^t)A$ =df $(\forall^mV^t)-A$

*9.03 $(\forall^mV^t)A(^mV^t)$ v p =df $(\exists^mV^t)(A(^mV^t)$ v p)

*9.04 p v $(\forall^mV^t)A(^mV^t)$ =df $(^mV^t)(p$ v $A(^mV^t))$

*9.05 $(\exists^mV^t)A(^mV^t)$ v p =df $(\forall^mV^t)(A(^mV^t)$ v p)

*9.06 p v $(\exists^mV^t)A(^mV^t)$ =df $(\exists^mV^t)(p$ v $A(^mV^t)$

These definitions require that p is an elementary wff – ie. one which contains no quantifier phrases. New definitions are needed for other cases. As we saw in our discussion of Russell's article 'Les Paradoxes', we shall have to stray from *Principia* here, adding *9.XX and *9.YY.

*9.07 $(\forall^{m}V^{t})A(^{m}V^{t}) \vee (\exists^{v}V^{n})B(^{v}V^{n}) = df$

$\qquad (\forall^{m}V^{t})(\exists^{v}V^{n})(A(^{m}V^{t}) \vee B(^{v}V^{n}))$

*9.08 $(\exists^{m}V^{t})A(^{m}V^{t}) \vee (\forall^{v}V^{n})B(^{v}V^{n}) = df$

$\qquad (\forall^{v}V^{n})(\exists^{m}V^{t})(A(^{m}V^{t}) \vee B(^{v}V^{n}))$

*9.XX $(\exists^{m}V^{t})A(^{m}V^{t}) \vee (\exists^{v}V^{n})B(^{v}V^{n}) = df$

$\qquad (\equiv]^{m}V^{t})(\exists^{v}V^{n})(A(^{m}V^{t}) \vee B(^{v}V^{n}))$

*9.YY $(\forall^{m}V^{t})A(^{m}V^{t}) \vee (\forall^{v}V^{n})B(^{v}V^{n}) = df$

$\qquad (\forall^{m}V^{t})(\forall^{v}V^{n})(A(^{m}V^{t}) \vee B(^{v}V^{n}))$

For the theory of deduction for quantified wffs, we find:

*9.1 Pp $A[^{m}pt_{|}^{|}^{m}V^{t}] \mathbin{.>.} (\exists^{m}V^{t}) A(^{m}V^{t})$

*9.11 Pp $A[^{m}pt_{|}^{|}^{m}V^{t}] \vee [^{m}Qt{:}^{m}V^{t}] \mathbin{.>.} (\exists^{m}V^{t}) A(^{m}V^{t})$

From *9.1 Russell proves *Universal Instantiation*:

*9.2 $\vdash (^{m}V^{t}) A(^{m}V^{t}) \mathbin{.>.} A[^{m}pt{:}^{m}V^{t}]$

where $^{m}Q^{t}$ is free for $^{m}V^{t}$ in A. The system continues with inference rules for wffs that are not elementary:

*9.12 Pp Modus Ponens[2]

If $\vdash A$ and $\vdash A > B$ then $\vdash B$

*9.13 Pp Universal Generalization[2]

If $\vdash A(^{m}V^{t})$ then $\vdash (^{m}V^{t})A$

The rule of variable rewrite is needed together with a version of the following rule:

(Switch)

From X[(∀μ)(∃v)Aμv], infer X[(∃v)(∀μ)Aμv,

> where all occurrences of μ in A bound by the
> quantifier are separated from those of v by a logical
> particle.

Reducibility completes the system.

The system *9 is designed to be sensitive to the philosophical distinctions relevant to Whitehead and Russell's
explanation of the order part of the order/type indices
on predicate variables. Central to that explanation is the
abandonment of Russell's former ontology of propositions. With a no-propositions theory, 'truth' and 'falsehood' no longer need be regarded as primitive
properties. Rather, there are now to be different sense
of 'truth' and 'falsehood' as applied to statements
differing in structure. The different sense, in turn,
explain and philosophically justify the order part of an
order/type indices on a predicate variable.

 The different senses of 'truth' and 'falsehood' are
generated by a recursive analysis which defines 'truth'
and 'falsehood' in terms of correspondence of belief
with fact. Whitehead and Russell write (*PM*, p. 42):

> That the words 'true' and 'false' have many different
> meanings according to the kind of proposition to
> which they are applied, is not difficult to see. Let us
> take any function øx̂, and let øa be one of its values.
> Let us call the sort of truth applicable to øa '*first
> truth*'. (This is not to assume that this would be first
> truth in another context; it is merely to indicate that
> it is the first sort of truth in our context.) Consider
> now the proposition (x) øx. If this has truth of the sort
> appropriate to it, that will mean that every value øx

has 'first-truth' ... thus if we call the sort of truth that is appropriate to (x).øx *'second* truth', we may define '{(x).øx} has second truth' as meaning 'every false for ø$\hat{x}$ has 'first truth', ie. '(x). (øx has first truth)' ... Similar remarks apply to falsehood.

This is unquestionably a recursive definition. But to fully understand how it is used to explain the order part of an order/type index, we must go a bit further than this rough sketch.

For the time being, let us introduce very finely grained indices. Instead of variables such as

$1_\emptyset(o\backslash o)$, $2_\emptyset(1(o\backslash o))$, etc.,

$1.sl;e.a_\emptyset(o\backslash o)$, $2.s2;1.s1;e.a_\emptyset(1.n1;e.m\backslash(o\backslash o))$, etc.

and so on. Here m≤a and each ni≤si for i∈N-{0}. The recursive characterization of 'truth' and 'falsehood' for quantified wffs would then be defined with respect to our finely indexed predicate variables as follows:

(o)   Where A is a genuinely atomic wff $\pi(a^1,...,a^n)$, [A] is true iff there is a complex (fact) consisting of $a^1,...,a^n$ and π with π occurring as concept.

(i)   For any statement A,
      −[A] is true$_{e.1}$ iff [A] is not true$_o$

(ii)   For any statements A and B,
      [A v B] is true$_{e.a}$ iff
         Either [A] is true$_{e.b}$ or [B] is true$_{e.c}$,
         for some b,c such that b+c = a.

(iii)a   For any wff A containing $^ox^o$ free,
      $[(\forall^ox^o)A]$ is true$_{z.s^z;...;k.s^k;...;1.s^1;e.a}$ iff
      $(\forall^ox^o)($ [A] is true$_{z.s^z;...;k.s^k;...;1.(s^1-1);e.a}$)

(iii)b   For any wff A containing $^ox^o$ free,

$[(\exists\,{}^{o}x^{o})A]$ is $true_{z.s}z;...;k.s^{k};...;1.(s^{1}\text{-}1);e.a$ iff
$(\exists\,{}^{o}x^{o})(\,[A]$ is $true_{z.s}z;...;k.s^{k};...;1.(s^{1}\text{-}1);e.a)$

We also need:

(iv)a For any wff A,

$[A]$ is $true_{z.o;...;k+1.o;k.s^{k};...;1.s^{1};e.a}$ iff
$[A]$ is $true_{k.s^{k};...;1.s^{1};e.a}$

(iv)b For any wff A,

$[A]$ is $true_{1.o;e.a}$ iff $[A]$ is $true_{e.a}$

Each of the indices s indicates the *number* of the sort of quantifiers that occur in the wff A in question. For predicate variables, we have:

(v)a For any wff A containing $k.sk;...;1.sl;e.a_{\varnothing}t$ free,

$[(\forall\, k.sk;...;1.sl;e.a_{\varnothing}t)A]$ is $true_q$ iff
$(\forall k.sk;...;1.sl;e.a_{\varnothing}t)[A]$ is $true_p)$.

(v)b For any wff A containing $k.sk;...;1.sl;e.a_{\varnothing}t$ free,

$[(\exists k.sk;...;1.sl;e.a_{\varnothing}t)A]$ is $true_q$ iff
$(\exists k.sk;...;1.sl;e.a_{\varnothing}t)[A]$ is $true_p)$.

(vi) For any wff A,

$[A]$ is $false_n$ iff $[A]$ is not $true_n$.

In (v)a and (v)b the index q is to a sequence of numerals appropriate to,

$z.s^{\circ}_{z};...;k+1.s^{\circ}_{k+1};...;1.s^{\circ}_{1};e.a^{\circ}$.

The index p is to be a sequence of numerals appropriate to,

$z.s^{\circ}_{z};...;k+1.(s^{\circ}_{k+1})^{-1};k.s^{\circ}_{k}+(s_{k}\text{x}d);...;1.s^{\circ}1+(s_{1}\text{x}d);e.$
$a^{\circ}+)a\text{x}d).$

where d is the number of occurrences of the bound

predicate variable in predicate positions in A when A is in primitive notation.

It should be noted that wffs with quantified statements subordinate to a propositional connective are to be defined in terms of their prenex equivalents. This is needed else the recursion would not apply to them. For example, where p is an elementary statement not containing μ free. The meaning of 'truth' for a statement such as $\lceil(\forall\mu)(A\mu \lor p)\rceil$ is to be the same as that for $\lceil(\forall\mu)(A\mu \lor p)\rceil$, because the former shall be defined in terms of the latter.

As we can see, the order indices of the predicate variables reflect the recursive definition of truth and falsehood. Whitehead and Russell's idea is that this philosophically explains them. The order part of an order/type index is designed to reflect the nature of the recursion.

Of course, such finely grained indices are not adopted in *Principia*. Nor could they have been, else Reducibility would have to fix the sub-orders as well as the orders. And where would they be fixed? Certainly not at 1. Fortunately *Principia*'s claim that the philosophical justification of orders lies in the recursive truth definition is not committed to the finely grained order indices above. The order indices on predicate variables reflect only the order of truth in the recursion, first, second, third, etc., and not also the sub-orders within first, second, third, etc., which reflect the *number* of quantifiers of the given order. Whitehead and Russell admit that the number is relevant to the meaning of 'truth' and 'falsehood', writing (*PM*, p. 162):

> First-order propositions are not all the same type, since as was explained in *9, two propositions which do not contain the same number of apparent variables cannot be of the same type.

Nonetheless, they dismiss this feature on grounds that 'no reflexive fallacies result' (*ibid.*). More exactly, the sub-orders are not reflected in the order indices of the variables because the sub-orders do not prevent the recursion from reaching its base case. An increase in the sub-order will not violate the recursive definition, but increase the order and the recursion cannot work. Accordingly, although the senses of truth and falsehood change relative to the number of quantifiers, and although the predicate variables of the formal language have order indices to reflect the recursive truth conditions of wffs, the finely grained order indices would not be warranted by the constraints of the recursion.

Returning then to the usual order and order/type indices on the variables as we find in *Principia*, we can see the relationship between the indices and the truth-conditions as follows. For the moment, put aside Reducibility comprehension principles in favour of a fully predicative type-theory. (Recall that in *Principia*, Reducibility principles are the only comprehension principles.) The present comprehension principles, (which will soon be obviated by the more general Reducibility principles) are now:

$$Pp_1 \quad (\exists 1_{\varnothing}(o\backslash o))(\forall o_Z o)(1_{\varnothing}(o\backslash o)(o_Z o) .\equiv. A),$$

where (i) $1_{\varnothing}(o\backslash o)$ is not free in A; and (ii) A has first order truth or first-order falsehood.

$$Pp_2 \quad (\exists 2_{\varnothing}(1\backslash(o\backslash o)))(\forall 1_{\theta}(o\backslash o))(2_{\varnothing}(1\backslash (o\backslash o))$$
$$(1_{\theta}(o\backslash o)) (o_Z o) .\equiv. A),$$

where (i) $2_{\varnothing}(1\backslash(o\backslash o))$ is not free in A; and (ii) A has second-order truth or second-order falsehood.

And so on. Whitehead and Russell are offering a philosophical explanations justification of the order part of the order/type indices on predicate variables by appeal to the fact that the comprehension principles employ wffs with fixed truth-conditions. The order part of order/type indices reflect the recursive truth-conditions of the wffs used in the comprehension principles.

Observe that this explains a feature of the formal grammar of ramified type-theory long thought to be unnecessary. Missing the relevance of the truth-definition to the justification of the order part of order/type indices, many have found it obscure when terms of the same type but differing in order cannot be arguments to the same predicate variable – so long as the order index of the predicate variable is higher than either. We saw the answer in the 1908 substitutional theory – viz., only entities of like order are intersubstitutable. In *Principia* it is generated by the recursive truth-definition. The definition defines higher sense of 'truth' and 'falsehood' in such a way that they collapse to the base of atomic 'truth' and 'falsehood' *step-by-step*.

8. *The Multiple-Relation Theory of Judgement*

In the above, we have seen how Whitehead and Russell's recursive definition generates senses of 'truth' and 'falsehood' and how these senses, in turn, were used to justify the order part of order/type indices on predicate variables. But there are further features of Russell's theory that need to be explained and this takes us to his controversial and much berated 'multiple-relation theory of judgement'.

Perhaps most immediate is the oddity that Whitehead and Russell's 'truth' (and 'falsehood') predicates flank statements and not names of statements. This may at first seem a use-mention confusion.[14] While Russell embraced an ontology of propositions, any declarative

---

[14] See Quine (1963).

statement ⌜A⌝ could be nominalized to form ⌜{A}⌝which is a name of a proposition. This in consort with Russell's early view that the sign '>' stands for the dyadic predicate 'implication' and is flanked by variables and nominalized wffs (ie. genuine names of propositions). This also makes sense of Russell's early view that 'truth' flanks statements themselves – for subject position can be regarded as sufficient to mark the nominalizing transformation. With propositions abandoned in *Principia*, however matters have changed significantly. The sign 'v' is a statement connective and is not flanked by names at all. It does not follow, however, that 'truth' and 'falsehood' must now flank the name of a statment. On the correspondence theory Russell envisions, when a genuinely atomic statement occurs in a subject position it is still to be viewed as a sort of name – viz., a disguised definite description. The predicate 'truth$_o$', then flanks a description. Since other senses or 'truth' are recursively defined in virtue of this base, the other expressions 'truth$_n$' are permitted to flank statements as well.

That a statement flanked by '... is true' is a disguised definite description is suggested by Russell in several passages. In 'On the Nature of Truth,' we find Russell saying that his new theory of 'truth' is '... an extension of the principle applied in my article, 'On Denoting' (*Mind*, October 1905), where it is pointed out that such propositions as 'The King of France is bald' contain no constituent corresponding to the phrase 'the present King of France' (*ONT*, p. 48). Compare the following from *Principia* (*PM*, p. 48):

> ... a statement in which a proposition appears as subject will only be significant if it can be reduced to a statement about the terms with appear in the proposition. A proposition, like such phrases as 'the so-and-so,' where grammatically it appears as subject, must be

broken up into its constituents if we are to find the true subject or subjects.

A reference is then made to *Principia*'s chapter 3, where the theory of definite descriptions is introduced. Moreover, Whitehead and Russell go on as follows (*PM*, p. 44):

> ... a 'proposition,' in the sense in which a proposition is supposed to be *the* object of a judgement, is a false abstraction, because a judgement has several objects not one. ... the phrase which expresses a proposition is what we call an 'incomplete' symbol; it does not have meaning in itself, but requires some supplementation in order to acquire a complete meaning. This fact is somewhat concealed by the circumstance that judgement in itself supplies a sufficient supplement and that judgement in itself makes no *verbal* addition to the proposition.

It seems, then, that a statement in the subject position of '... is true' is to be a disguised definite description. It is far less clear, however, what sort of description is disguised. Help comes when we better understand Russell's new definition of 'truth' as correspondence.

While there were propositions, Russell regarded belief as a dyadic relation between a mind and a proposition. Truth and falsehood were taken as unanalysable properties of propositions. Russell became dissatisfied with propositions as entities, and this required a new account of belief and truth. It is important to realize, however, that his dissatisfaction did not turn on the matter of the unity of a proposition. Propositional unity is fully accounted for by Russell's view in *Principles* that a concept (property or relation) is capable of an indefinable 'two-fold' occurrence in a proposition.

It is, for example, the occurrence of the relation R *as relating* that accounts for the unity of the proposition {aRb}. The issue of unity is divorced from the issue of truth. There is no hint at all that insofar as it contains a relating relation, the proposition must be true. It is sometimes argued that this changed for Russell in 1910. When a relation relates we get truth, so false propositions become unintelligible since there is nothing which could account for unity in such a case. This is mistaken.

The reason Russell abandoned propositions in 1910 was because of the paradoxes of propositions and his desire to avoid introducing a hierarchy of orders and a calculus for logic with restricted variables. By abandoning propositions, Russell can hold that 'truth' and 'falsehood' are definable in terms of 'correspondence'. The meanings of 'correspondence', in turn, generate senses of 'truth' and 'falsehood' and explain order indices. The entities that Russell calls 'facts' (or 'complexes') come in as part of this new correspondence definition of 'truth' and 'falsehood'. It is, therefore, mistaken to think of complexes as 'true propositions'. The very meaning of 'true' in the phrase 'true proposition' is distinct from that in the later correspondence theory. Complexes ('facts') are not really 'true' in the sense that propositions were. The right phrase is that some facts (belief complexes) correspond to others. Possible facts, whose unity would lie in their relating relations, would be entirely compatible with the idea of defining 'truth' as correspondence. To be sure, Russell did not embrace possible facts in 1910, preferring to count falsehood as simply lack of a corresponding fact. But possible facts are entirely consistent with Russell's abandonment of propositions.

As we see, 'truth' (in the simplest case) is the correspondence between a belief complex and another complex composed of the objects of the belief complex. When a person judges (believes) that *a* is R to *b*, there is a complex entity composed of a mind in a belief relation to the entity *a* and the relation R and the entity *b*. To say that the belief complex is true is to say that there is a corresponding complex composed solely of *a* and R and *b*. Russell uses the expression 'a-R-b' or '*a*-in-the-relation-R-to-*b*' to name the corresponding complex. (The expression 'a-R-b' is a term, not a statement.)   More perspicuously, this simple sort of correspondence is as follows.   When Othello (whose mind is *m*) believes that Desdemona loves Cassio, there is a complex mental state

> m-in-a-relation-belief-with-respect-to-
>   Desdemona-and loves-and-Cassio.

This complex (fact) is true insofar as there is a corresponding complex (fact),

> Desdemona-in-the-relation-loves-to-Cassio.

It is false insofar as there is no such complex.

What then is to be the definite description that the statment '*a* is R to *b*' disguises when occurring in '[*a* is R to *b*] is true'?   The simplest approach is to take '[$\pi(a^1,...,a^n$] is true' to disguise the description

> the complex (fact) consisting of the relation (property) π, and a^1, and,..., and, a^n.

And then regard '... is true' as functioning just the way 'E!' functions in the theory of descriptions.   But this neglects Russell's emphasis on atomic truth as correspondence with a mental state.   Russell's idea is partly captured if the disguised description we are seeking is[15]

---

[15] I adopted the view in Landini (1991).

the complex (fact) corresponding to m-in-a-belief-relation-to-π-and-a^1-and...and-a^n, for some mind *m*.

Unfortunately, this causes difficulties for the recursion. In the case of true$_1$, for instance, it requires that for each object in the range of quantifier, there is some mind (and some belief complex). But there may be two few minds. An alternative is to put:

the belief complex consisting *m* related to π and a^1, and,..., and a^n.

On this construal, the disguised description purports to refer to a belief complex rather than the purported complex (fact) that would correspond to it.

Whose belief complex? The person making the judgement. Thus if we unguise the description in '[Desdemona loves Cassio] is true' when asserted by Othello, we get,

the belief complex consisting of Othello related to Desdemona and loves and Cassio.

This serves to avoid the above problem of too many minds that Russell's recursive truth definition would otherwise face. For instance, we would have:

[(x)(x loves Cassio] is ^{m}true$_1$ iff

the general belief complex consisting of *m* related to 'loves' and Cassio is true^1 iff

For every x there is a complex (fact) consisting of x, 'loves', and Cassio.

Our problem is solved. We see, however, that a new difficulty looms . What are the constituents of m's general belief (judgement)? A similar problem arises for the question as to the constituents of a belief complex whose apparent object is a molecular proposition. As

Anscombe put it: '... what happens when I judge that A is *not* to the right of B?   Do I stand in the judging relation of A,B, *to the right of*, and *not*?   Similar questions arise for the other logical constants "if", "and", "or"' (Anscombe, 1959, p. 46).

The judgement 'All men are mortal,' Whitehead and Russell explain, 'collects together a number of elementary judgements' though it is not composed of them, and is of a 'radically new kind' (*PM*, p. 45).   But what constituents are severally before the mind in a general belief?   Whitehead and Russell are naggingly silent about such questions.   This is unfortunate.   For it has led interpretations of *Principia* to entirely miss its recursive truth definition and thereby obliterate *Principia*'s philosophical justification of orders.

Consider, for example, Cocchiarella's excellent solution of Anscombe's question.   Cocchiarella begins from the interpretation that *Principia* assumes that every open wff stands for a Platonic attribute (ie. a 'propositional function' in the ontological sense), Cocchiarella takes a belief as a multiple relation between a mind and the objects, including propositional being judged (Cocchiarella, 1980, p. 102).   Accordingly, he offers the following as the mental-state for the judgement 'All men are mortal'.

$$J\{m,(x)(\hat{\emptyset}x > \theta x), \hat{x} \text{ is a man}, \hat{x} \text{ is mortal}\}.$$

In Cocchiarella's view, judgements (mental states) are arranged into a hierarchy of orders.   The order of the judgement's truth or falsehood is the maximum of the orders of the propositional functions occurring as objects of the judgement.   'Instead of taking propositions of different orders as being single entities that are themselves objectively true or false', Cocchiarella writes, 'Russell now assumes that judgements as particular occurrences, or statements as potential judgements, are vehicles of a hierarchically ordered system of truth and falsehood' (Cocchiarella, 1980, p. 104).

Cocchiarella then determines the notion of 'correspondence' appropriate to the judgement in accordance with the order of the judgement. The judgement (above) contains a second-order propositional function, says Cocchiarella, so the judgement has *second-order* truth or *second-order* falsehood. The judgement is true when it corresponds to several complexes – viz., *the mortality-of-x_1, the mortality-of-x_2*, etc., where all the x's are men.

Cocchiarella has things top-down, establishing orders of judgements (complexes) on the basis of an independently established hierarchy of orders of propositional functions. Faced with the problems of the contents of belief complexes, Cocchiarella allows propositional functions as objects of belief complexes. Indeed, he says that '... without including propositional functions among the single entities contained in a judgement or belief complex, there would simply be no multiple-relation theory of belief at all' (Cocchiarella, 1987, p. 189). This cannot be correct. Whitehead and Russell have things 'bottom-up'. They explain that the *second truth* of

$$(x)(Man(x) > Mortal(x))$$

is to mean

(x)(if 'x is a man' has elementary truth then 'x is mortal' has elementary truth),

where *elementary truth* was previously defined as the correspondence of belief with fact in accordance with the multiple relation theory (*PM*, p. 46). Unlike Cocchiarella's interpretation, we find no hierarchy of orders of belief complexes ('judgements') at all; and no independently conceived hierarchy of orders of propositional functions used to generate them. All complexes are on a par with individuals. Quite clearly, the multiple-relation theory is meant to comport with the recursive definition and it is the recursion that generates the meanings of 'truth' (and accordingly the notion or 'order'). We must not, therefore, construe the multiple-relation theory in a way that dislodges recursion as the centrepiece of Whitehead and Russell's philosophical explanation of orders. Cocchiarella's interpretation does just this.

Once we see that it was a recursive truth definition that generates orders, we get an entirely new perspective on *Principia*. The 'direct inspection' argument and the recursive truth definition (of which the multiple-relation theory is a component) now find their proper positions in the work. Far from being a system of genuinely restricted variables ranging over a ramified hierarchy of Platonic entities (propositional functions), the system aims at capturing (at least in spirit) the philosophical ideas that have exercised Russell ever since his *Principles of Mathematics* – viz., the doctrine that the unrestricted variable is essential to any calculus for logic. At last the real *Principia* has stood up.[16]

---

[16] This interpretation has important consequences for the Introduction to the 1925 second edition of *Principia* and Russell's attempt (in the new Appendix B) to show that mathematical induction is recoverable if the system of *Principia* is modified in accordance with certain ideas which occurred to him in discussions with Wittgenstein (see Landini, 1995, forthcoming).

BIBLIOGRAPHY OF WORKS CITED

Chiahara, Charles, 1973. *Ontology and the Vicious Circle Principle* (Ithaca).

Cocchiarella, Nino, 1980. 'The Development of the Theory of Logical Types and the Notion of a Logical Subject in Russell's Early Philosophy,' *Synthese*, vol. 45, pp. 71–115.

—— 1987. 'Russell's Theory of Logical Types and the Atomistic Hierarchy of Sentences', in Nino Cocchiarella, *Logical Studies in Early Analytic Philosophy* (Columbus, Ohio State University Press).

Copi, Irving, 1971. *The Theory of Types* (London, Routledge and Kegan Paul).

Church, Alonzo, 1956. *Introduction to Mathematical Logic* (Princeton, Princeton University Press).

—— 1976. 'A Comparison of Russell's Resolution of the Semantical Antinomies with that of Tarski', *Journal of Symbolic Logic*, vol. 41, pp. 747–60.

Grattan-Guinness, Ivor, 1977. *Dear Russell – Dear Jourdain* (London, Duckworth).

Hatcher, William, 1982. *The Logical Foundations of Mathematics* (Pergamon Press).

Hylton, Peter, 1990. *Russell, Idealism and the Emergence of Analytic Philosophy* (Oxford, Oxford University Press).

Landini, Gregory, 1995. 'The *Definability* of the Set of Natural Numbers in the 1925 *Principia Mathematica*', *Journal of Philosophical Logic* [forthcoming].

Russell, Bertrand, *POM, The Principles of Mathematics*, (London, 1903; 2nd edn., W. W. Norton and Co, London, 1937).

—— 1908. 'Mathematical Logic as Based on the Theory of Logical Types', *American Journal of Mathematics*, vol. 30, pp. 222–62.

—— 1906, 'On "Insolubilia" and Their Solution By Symbolic Logic', in by D. Lackey (ed.), *Essays in Analysis* (New York, Brazillier), pp. 190–214.

Schutte, Kurt, 1960. *Beweistheorie* (Berlin).

Whitehead, Alfred and Bertrand Russell, *PM*, *Principia Mathematica*, 1910–1913, vols. 1–3 (Cambridge, Cambridge University Press).

BERTRAND RUSSELL:
A NEGLECTED ETHICIST[1]

Charles R. Pigden
University of Otago

1. Russell Underrated

Russell is underrated as a moral philosopher. This is odd since he was perhaps best known to the general public as a practical moralist. His writings on sex, love, war and politics brought both fame and notoriety. But philosophers have tended to ignore them. This is partly Russell's fault. He adhered to (and argued for) a rather strict interpretation of 'philosophy' which disqualified many of his own ethical writings. Subsequent philosophers have taken him at his word without realizing that their own conceptions of what counts as philosophy were rather more relaxed. For although Practical or Applied Ethics is now a respectable philosophic enterprise, Russell's writings on the topic have not returned to philosophical favour. His name does not even occur in the index to Singer's *A Companion to Ethics*,[2] despite the space devoted to practical concerns. One reason, I suspect, is that what is nowadays done solemnly in philosophical seminars, Russell did flippantly for a wider public. However that may be, it remains a singular fact

---

[1] The various volumes of *The Collected Papers of Bertrand Russell* are cited thus: *CPBR* 1, 8 or 13 as the case may be. Paper 38 in vol. 1 would be cited thus: *CPBR* 1. 38. Publication details are given in the final note.

[2] Peter Singer (ed.), *A Companion to Ethics* (Oxford, Blackwell, 1991).

that one of the most influential practical ethicists of the century is largely excluded from the canon of Practical Ethics.

But Russell has suffered a double injustice. It is not just that he is neglected as a practical ethicist. He is ignored as an ethical theorist as well. Again, he may have brought this injustice on himself. 'I do not myself think very well of what I have said on ethics', he wrote in 1963.[3] And most ethical theorists have agreed with him. Either they do not think very well of what he said or they do not think of it at all. But he was wrong in his low estimate and so are they. Of course I do not want to claim for Russell the same status as an ethical theorist that he very properly enjoys as a logician and philosopher of mathematics. Nevertheless, his achievement is not to be sneezed at. To begin with, he was first in the field with emotivism[4] and the error

---

[3]   In a letter to Elizabeth Aiken 26 August 1963 in Feinberg and Kasrils (eds.), *Dear Bertrand Russell* (London, Allen and Unwin, 1969), p. 130. He made the same point in his brief reply to D. H. Munro in *Philosophy*, vol. 35 (1960): 'I am not myself satisfied with what I have read or said on the philosophical basis of ethics.'

[4]   Russell claimed to have abandoned his belief in the objectivity of good and evil because of Santayana's criticisms in *The Winds of Doctrine*, though he was 'never ... able to be as bland and comfortable without it as [Santayana] was'. (Russell, *Portraits from Memory*, London, Allen and Unwin, 1958, p. 91.) Russell's recollections are borne out by the evidence. The first paper in which there are hints of emotivism is his 'The Place of Science in a Liberal Education' (*CPBR* 12, pp. 390–97 especially p. 395) written in early 1913 (*CPBR* 12, p. liv) at which time he was reading Santayana, as we know from a letter to Goldsworthy Lowes Dickenson dated 13 February 1913 (*Autobiography*, vol. 1, p. 222). Something like emotivism is elaborated in 'Mysticism and Logic' (*CPBR* 8.2) and in 'On Scientific Method in Philosophy' (*CPBR* 8.4) both of which predate 'The Ethics of Warfare' (*CPBR* 13.14) written in late 1914 which is generally supposed to mark his conversion to emotivism. The theory was developed in a series of writings in the twenties and thirties, perhaps the clearest formulation being chap. 9 of his (1935) *Religion and Science*, London, Home University Library. All this is worth stressing since later authors such as Ayer and Stevenson are generally given the credit (if credit it be) for inventing emotivism. Mark Sainsbury , who should know better,

theory,[5] the two anti-realist theories that have dominated the twentieth-century debate. His writings reveal the anguish of a philosopher with a yearning for moral truth who cannot reconcile the objectivity of ethics with his philosophical conscience.[6] (And what are Simon Blackburn's writings on the topic but attempts to scratch this itch?)[7] Earlier on Russell was an expositor and critic of the ethical doctrines of G. E. Moore and played a major part in the Apostolic debates in which those doctrines were developed.[8] He was also a pupil of Henry Sidgwick, whose writings continue to loom large in twentieth-century ethics,[9] and his reactions to Sidgwick's teachings are well worth preserving, dealing as they do with such hot topics as virtue ethics, the Is/Ought question, and the ethical implications (if any) of Darwinism.[10] Even his revolt against Hegelianism

remarks rather dismissively that Russell's moral philosophy is 'too derivative to justify a discussion of it' (Mark Sainsbury, *Russell*, London, Routledge, 1979, p. x). The kindest thing to say about this is that it simply isn't so.

[5] See 'Is There an Absolute Good', (*CPBR* 9.58, 1922) a paper which remained unpublished in Russell's lifetime. The theory was arrived at independently by J. L. Mackie and expounded in his (1946) 'The Refutation of Morals', *Australasian Journal of Psychology and Philosophy*, and most influentially in his *Ethics: Inventing Right and Wrong* (Harmondsworth, Penguin, 1977).

[6] See Bertrand Russell, 'Reply to My Critics', in P. A. Schilpp (ed.), *The Philosophy of Bertrand Russell* (Evanston, Northwestern University Press, 1944).

[7] See Essays 3, 6, 7, 8, 9 & 10 in Simon Blackburn, *Essays in Quasi-Realism* (Oxford, Oxford University Press, 1993).

[8] See Russell's 'The Elements of Ethics' in *CPBR* 6. 19 (1910), and the two reviews of *Principia Ethica* (1903) and (1904) *CPBR* 4. 27 & 28, for the Apostolic debates see below.

[9] Specifically his masterpiece, Henry Sidgwick, *Methods of Ethics* (London, Macmillan, 1907).

[10] See *CPBR* 1, papers 31, 32, 33, 34 & 35.

had an ethical dimension to it and (as we shall see) his essay, 'Seems Madam? Nay, It Is',[11] can be deployed against any attempt to reconcile the claims of morality and self-interest by positing a metaphysical unity of selves. He had some sharp things to say about morality considered as a social institution,[12] though unlike such nihilists as Max Stirner,[13] he did not argue that we should give it up. Although his moral psychology was largely derived from Spinoza and Hume,[14] (reason being the slave of the passions) he gave it an original twist. Much of what we do – in civilized societies at least – is done out of what Butler called 'cool self-love', a sort of settled desire for our long-term survival and satisfaction. Russell thought that a life wholly dominated by this desire is liable to be frustrating and boring and that a place must be found for what Frankfurt[15] would describe as 'wanton' impulses.[16] The problem is to ensure that such impulses are creative rather than destructive. Russell's conception of the human good (and hence the end of moral action) seems to me far

[11] *CPBR* 1. 16.

[12] See his 'What Is Morality', *CPBR* 9. 59 (1922) and Bertrand Russell, *Power: A New Social Analysis* (London, Allen and Unwin, 1938), chap. 15.

[13] Some of Russell's opinions are strikingly similar to those of Max Stirner, though so far as I can determine, Russell had not read him. See Max Stirner, *The Ego and Its Own*, trans. Byington, ed. by Leopold, (Cambridge, Cambridge University Press, 1995), originally published 1844.

[14] For Russell's allegiance to Spinoza see *CPBR* 1. 14 , p. 92. For Russell's deference to Hume see the preface to Bertrand Russell, *Human Society in Ethics and Politics* (London, Allen and Unwin, 1954), pp. 8–11, where the Humean slogan that reason is and ought only to be the slave of the passions is enthusiastically endorsed.

[15] See chap. 2, 'Freedom of the Will and the concept of a Person', in Harry G. Frankfurt, *The Importance of What We Care About* (Cambridge, Cambridge University Press, 1988), especially pp. 16–17.

[16] This view is expressed in many of Russell's writings but appears for the first time in 'Cleopatra or Maggie Tulliver', *CPBR* 1. 14.

more intelligible and at least as interesting as the rival conceptions of Marx and Aristotle to which so many weighty tomes have been devoted. Finally, Russell had some interesting things to say in defence of consequentialism, or, to be more precise, in criticism of its rivals.[17] In short, Russell had something to say about most of the questions that have exercised twentieth-century ethical theory. And quite often he was the first to say it.

If I am right, there is more to Russell as an ethical theorist than has met many a philosophic eye. But by the same token, there is rather more than I can cover in a single paper. So I must be selective. Taking my cue from the title of this conference, I shall concentrate on Russell and the origins of the analytic tradition in ethics. This means that there will be rather more about Moore than some of you might like. But this is unavoidable. *Principia Ethica* (henceforth intermittently *PE*)[18] dominated Russell's destiny as an ethical theorist. There was a Before, a During and an After *Principia* period (this last being rather protracted) and each phase needs to be understood in those terms. Today I will confine myself to the Before, leaving the During and the After to one side. But the During and the After should not be forgotten. In 1903 Russell became an enthusiastic (though not uncritical) convert to the doctrines of *Principia Ethica*. In 1913 he lost his faith in the Moorean good and remained a moral sceptic thereafter, vacillating between various forms of moral anti-realism. Even so he was very much a post-Moorean moral sceptic.

---

[17] See for example his criticism of Stoicism in Bertrand Russell, *A History of Western Philosophy* (London, Allen and Unwin, 1946), pp. 272–5.

[18] Originally published 1903. Revised edition with a substantial introduction by Thomas Baldwin, plus a cancelled preface by Moore himself plus additional material (Cam bridge, Cambridge University Press, 1993). All references to the revised edition.

2. *G. E. Moore and the Origins of Analytic Ethics*

The Comic Book History of Philosophy says that analytic philosophy was born when Moore and Russell revolted against the absolute idealism they imbibed from McTaggart and Bradley. The Comic Book History is of course a crude work and needs to be corrected in detail. To begin with, the analytic revolt was as much a rebellion against Kant as against Hegel's British disciples. And before they were rebels, both Moore and Russell were enthusiastic converts, Moore from something like common sense and Russell, from the doctrines of Mill. Russell's period as convert, his 'idealist apprenticeship', was no flash in the pan but lasted several years during which he embarked upon a vast program in metaphysics and the philosophy of science.[19] The revolt likewise, was a rather protracted affair, during which the revolutionists temporarily occupied some rather untenable positions. (I sympathize with Russell's puzzled friend Maurice Amos: 'What ... Moore means by saying the world consists of concepts alone, I do not know.'[20] Indeed, when I read about the origins of analytic philosophy, I am amazed that it turned out so well!) In consequence it is difficult to pitch upon a single text which ushers in the new era ('The Refutation of Idealism', *The Philosophy of Leibniz*, *The Principles of Mathematics*, 'On Denoting' – which do we select?). But with ethics it is otherwise. Here, there is *one* text which set the agenda for twentieth-century debate and still dominates discussion down to this day – G. E. Moore's *Principia Ethica*. If Russell

---

[19] See N. Griffin, *Russell's Idealist Apprenticeship* (Oxford, Oxford University Press, 1991).

[20] Amos to Russell, 6 November 1898, in Bertrand Russell, *The Autobiography of Bertrand Russell* (London, Allen and Unwin, 1967), vol. 1, p. 141.

played a part in the creation of analytic ethics it consisted in his contributions to the Apostolic debates which led up to Moore's meta-ethical masterpiece.

But there is a problem with *Principia Ethica*. Although a founding document in the analytic tradition, it does not really conform to the Comic Book History. It is true that there is a vestigial chapter on 'metaphysical ethics' in which some more or less Hegelian doctrines are glanced at (though Moore is so unspecific about his targets that it is very difficult to evaluate his attack). And it is true too that the book had its origins in a set of extended meditations on Kant beginning with Moore's failed fellowship dissertation of 1897. But the revolt against Hegel and Kant is not Moore's major preoccupation in *Principia*. His chief targets are empiricist and naturalistic thinkers who want to define goodness in terms of something else such as happiness or what we desire to desire. His consequentialism (which he makes implausibly analytic, *defining* what we ought to do as what will produce the best consequences) is borrowed from the utilitarians he attacks. His central thesis, that moral concepts cannot be reduced to concepts of any other kind, was anticipated by Sidgwick[21] and before him by Richard Price.[22] Even the Open Question Argument, his prime polemical weapon, is something of a reinvented wheel, since Price put forward a very similar argument in 1758 (as Moore might have discovered had he bothered to read

---

[21] As Moore himself acknowledges, *PE*, chap. 1, sec. 14. He refers the reader to Sidgwick, *Methods of Ethics*, book 1, chap. 3.

[22] See Richard Price, *A Review of the Principal Questions of Morals*, in Raphael (ed.), (Oxford, Oxford University Press, 1974), originally published 1758, chap. 1.

Sidgwick's *Outlines of a History of Ethics*).[23] So what is novel about the book? First its *emphasis*. As Baldwin points out in his introduction to the new edition, 'Moore is primarily concerned to articulate a metaphysical [and I would add *semantic*] thesis about the status of ethical values which he takes to have absolutely fundamental significance ... Sidgwick [by contrast] was not much interested in the metaphysics of value'.[24] In particular, Moore argues (or can be reconstructed as arguing) that if moral concepts cannot be reduced to the non-moral, then a peculiarly moral property of goodness is required to make moral judgements true. And this property cannot be neatly fitted into a naturalistic ontology. To my mind the chief merit of the book consists in posing the matter so starkly. Before Moore people might not have realized that there was something ontologically odd about goodness. (Sidgwick, as Baldwin suggests, was inclined to fudge.) After Moore the problem could not be ignored. Secondly, *Principia* is notable for its rejection of hedonism and its pluralism about the good. In Moore's opinion there are other good things besides pleasure, indeed pleasure can even contribute to the badness of a whole when accompanied by something vile like lasciviousness, he proves this by asking us to imagine a Paradise of Ecstatic Bestiality. Moore even thinks that worlds without minds can be the bearers of value although 'by far the most valuable things which we know or can imagine, are certain states of consciousness, which can be roughly described as the pleasures of human intercourse and the enjoyment of

---

[23] See Price, *Review*, pp. 16–17; Henry Sidgwick, *Outlines of a History of Ethics* (London, Macmillan, 1888), p. 216. Baldwin in his Introduction to *PE* (p. xix) quotes Rashdall as making the same point.

[24] Thomas Baldwin, Introduction to the revised edition of *PE*, p. xv.

beautiful objects'.[25] Finally *Principia Ethica* is remarkable for what it leaves out. It is possible to portray the 'British Moralists' of the seventeenth and eighteenth centuries as concerned with the questions that interested Moore. The empiricists believed that words are meaningless unless they can be defined in terms of impressions or combinations of copies of impressions. Accordingly they tried to construct analyses of the moral concepts that met this constraint, thus committing what Moore would call the Naturalistic Fallacy.[26] Their rationalist opponents disputed these analyses, proposed rival, often Platonistic, accounts of value, and in some cases went on to contest the empiricist theory of meaning. Thus far their debates were within Moore's intellectual purview. But they were interested in other matters besides. To begin with the empiricist theory of meaning was a psycho-semantics, a theory of meaning based on a theory of mind. In opposing it, Price and Reid were compelled to construct a counter-psychology of their own. Neither side supposed that you could construct a theory of meaning (which must, at least, *include* an account of understanding) without some reference to the understanding mind. Moreover, both parties to the debate were concerned with the following questions: What must

---

[25] *PE*, p. 237.

[26] That the empiricists had a psychosemantic theory and that they used it to dispose of their opponents is of course well known. (It is a major theme of Bennett's, *Locke, Berkeley, Hume: Central Themes* (Oxford, Oxford University Press, 1971).) It is less well known that their moral theories can be construed as attempts to give analyses of the moral concepts which conform to the psychosemantics. Contemporaries were aware of the fact however. Thus Price does not think it enough to criticize the response-dependent theories of Hume and Hutcheson. He has to dispose of the psychosematic theory which makes such analyses necessary. See his *Review*, chap. 1, sec. 2.

men be like if they are to respond to the demands of morality? And what must morality be like if men are to respond to its demands? Given that moral truths are of such-and-such a character, how can we know them?[27] These questions scarcely seem to have occurred to Moore. So far as he is concerned, goodness is just *there*. When our minds are uncluttered we can see what is good and good people (at any rate) will want to instantiate good things. Why this should be so, he does not bother to enquire. The sociological, psychological and epistemic questions that preoccupied philosophers from Hobbes to Sidgwick scarcely exist for him. Indeed, one might argue that the net effect of *Principia Ethica* has been to impoverish ethical debate. If so, it is a book from which we have but recently recovered.

Russell, both early and late, *was* interested in the kinds of question that Moore neglected. But his gradual conversion to the doctrines of *Principia Ethica* sent his interest to sleep. It took him about ten years to awake from his dogmatic slumbers.

3. *The Prehistory of 'Principia Ethica': Russell's Role*
During the 1890s Russell thought more about ethical theory than he ever did thereafter. About a third of the papers in *CPBR* 1 are devoted to ethics. Many of Russell's subsequent concerns are prefigured in these writings. This is partly because he did a course with Sidgwick and partly because he seems to have been carrying on a sort of running debate with G. E. Moore at meetings of the Apostles. Interestingly what he was opposed to seems to have been Moore's non-naturalism and his anti-Sidgwickian thesis that there could be

---

[27] See Raphael (ed.), *The British Moralists* (1969), 2 vols. (henceforward *BM*) for a comprehensive anthology.

valuable things besides states of consciousness. Although Russell became a convert to Moorean orthodoxy in the early 1900s it obviously took him some time to quell his subjectivist and utilitarian misgivings. This debate would be of interest if we were solely concerned with *Russell's* philosophical development, but it seems to me that some of the exchanges may have been crucial in the evolution of *Moore's* ideas.

Two papers in particular are worthy of remark: 'Is Ethics a Branch of Empirical Psychology?',[28] in which Russell seems to define the good in terms of what we – or I the speaker? – desire to desire, and 'Was the World Good before the Sixth Day?'[29]

'Is Ethics a Branch of Empirical Psychology?' (February 1897) seems to be a response to Moore's paper 'Can We Mean Anything When We Don't Know What We Mean?' read on 23 January 1897. In this paper Moore criticizes hedonistic definitions of the good using arguments which foreshadow *PE*.[30] These arguments could easily be applied against the identification of the good with the desired. Russell defends such a theory in a sophisticated version: the good is what we (I, the speaker?) desire to desire. But the essay ends with a challenge or perhaps a request: 'If our brother Moore will give me an unexceptionable premiss for his definition of the good, or even a hint of where to find one, I will retract.'[31] Could it be that at this meeting, or shortly thereafter, Moore responded with his famous no-definition definition of 'good'? And did

---

[28] *CPBR* 1.15.

[29] *CPBR* 1.17.

[30] See Paul Levy, *Moore: G. E. Moore and the Cambridge Apostles* (Oxford, Oxford University Press, 1979), pp. 192–3.

[31] *CPBR* 1, p. 104.

Russell consider himself answered? I am inclined to think so given the annotation in Moore's hand ('Good = good') on the back of the paper 2[32] and the content of a later essay 'Was the World Good before the Sixth Day?

'Was the World Good before the Sixth Day?' (February 1899) is clearly a response to Moore's lecture series 'The Elements of Ethics' delivered in 1898.[33] Russell had read the typescript of Moore's lectures and had even written some comments.[34] In these lectures, substantial portions of which are reproduced in *Principia Ethica*, Moore explicitly adopts his famous no-definition definition of 'good'. He also discusses Sidgwick's thesis that only states of consciousness are good. Indeed Moore's lengthy and explicit critique of Sidgwick on pages 135–6 of *PE* first appears in 'The Elements of Ethics'.[35] Moore argues, against Sidgwick, that a lifeless but beautiful world would be better than a similarly lifeless world which was 'one heap of filth containing everything that is most disgusting to us'. And since beautiful things can be good even if they are not appreciated, the promotion of beauty must be, for Moore, an end in itself, though the creation of beautiful things which *will* be appreciated will tend to take precedence. But Russell attacks a different argument for the same conclusion: that beauty cannot be good only as a means since the man who derives aesthetic pleasure from the ugly is somehow worse than the man of refined taste who only derives aesthetic pleasure from the

---

[32] *CPBR* 1, p. 99.

[33] These have been recently published; G. E. Moore, *The Elements of Ethics*, in T. Regan (ed.), (Philadelphia, Temple University Press, 1991).

[34] *CPBR* 1, p. 112.

[35] See Baldwin's Appendix to the revised edition of *PE*, pp. 312–13, in which he details which bits of *PE* are borrowed from 'The Elements of Ethics'.

beautiful. If beauty were valuable merely as a means, then the state of the clod savouring Tammy Wynette's 'Stand By Your Man' would be as valuable as the state of the aesthete savouring Mozart. Since this is not so, beauty is not valuable merely as a means. (See Moore *The Elements of Ethics*, pp. 90–91.) This argument does not reappear in *Principia* so far as I can tell, though Moore is much preoccupied by the value of wholes in which evil or ugly things are admired. ('When we admire what is ugly or evil believing that it is beautiful and good, this belief seems also to enhance the intrinsic vileness of our condition' he declares with aesthetico-moral fervour.[36] Tammy Wynette fans, please take note!) Perhaps Moore withdrew the argument in the face of Russell's criticisms. In 'Was the World Good before the Sixth Day?', Russell concedes that beauty is an objective property (perhaps a non-natural one?) but opposes Moore's view that a world devoid of conscious beings could be good in virtue of its beauty. His counter-argument seems to me a bit of a quibble – though it must be admitted that the argument he attacks isn't much better. He denies that the man of low tastes who derives pleasure from the ugly is really experiencing the same emotion as the refined gent who appreciates the beautiful. Since the states of the Mozart fancier and the Tammy Wynette fan are distinct, we cannot argue that the difference in the value of their states must be due to the difference in the value of their objects (the produc-tions of Mozart and Tammy Wynette respectively). I am not sure why the 'heap of filth' argument is neglected. Perhaps Russell thought it impossible to base a paper on a mere clash of intuitions. However Moore does not

[36] *PE*, p. 259.

appear to have been persuaded by Russell's arguments. In *PE*, p. 257, he considers states in which people have 'the very same emotions' towards an ugly thing as they ought to have towards a beautiful thing (he considers such states among 'the greatest positive evils'!) But if Russell is to be believed, the emotions of the Mozart fancier and the Tammy Wynette fan cannot be the very same, so such states are impossible.

Although the argument of the paper is clear enough, Russell's strategic purpose in writing the piece is a little obscure. The thesis that the only good things are states of consciousness is distinct from the claim that goodness can be defined in terms of states of consciousness, but I am not entirely sure that Russell can be cleared of confusion on this point. His strategy may be to argue that because only states of consciousness can be good, goodness can be defined in terms of states of consciousness (eg. desire). On the other hand the paper may be a rearguard defence of Sidgwickism on the part of someone who has been converted to the existence of non-natural properties but cannot believe that goodness in particular attaches to anything besides conscious states. (Moore himself reverted to Sidgwickian orthodoxy in his *Ethics* of 1912.)[37] Or maybe Russell had to do the paper in a hurry and simply pitched upon an argument he thought he could refute.

But if 'Was the World Good before the Sixth Day?' represents a partial conversion to Moore's views, 'Is Ethics a Branch of Empirical Psychology? is even more interesting since it represents a position that Moore reacted against. In *PE*, much, of which is borrowed from *The Elements of Ethics*, Moore denounces a great many naturalistic definitions of 'good. But he is partic-

[37] G. E. Moore, *Ethics* (London, Home University Library, 1912), chap. 7.

ularly severe with philosophers who attempt to define goodness in terms of desire. Who are these unnamed miscreants? Well Hobbes, of course, said something of the sort but you get the impression that the desire-fixated philosophers that Moore has in mind are rather more recent. One of them I suggest is Russell. Moreover, the view that Russell explicitly defends in 'Is Ethics a Branch of Empirical Psychology?', namely that ethics is a branch of empirical psychology, is explicitly denounced by Moore in *The Elements of Ethics* along with similar attempts to reduce ethics to sociology.[38] (Here the reprobate is that notorious epistemic puritan W. K. Clifford, like Russell, a fellow-apostle.) Finally, in section 13 of *Principia*, in which Moore develops his famous Open Question Argument, the definition he selects for dissection ('one of the more plausible, because one of the more complicated of such proposed definitions') is Russell's: '"good" means "what we desire to desire".' Besides 'Is Ethics a Branch of Empirical Psychology?', Russell put forward this definition in several other papers of the nineties and no doubt in conversation as well. Of course, Moore may have had someone else in mind when he penned this passage. But given his marked tendency not to look beyond the confines of Cambridge for philosophical opponents, I rather doubt it.

4. *Analysis, Paradox and Desiring to Desire*
But 'Is Ethics a Branch of Empirical Psychology?', together with what appear to be preparatory papers 'A Note on Ethical theory' and 'Are All Desires Equally Moral?',[39] are now of more than historical interest. For

---

[38] The passage reappears in *PE*, p. 92.

[39] *CPBR* 1.38 & 39.

what did away with Russell's Apostolic theory was the Open Question Argument. And this argument proved to be incompatible with Moore's philosophic practice. For the Open Question Argument relies on a publicity condition – that for B to constitute an analysis of A (or for A to be synonymous with B), the equivalence must be obvious to every competent speaker. Moore assumes that if goodness were identical with some other property such as what we desire to desire, 'good' and 'what we desire to desire' would be synonymous. So all he has to do to prove that goodness is not identical with what we desire to desire (or indeed with anything else) is to prove that 'good' and 'what we desire to desire' are not synonyms. How does he do this? He argues that if 'good' were synonymous with 'what we desire to desire' the question 'Is what we desire to desire, good?' would be a silly one, since the answer would be very obvious – yes. The question would be an interrogative tautology, a linguistic truism with a question mark tacked on the end. Nobody *who understood the words of which it was composed* would bother to ask it, and there could be no two opinions among competent speakers as to what the answer was. Moore takes it to be obvious that 'Is what we desire to desire, good?' is *not* like this; that the question is open; that it makes sense to ask it; and that competent speakers can, and do, disagree about what the answer is. Hence 'good' and 'what we desire to desire' are not synonymous. And the same trick can be used to dispose of alleged synonymies between 'good' and other naturalistic predicates. But note the publicity condition. Moore assumes that *if* 'good' were synonymous with 'what we desire to desire', this would be obvious to all. That is why the open question would not then be open, and why the actual openness of the question disproves the synonymy.[40]

This publicity condition came back to haunt Moore in later life. His stock in trade was *analysis*; the breaking down of more complex concepts into their components. (That is why he was known as an analytic philosopher.) C. H. Langford proposed a paradox.[41] Analysis as Moore conceives it is either useless or productive of falsehoods. For suppose the *analysans*, or analysing phrase, means the same thing as the *analysandum*, or thing to be analysed. Then, by the publicity condition, everyone would know this, and the analysis would teach us nothing new. Suppose on the other hand that the analysis is informative. Then (again by the publicity condition) the *analysans* and the *analysandum* are *not* really synonymous and the analysis is *false*. Indeed the naturalistic fallacy can be seen as an instance of the Paradox of Analysis. Moore argues, in effect, that any naturalistic analysis of 'good' must either be redundant, because widely known, or false, because not evident to all. It is just that he denies the naturalist the redundant horn of the dilemma. It is rather as if someone argued that 'The King of France is bald' cannot, as Russell supposes, mean that there is something which is both King of France and bald, that all things which are Kings of France are identical with that thing. For not only is this definition rather startling, thus failing the publicity

---

[40] My reconstruction of Moore's argument would probably not have met with his approval. To begin with he did not like to think of himself as proceeding form linguistic premises (since 'verbal questions are properly left to the writers of dictionaries', *PE*, p. 54) and he did not regard two expressions as synonymous if one 'contained an analysis' of the other even though (if the analysis were correct) they would have to mean the same thing (*PE*, p. 9).

[41] See C. H. Langford, 'On the Notion of Analysis in Moore's Philosophy', in P. A. Schilpp (ed.), *The Philosophy of G. E. Moore* (Evanston, Northwestern University Press, 1942), p. 323. Thomas Baldwin suggests that it may have been Moore who first formulated the paradox. See T. Baldwin, *G. E. Moore* (London, Routledge, 1990), p. 208.

condition, but it has actually been disputed, for instance by Sir Peter Strawson.

It seems we must choose between the Paradox of Analysis and the Open Question Argument. Either the Paradox is veridical and informative philosophical analyses are impossible, or there is something wrong with the assumptions that generate the paradox and the Open Question Argument is called into question.[42]

Now it does not seem plausible that Moore's method of analysis (or Russell's for that matter) is *entirely* worthless. Analysis in something like Moore's sense is surely capable of turning up results that are both true and interesting. Which means that Moore is implicitly operating with a notion or notions of equivalence that fall short of the strict and public synonymy he demands of his naturalistic opponents. We may allow that in this strict and public sense, 'good' is not synonymous with any other predicate, including 'what we desire to desire'. But this does not prove that 'good' cannot be *analysed* as what we desire to desire. For the purpose of analysis – *one* of the purposes at any rate – is to disinter the buried rules, presuppositions or primitive concepts that govern the use of a word and to express them in a perspicuous definition. (This can, of course, be a definition in use as with Russell's analysis of definite descriptions.) Such an analysis need not be obvious to every competent speaker, since we are not, in general, conscious of the rules, presuppositions or primitive concepts which determine the way we speak. Thus the Paradox of Analysis can be dissolved but only by reducing the Open Question Argument to impotence.

---

[42] I owe this point to conversations with David Lewis and John Burgess, though it is now becoming something of a commonplace. The issue is addressed in Lewis, 'Dispositional Theories of Value II', *Proceedings of the Aristotelian Society Supplementary*, vol. 63 (1989), pp. 129–32.

Russell's analysis of good as what we desire to desire may be correct after all and ethics a branch of empirical psychology!

Whether or not it is correct, it is at least a going concern. For a variant of Russell's theory has recently found a distinguished champion in David Lewis.[43] Lewis argues that values can be defined as what we are ideally disposed to desire to desire. Although I do not agree with this theory it is perhaps worth noting that Lewis's account, like Russell's is immune from another argument of Moore's. (Sometimes supposed to be *the* argument for the Naturalistic Fallacy.) Suppose that 'good' *is* synonymous with some natural predicate X. Then the assertion that X-things are good, provides us with no extra reason for promoting them. We are to produce states of affairs of such and such a character, and for no better reason than that 'goodness' is a synonym for the characteristic in question. By defining goodness in terms of X-ness, the naturalist deprives the proposition that X things are good of motivating power. For it now amounts to the tautology that X things are X. Since the assertion that X things are good *does* have some sort of influence on the will (at least when it is believed) and is propounded by the naturalist with the object of *exerting* such an influence, this indicates that the definition is false.[44] But this argument presupposes that 'good' is being defined in terms of some good-making-property, as when Bentham, for instance, defines goodness in terms of pleasure.[45] Many naturalistic

---

[43] See Lewis, *ibid.*

[44] See *PE*, chap. 1, sec. 11, pp. 63–4.

[45] Actually Bentham implies but does not state that 'good' means pleasurable. What he says is that 'pleasure, good or happiness' 'all ... comes to the same thing' (*BM*, p. 948). However he does give a utilitarian definition of 'ought', 'right' and 'wrong' and goes on to say that 'when thus inter-

definitions are in fact like this. The naturalist defines goodness as the property or disjunction of properties he wants to promote. But not all naturalists confuse analysis with advocacy. Hume for example does not. Although, like Bentham, he is a utilitarian (though of a rather refined and gentlemanly sort) he does not define goodness in terms of pleasure or happiness. In effect (and I am slurring over some complications here)[46] he defines goodness as what an informed and dispassionate observer would approve of, or would approve of promoting. This means that when *Hume* gets around to saying that pleasure is good, he is saying something more than that pleasure is pleasure. By distinguishing between analysis and advocacy, Hume makes his advocacy of utilitarianism more rationally persuasive. In so far as our dispositions to approve track those of the ideal observer, we too will approve of pleasure and thus are more likely to promote it. The approbation of the ideal observer may not be much of an added inducement for the pursuit of utility, but at least it is better than a tautology. In much the same way, Russell and Lewis are immune to this version of Moore's argument. When they define goodness or value as what we desire to desire (or are disposed to), they are not trying to promote what we desire to desire. (Hence it

---

preted [these words] and others of their stamp have a meaning; when otherwise they have none' (*BM*, p. 951.)

[46] In fact Hume defines a *virtue* (rather than goodness) as 'whatever action or quality gives to a spectator the pleasing sentiment of approbation' and then proceeds to examine a 'plain matter of fact, to wit, what actions [or qualities] have this influence' (*BM*, p. 600). The qualities which have this influence are those 'mental qualities [which are] useful or agreeable to theperson himself or to others' (*BM*, p. 586). But this makes no difference to the point I am trying to make in the text. Hume does not *define* virtue in terms of utility and it is for this reason that his claim that utilitarian actions are virtuous is not an impotent tautology.

does not matter to them that 'What we desire to desire is good' is tautologous or analytic.) They are trying to explain why predicating goodness of something else gives us some sort of reason to promote it. As Lewis puts it, the aim is to secure 'a conceptual connection between value and motivation'. And like Russell he wants the connection to be 'multifariously iffy'. After all we do not always choose the good.

The history of philosophy, like history in general, has its little ironies. G. E. Moore, one of the founding fathers of analytic philosophy, rose to fame with an argument which, if it had been a success, would have rendered the analytic project unworkable. Luckily nobody noticed. He had another argument for the fallaciousness of the Naturalistic Fallacy which does not subvert the analytic enterprise. But it does prove to be impotent against one of its principal targets – Russell's definition of the good as what we desire to desire. Luckily – or perhaps unluckily – Russell did not notice and became a convert to the doctrines of *Principia Ethica* anyway. Russell prided himself on his willingness to change his mind in the face of counter-arguments. This is indeed a virtue but it can be carried to excess, and Russell frequently did so, giving up good theories in the face of bad counter-arguments. His giving up on what we desire to desire is a case in point.

5. *More Prehistory: Intellectual Adventures of a Young Hegelian*
Despite the vestigial chapter on 'Metaphysical Ethics', *Principia Ethica* does not read like the work of a recently liberated Hegelian. Russell's references to Hegelian doctrine in his 'Elements of Ethics' are even more vestigial, and noone would guess, from this paper, that he had recently emerged with relief 'from a bath of

German idealism' in which he had languished for some years. In so far as either piece reads like a manifesto of revolt, it is a revolt against Sidgwick not Hegel (and even here it is a case of reform rather than revolution). But in Russell's case, the conversion to Hegelianism (the famous throwing up of the tobacco tin) *did* have an effect on his development as an ethicist, and his revolt against Hegel had an ethical dimension to it too. So in fact, the emergence of analytic ethics conforms rather more closely to the Comic Book History than might at first appear. But most of the materials for this history remained unpublished in Russell's lifetime. What I want to suggest is that Russell sought in Hegelian metaphysics the solution to a problem posed by Sidgwick. The paper which announced his rejection of Hegelianism, though superficially concerned with another topic, can easily be converted into a proof that such a solution cannot be found.

Neither Moore ('His personality did not attract me')[47] nor Russell ('We called him "old Sidg" and regarded him as merely out of date')[48] took to Sidgwick with much enthusiasm. But he had a greater influence on them than they seemed to realize at the time. This is

---

[47] G. E. Moore, 'An Autobiography', in Schilpp (ed.), *The Philosophy of G. E. Moore* (1942), p. 16.

[48] Bertrand Russell, *My Philosophical Development* (1959), p. 38. Both Moore and Russell talked of Sidgwick both in the nineties and later as if he was a doddering old fellow on the edge of senility. In this they have been followed by commentators who should have known better. Baldwin in his Introduction to *PE*, p. xiv, writes that 'Sidgwick was by then [that is at the time Moore was attending his lectures] an old man (he died in 1900)'. But at the time Moore was attending his lectures, Sidgwick was in his middle fifties and hence middle-aged rather than old. It is true that he died in 1900, but he died relatively young at the age of sixty-two. That Moore and Russell have managed to foist there adolescent perceptions of a supposedly aged Sidgwick on subsequent writers is a triumph of the auto-biographer's art.

evident in the case of Moore. In Russell's case the influence is more subtle but it is there nevertheless. In particular, I suspect Sidgwick was important in setting a problem which Russell tried to solve with the aid of Hegelian metaphysics. Sidgwick, notoriously believed in 'the Dualism of Practical Reason'. He thought that 'ought'-judgements express dictates of reason.[49] But reason sometimes speaks with a divided voice. It is rational to promote the public interest and rational to promote ones private interest. And where they come into conflict, you cannot say that the one is more reasonable than the other. Sidgwick considered this 'the profoundest problem in Ethics' and did not profess to have a solution.[50] Now, of course, Sidgwick is not alone in seeing this difficulty. Plato's *Republic* can be seen as a not very successful attempt at what Kavka calls 'the reconciliation project',[51] since Glaucon's Ring of Gyges suggests that justice and self-interest do not always coincide. But if Russell was interested in the problem it seems reasonable to suppose, given his intellectual background, that it was Sidgwick who set the agenda.

And Russell *was* interested in the problem. 'On the Foundations of Ethics' (September 1893)[52] is an essay written for Alys Pearsall Smith, to whom he had just proposed. This was some time before the famous incident with the tobacco tin, but he is clearly well on

[49] H. Sidgwick, *Methods of Ethics* (1907), 7th edn., pp. 34, 105.

[50] *ibid*, pp. xviii–xxiii, 162–175, 506–509. J. L. Mackie's 'Sidgwick's Pessimism' in his *Persons and Values* (Oxford, Oxford University Press, 1985), is an excellent essay on the topic.

[51] See Gregory S. Kavka, 'The Reconciliation Project', in D. Copp, and D. Zimmerman (eds.), *Morality, Reason and Truth* (Totowa, Rowman and Allanheld, 1985).

[52] CPBR 1.31.

the way to neo-Hegelianism. In a letter he says that 'instead of systematically criticizing Green I have set forth my own views [which] have no philosophic interest'.[53] It is sad to have to contradict the one modest remark in what is otherwise a horribly conceited letter, but if, as Russell says, 'the view I have put forward is that of most of the younger men at Cambridge' then it *is* of philosophic interest. For the young men in question included Russell himself, Moore and McTaggart. As Russell realizes the view is really a modified form of utilitarianism. What distinguishes Russell and his *confreres* from standard-order utilitarians is an assumption derived from McTaggart's version of Hegelian metaphysics, that there is a 'most perfect form into which it is metaphysically possible for the universe to develop' and that this consists of an absolute – and, one gathers, blissful – harmony among spirits. It is important that the harmony which Russell believed in 1893 was a *future* harmony rather than a current harmony (if that is the right way to put it) existing in a timeless reality. For such a harmony can perhaps be promoted or retarded and hence can be an end for rational action. Not so a harmony that already exists in some timeless supersensible realm. Moreover, (since at this time Russell accepted McTaggart's arguments for personal immortality)[54] this future harmony is one in which I can hope to participate. Hence I have a selfish motive for the pursuit of this collective end. Ultimately, as 'sympathy [becomes] more developed ... selfishness and unselfishness will become indistinguishable and the end of each will become the end of all'. Thus Sidgwick's problem is neatly solved – though

---

[53] Quoted in *CPBR* 1, p. 206.

[54] See N. Griffin, *Russell's Idealist Apprenticeship* (1991), p. 50.

at the cost of some metaphysical implausibilities. But McTaggart's solution did not satisfy Russell for long since it relied on personal immortality and a *future* state of absolute harmony and he soon ceased to believe in either. Reality – the Absolute – may be harmonious, but there is no reason to expect such harmony in the world of Appearance.

The problem is addressed again in an Apostolic paper 'Cleopatra or Maggie Tulliver'[55] (chosen as representatives of passion and duty respectively) delivered in November 1894. This represents Russell's first foray into moral psychology. Here Russell develops certain characteristic theses about reason and the passions which remained with him for the rest of his life. He claims 1) that 'as Spinoza says' a passion can only be overcome by another passion; 2) that the 'greatest passions, those which most influence our actions' are not necessarily those of the greatest intensity; and 3) that the greater a passion is the more it ought to be followed.[56] As stated these theses look as if they might generate the kind of absurd philosophical precept that Russell criticizes in others, where the philosopher denounces as wrong the very things his philosophy professes to prove impossible. After all if the greatest passion at any moment is the one which determines my actions, then I *cannot* give the victory to a lesser passion. If I do, then what this proves is either that the greatest passion was not the greatest passion after all, or that Russell's theory is false. Like Bergson, who Russell accuses of just such an intellectual crime, Russell appears to condemn as wrong those actions which condemn his theory to

[55] *CPBR*, 1.14.

[56] *CPBR* 1, pp. 92–3.

falsehood.[57] However, the context suggests that Russell is equivocating here. Though in 2) the greater or greatest passion is simply the one which predominates, in 3) a passion is great if it is permanent and comprehends a larger 'universe'. Thus the greatest passion in sense 2) might not be one of the greater passions in sense 3). In the end the practical message seems to be as this: A. We should not stifle our passions lightly, since this leads to frustration, lassitude or maybe even madness(!).[58] Rather we should cultivate those passions which admit of a harmonious realization and only do away with those which are inimical to the others. B. That as moral beings, concerned for the welfare of creatures besides ourselves, we should cultivate those passions which harmonize with the desires of other people.[59] In other words, we should cultivate compossible desires, which is pretty much the ethic of *Human Society in Ethics and Politics* (1954)[60] and most of the books and essays written in between. The essay ends up dogmatically asserting that 'the Satisfaction required to make [desires] ethically good is not of the self'.[61] This is simply an appeal to the humanity or the moral feelings of his audience, and does not really solve Sidgwick's problem. For it has not been shown that it is *reasonable*, and hence obligatory, to pursue socially rather than individually harmonious desires when the two come into conflict. But Russell does try for something better.

---

[57] See 'Behaviourism and Values', *CPBR* 9, especially pp. 70–71.

[58] *CPBR* 1, pp. 95–6.

[59] *ibid.*, pp. 96–8.

[60] Bertrand Russell, *Human Society in Ethics and Politics* (London, Allen and Unwin, 1954).

[61] *CPBR* 1, p. 98.

After dismissing McTaggart, he flirts with the idea that individual selves can be somehow seen as aspects of the one, so that the prudential arguments for cultivating harmonious desires will rule out harmonious but antisocial passions such as those of Napoleon and Iago. 'I am vastly tempted to regard the subject, as apparently Bradley does, as a mere fluid nucleus of Feeling ... and so to adopt an almost Spinozistic monism, in which our terms become merely Desire on the one hand and Satisfaction on the other – this would obviate all these ethical difficulties, and reduce Hatred and similar passions to my former case of a conflict.'[62] The idea is that *really* different selves are not distinct, so that if I have a reason to cultivate desires which are harmonious *inter se*, I have a similar reason to cultivate desires which harmonize with everyone else's.[63] But though Russell professes himself 'vastly tempted' to adopt this hypothesis, he does not do so in the paper (though he may have done so in discussion).[64]

Why shouldn't he have given in to temptation? An answer is suggested by 'Seems Madam? Nay, It Is' (December 1897),[65] the paper which marks his exit from Hegelianism. Although Russell describes it in a letter to Moore as a 'scratch sort of paper' due to the

---

[62] *ibid.*, p. 98.

[63] This idea is fairly common one in the history of philosophy. See for example Arthur Schopenhauer, *On the Basis of Morality*, trans F. J. Payne (Indianapolis, Bobbs-Merrill, 1941), originally published 1841, p. 207.

[64] See the letter to Alys Pearsall Smith, 4 Nov. 1894, quoted *CPBR* 1, p. 91.

[65] *CPBR* 1.16.

fact that he was having 'a dry time',[66] it is a glittering piece which marks a new high in stylistic sophistication. (It is the only one of his Apostolic papers which Russell saw fit to reprint in his lifetime.)[67] Its theme is concisely summed up in a letter to Moore: 'that for all purposes which are not *purely* intellectual, the world of Appearance is the real world.' The paper is a morally based critique of the consolatory pretensions of Hegelian philosophy. Its basic thesis is this: If the world of Appearance is bad, it is no consolation to be told that the world of Reality is good since what we experience is the world of Appearance. (Again, Russell rejects the idea of the Absolute as 'a future state of things "a harmony which must some day become explicit"'.[68] If Reality really is timeless, it has no more intimate connection with the future than the past – 'there is, indeed every likelihood that God will stay in his heaven'.)[69] Although Russell does not discuss the matter explicitly, the application of all this to the tempting Bradleian hypothesis of 'Cleopatra or Maggie Tulliver?' is plain. What does it matter if really you and I are one, if our experience is confined to the world of Appearance rather than Reality? Since I do not experience the pains I inflict on you when pursuing my harmonious but evil desires, why should I worry about the fact that in reality I am inflicting them on myself? After all, it is the phenomenal self that feels, or for that matter desires, and phenomenal selves are distinct. Thus we cannot reconcile self-interest with the public interest by positing

[66] 7 December 1897, quoted in *CPBR* 1, p. 105.

[67] In Bertrand Russell, *Why I am Not a Christian*, in Edwards (ed.), (London, Allen and Unwin, 1957).

[68] *CPBR* 1, p. 107.

[69] *ibid.*, p. 107.

a metaphysical unity of selves. The paper puts the kybosh on the neo-Hegelian version of 'the reconciliation project'.

Thus Sidgwick's problem remains unsolved and the Dualism of Practical Reason reasserts itself. Three years before, at the time of 'Cleopatra or Maggie Tulliver?', Russell had written that 'My paradox [by which, I take it, he means Sidgwick's problem] has been for years a worry – a solution would be a real solid addition to my happiness'.[70] However, he thought that there was 'no solution short of the Hegelian Dialectic'.[71] Once he came up with an argument which implied that even Hegelian Dialectic would not do the trick, he soon gave it up. Why then should we be moral? Russell has no answer besides the hope that the right sort of upbringing will instill the right motivations. And like a more enlightened version of James Mill, he tried to supply his children with just such an upbringing. The right motivations were not always forthcoming however. Katharine Tait in *My Father Bertrand Russell* records the following exchange (Kate is the first speaker):

'I don't want to! Why should I?'
'Because more people will be happier if you do than if you don't.'
'So what? I don't care about other people.'
'You should.'
'But why?'
'Because more people will be happier if you do than if you don't.'[72]

---

[70] 29 October 1894, quoted *CPBR* 1, p. 91.

[71] Letter to Alys of 26/10/94, quoted *CPBR* 1, p. 90.

[72] Katharine Tait, *My Father Bertrand Russell* (New York, Harcourt Bruce Jovanovich, 1975; reprinted by Thoemmes Press, 1996).

Little did she know that in this dialogue she was displaying the Dualism of Practical Reason. Russell's answer is, of course, a dusty one, but given the Dualism of Practical Reason there is probably no better answer to be had.

Now I could go on – indeed I would like to go on – to examine Russell's period as a Moorean and his subsequent conversion to non-cognitivism and (briefly) to the error theory. But not many us of are likely to live as long as he did, and we do not have world enough and time. However, I hope I have said enough to stimulate your interest in Russell as an ethical theorist. Reading Russell is not a mere exercise in what is known in the Antipodes as *text-fondling*, the shameful vice of history-for-history's-sake scholarship.[73] He is far too stimulating and far too inventive for that. At the very least, Russell is often interestingly wrong. And not many of us can hope to do better than that.

---

[73] The term is due to that quintessentially Australian philosopher, Kim Sterelny.

BIBLIOGRAPHY OF WORKS CITED

Russell, Bertrand, 1983. *The Collected Papers of Bertrand Russell, Cambridge Essays 1888–1899*, vol. 1, ed. by Blackwell, Brink, Griffin, Rempel & Slater (London, Allen and Unwin).

—— 1985. *The Collected Papers of Bertrand Russell, Contemplation and Action 1902–1914*, vol. 12, ed. by Rempel, Brink and Moran (London, Allen and Unwin).

—— 1986. *The Collected Papers of Bertrand Russell, The Philosophy of Logical Atomism and Other Essays 1914–1919*, vol. 12, ed. by Slater (London, Allen and Unwin).

—— 1988. *The Collected Papers of Bertrand Russell, Essays on Language, Mind and Matter, 1919–1926*, vol. 9, ed. by Slater and Frohman (London, Allen and Unwin).

—— 1988. *The Collected Papers of Bertrand Russell, Prophecy and Dissent 1914–1916*, vol. 13, ed. by Rempel with Frohman, Lippincott and Moran (London, Unwin Hyman).

—— 1992. *The Collected Papers of Bertrand Russell, Logical and Philosophical Papers 1909–1913*, vol. 6, ed. by Slater and Frohman (London, Routledge).

—— 1994. *The Collected Papers of Bertrand Russell, Foundations of Logic 1903–05*, vol. 4, ed. by Urquhart with Lewis (London, Routledge).

THE HISTORY OF WESTERN PHILOSOPHY
– FIFTY YEARS LATER

Louis Greenspan
McMaster University

We have passed the fiftieth anniversary of the publication of Bertrand Russell's *History of Western Philosophy*, without any suggestion of a commemoration or announcements to mark the occasion. Russell himself would not be surprised at this. This year of 1995 has also been the fiftieth anniversary of the end of the war in Europe and the dropping of the atomic bomb in Hiroshima, events that overshadowed this anniversary. Any effort to mark Russell's *History* could only have been a reminder that his pen was 'neither mightier nor busier than other people's swords'. Aside from this however, Russell's history is rarely to be found in the curricula of philosophy departments. It is still a popular success. It remains a favourite with Book Clubs, it is the book by a major philosopher most likely to be found in Airport book stores, but it has not become, what he hoped it would become, the text of choice for professional philosophers.

Russell may have been unduly optimistic in entertaining such hopes for the book. In composing the book, in choosing the figures that he thought to be most important, and in the historical schema that he chose, Russell followed his own lights, and in this book these lights shone differently and on different places than everyone else's. The criteria that he used for selecting his canon remains puzzling even to his most enthusiastic followers. Russell devotes almost as much space to the social structure of Sparta as he does to the philosophy of Thomas Aquinas, he tells us little about what he knew best, the development of philosophy in the twentieth century – George Boas, protested that in a work that purported to emphasize

> political and social circumstances ... the philosophers of the eighteenth century are given a few lines more than a page ... . The Encyclopedists as a group appear only once (p. 599) along with the 'English Eighteenth Century' and the founders of the American Constitution, as people 'dominated' by early liberalism. (Boas, 1947, p. 123)

He devotes a complete chapter to Lord Byron, a writer who does not appear in any other work in philosophy, while Frege is mentioned *en passant* and Heidegger doesn't even merit a line in the index.

Russell insists that he is writing as an Historian of Ideas especially sensitive to social and historical context yet he has no difficulty in finding twentieth-century phenomena in ancient Greece. Thus he introduces Plato by announcing that 'I wish to understand him, but to treat him with as little reverence as I would treat him if he were a contemporary advocate of totalitarianism' (Russell, 1961, p. 122). But he does not describe the concept of totalitarianism as having any historical specificity and uses it almost indiscriminately. Even if we thought we fathomed its meaning we learn in another passage on Plato that Plato's later dialogue *Parmenides* 'contains one of the most remarkable cases in history of self criticism by a philosopher' (Russell, 1961, p. 142). Most of us do not associate totalitarianism with ruthless self-criticism and will therefore remain baffled about what model of totalitarianism Russell is guided by.

But even if we ignore his criteria for selection and some of his critical vocabulary, his basic narrative structure is like everything else in Russell: unique and *sui generis*. Histories of Philosophy usually have some narrative line; for example there are those who believe that ancient Greece was the high point in the history of thought and from there philosophy went downhill; others, mainly Catholic historians, believe that Ancient Greece was but an introduction to the Christian Philosophy of the Middle Ages. This period they maintain was the high point of human civilization which began to deteriorate with the advent of modernity. Finally there are those who from Hegel to Compte find the history of philosophy follows a line of evolutionary development in which each age is an improvement over the one that it succeeds.

Russell's schema does not fit comfortably with any of these. He admires the Greeks, but writes more favourably of the presocratics than of Plato and Aristotle. Like the Catholic philosophers he admires some of the Medievals but dismisses Thomas Aquinas, maintaining that 'I cannot feel that he deserves to be put on a level with the best philosophers of modern times' (Russell, 1961, p. 454). It would be reasonable to suppose that a modern sceptic, agnostic and champion of the scientific outlook would favour an evolutionary schema in which the modern world is the culmination of all that went before. But as is evident from the text, Russell despised Hegel, and does not follow a progressive schema at all. The unfolding of culture in Russell's historical narrative is not nearly as neat as anyone else's. In his schema philosophy receives a jump start with the Greek cosmologists, but beginning with

Pythagoras takes a wrong path from which it doesn't return until the scientific revolution in the sixteenth century. After that there are leaps forward, as with Leibniz, admirable way stations as with Spinoza, and jumps into the abyss as with Nietzsche and other German Idealists, but nothing that matches the historical narratives that might be familiar to others.

The key to the historiography of this work is the influence of Marxism. Commentators on Russell and on this work have failed to notice this. When Russell wrote this book he was one of the most outspoken critics of Bolshevism. Few had criticized Marxist politics and Marxist dialectic as persistently and as effectively as had Russell. Yet he tells us unambiguously that work is a variation of the Marxist agenda that connects philosophies to social and historical systems. Marxism, Russell writes, conceives of the history of philosophy and of culture in general as 'the outcome of its methods of production and, to a lesser extent of its methods of distribution' (Russell, 1961, p. 750). Russell does not 'accept the thesis as it stands but, I think it contains an important element of truth and *I am aware that it has influenced my own views of philosophical development as set forth in this work*' (Russell, 1961, p. 750, my italics). This is a candid and accurate statement. Russell, the historian is not concerned about the truth of the philosophies that he describes but their role as expressions of certain social and political orders. In the paragraphs that follow he provides an excellent summary of the entire work. He writes:

> We may say in a broad way, that Greek philosophy down to Aristotle expresses the mentality appropriate to the City State: that Stoicism is appropriate to a cosmopolitan despotism; that scholastic philosophy is

an intellectual expression of the Church as an organization; that philosophy since Descartes, or at any rate
since Locke tends to embody the prejudices of the
Commercial Middle Class and that Marxism and
fascism are philosophies appropriate to the modern
industrial state. (Russell, 1961, p. 751)

Russell the historian conceives of the philosophies of the
past as ideologies. In treating these philosophies as
ideologies he is not concerned with their truth, their
inner coherence or their inner consistency. He is
concerned primarily with the manner in which they are
connected, serve the interests of or express social and
historical systems. Russell's argument echoes that of
Marx but it is Marx without the dialectic.

Russell also follows Marx in declaring that once the
ideological character of the history of philosophy is
exposed we can advance from ideology to science. In
Russell's account as well as in Marx's the essential point
about the philosophy of the past is that it has been
overcome. His history, then, is an obituary and a call for
a new beginning. In the closing pages of his history he
announces that 'a method has been discovered by which
in philosophy we can make successive approximations
to the truth, in which each stage results from an
improvement, not a rejection, of what has gone before'
(Russell, 1961, p. 789). He cites the philosophies of the
past for their dependence on religion, a dependence that
forced them to 'falsify logic, to make mathematics
mystical and to pretend that deep seated prejudices were
heaven sent intuitions' (Russell, 1961, p. 789). Russell
declares an end to philosophy as ideology and a
beginning as science and technical analysis. He shares
in the movement that brought forward the works of
Daniel Bell's *End of Ideology* and even Camus' *The*

Rebel who also called for an end to the ideological extravagance of the past.

Russell's *History* then was meant to be one of the crowning achievements in a revolution in philosophy. It was a triumphant conclusion to the past which, it proclaimed, had been overcome. It is no wonder that traditionalist critics as well as admirers concluded that Russell's aim was to make the History of Philosophy redundant. The critics were outraged. The anonymous reviewer in the *Times Literary Supplement* spoke for many of these when he stated that

> when Russell comes to us to display his talents and his productions, we are tempted to treat him as the citizens of Plato's Republic treated the poet, paying him reverence as a sacred, admirable and charming personage, but sending him away to another city after pouring perfumed oil upon his head and crowning him with woolen fillets ... while we owe him a debt for entertainment, we must turn from him and look for something of greater weight and substance. (*Times Literary Supplement*, 1946)

The views of his admirers is aptly summarized in the review by T. D. Weldon, who in his discussion of Russell's volume, notes that 'After all Life is short, and, unless some positive argument for studying them can be produced, we had surely better send Aristotle and Aquinas to join Lucretius and Copernicus in the museum of distinguished antiquities'. Weldon goes on to note that such study might be useful as a study of the effect of past philosophies on society and as a compendium of errors for all philosophical beginners. They believed that Russell had done his work too well.

In today's philosophical climate few would accept Russell's historiography as it stands. Few would defend the view that the history of philosophy is a drama of ideology versus science. There is too much scepticism about the privileged view of science, and too much eclecticism concerning philosophical legitimacy. The German philosophers whom Russell had undermined, especially Hegel and Nietzsche, are back in full force. There is an extensive and to my mind inconclusive discussion of the relationship between ideas and social structures. The end of philosophy is proclaimed not by logicians but by students who, like those in the famous demonstrations in Stanford in 1988 chant 'Heigh Ho Heigh Ho western thought has got to go'. Russell's work retains its charm but not its authority.

But this does not end our consideration of this text, for Russell's history contains a subplot. Earlier I noted that Russell writes sometimes as a historian of ideas and sometimes as a philosopher. Often he forgets that he is a historian. He seems to lose sight of his goal to present the history of philosophy as ideology and engages in purely philosophical discourse with the thinking he is considering, treating their ideas on their own merits and without reference to their connection with the social structure. The pattern of such discussions is different from the pattern of his historiography. When Russell writes as an historian he writes of the triumph of analytic philosophy as the triumph of science, when he writes as a philosopher he is engaged in a struggle to define, to defend and uphold analytic philosophy against formidable foes. This point will become clearer if we examine Russell's engagement with his fellows.

In practice Russell does not treat the individual philosophers as dead letters. In the one passage in the book when he describes his methodology, he urges that we follow the method of philosophers not historians – that we begin by treating each philosophy as though it were true and then gradually finding errors and mistakes if they are there. This method, by the way, echoes the method of Hegel but in Russell leads to very different results. Hegel studies a philosopher, finds what is living and what is dead, translates the living into his own language so that in the end philosophers are placed on pedestals of ascending importance as contributions to his own thought. Russell's results are different. Some philosophers are disposed of but a much larger number are left standing – his controversies with them unresolved. Thus he concludes his discussion of Plato's views on the objectivity of morality with 'this is one of the issues in philosophy that is still open' (Russell, 1961, p. 134). He concludes his discussion of the twelfth-century philosopher Abelard's views on logic with 'The most modern discussions of the problem of universals have not got much further' (Russell, 1961, p. 430). Russell also presents a number of excellent discussions of ethical and religious systems, such as those of Epictetus and Plotinus, or the philosophical retreats into private mysticisms, a tendency so common in the Hellenic and Roman world which, in his view are convincing responses to chaotic social and political conditions, and which leave open the question of whether in similar circumstances such systems of thought might again be live options. In his discussion of the Stoics and Epicureans Russell asks whether Stoic can be determinists and still consider acts of resistance in concentration camps as examples of human freedom. This is still a powerful question. In short Russell has not given us what so many thought he had, a story in which the human race has groped through the darkness until it came to the light of philosophical analysis. Instead we have a story in which a number of characters, admirable as well as villainous seem to have made a temporary exit and could very well emerge again.

Russell's historiography suggests that he was inspired by the most militant versions of positivism which insisted on a demarcation between meaningless metaphysical speculation and fruitful scientific theorizing. This dichotomy does indeed throw light on one of the principle themes in the book but in Russell's hands the division is not a very neat one. Russell's history does feature a tension between the scientific philosophers, such as the early Greek cosmologists whose theories tried to account for what they had observed in nature and the works of philosophers such as Pythagoras who according to him were merely articulating the religious visions of the Orphic. But anyone who expects to find a detailed articulation of the dualism announced by the positivists will find the book profoundly confusing. They will not find a rote schema of praise for empiricists and indictments of speculators. The accusation that used to be hurled at the metaphysical systems of the past as a succession of offerings of science fiction is not to be found in Russell. On the contrary, he treats Bacon and Locke with much more reserve. Russell's bias is towards adventurous speculations rather than cautious induction. He does not give wholehearted endorsement to those who have brought us down to earth. Thus in his account of the Greeks he describes a philosopher who could easily be dubbed as a Russellian alter ego, the philosopher Xenophanes, with cool reserve. Russell quotes Xenophanes' most Russellian remark

> Mortals deem that gods are begotten as they are, and have clothes like theirs, and voice and form ... yes and if oxen and horses and lions had hands and could paint with their hands and produce works of art as

men do, horses would paint the forms of gods like
horses, and oxen like oxen'. (Russell, 1961, pp. 58–9)

But instead of rejoicing that he had found a precursor,
sums him up as follows:

> Xenophanes has his place in the succession of ratio-
> nalists who were opposed to the mystical tendencies of
> others, but as an independent thinker he is not in the
> first rank. (Russell, 1961, p. 59)

Russell reserves his admiration for great and fruitful
speculations. Throughout the work he shows his
admiration for great leaps such as Augustine's theories
of time, Descartes' division of the world into thought
and matter and even Plato's theory of the good. Plato's
theory, Russell argues, required that the heavens be
shown to exhibit a circular pattern of planets around the
sun: such a pattern was finally demonstrated by
Copernicus (at which point Plato's theory became
redundant). Nevertheless such speculations of the philosophical hares then were more fruitful than the slow
hoarding of evidence of the empirical tortoises. Of the
Greek cosmologists Russell writes

> To learn to conceive the universe according to each of
> these systems is an imaginative delight and an antidote
> to dogmatism ... The imaginative inventiveness of the
> Greeks can hardly be too highly praised. (Russell,
> 1961, p. 57)

In his section on the philosophies of the seventeenth
century his accounts of the rationalists, though critical,
are often more enthusiastic than his accounts of the
empiricists. In a later section he insisted that it was a
mistake to try to ground the principle of induction with
arguments derived from experience.

The perspectives on the history of philosophy that were so common among empiricists and which influenced the reception of this work do not go to the heart of this work. It is not a history that lays the past to rest, nor is it a sustained exposé of the follies of metaphysics.

Modernity Revisited

A careful examination of Russell's account of the modern period reveals an account that is at variance with the triumphalism of his History of Ideologies. It is possible to reconstruct Russell's account of modernity as a struggle of contending forces where we cannot know the outcome.

For Russell, the modern world resembles the ancient and medieval worlds in that it is a product of religious ideas. Ancient philosophy is the story of the unfolding of the Orphic religion, medieval philosophy is the story of the unfolding of Christianity and the modern world is the story of the unfolding of Protestantism. Russell writes 'From the sixteenth century onward, the history of Europe is dominated by the Reformation ....' When Protestants 'rejected the Church as a vehicle of revelation; truth was to be sought only in the Bible, which each man could interpret for himself. If men differed in their interpretation, there was no Divinely inspired authority to decide the dispute' (Russell, 1961, p. 20). The consequences of this development were 'momentous ...'.

> there was a tendency towards anarchism in politics and mysticism in religion ... the result, in thought was literature was a continually deepening subjectivism, operating at first as wholesome liberation from spiritual slavery, but advancing steadily towards a personal isolation inimical social sanity. (Russell, 1961, p. 20)

The logic of Protestantism leads to Romanticism, a rapturous philosophy made more rapturous by the possession of modern technology. Russell says of Romanticism that

> the typical Romantic removes the bars and enjoys the magnificent leaps with which the tiger annihilates the sheep. He exhorts men to imagine themselves tigers, and when he succeeds the results are not wholly pleasant. (Russell, 1961, p. 21)

These long quotations help establish the cultural and philosophic framework of the modern world, its problematic milieu. It also helps account for some of the characteristics and even eccentricities in Russell's history. The most important characteristic is that Russell's celebration of the development of modern science does not imply for him a Comptean schema of history whereby modernity is a triumphant conclusion to the ordeal of history or even a narrative which applauds the advance of freedom. He applauds science as one of humanity's triumphs but remains apprehensive about its reception because he feared that the mixture of science, Protestantism and Romanticism is potentially lethal. Modern philosophy then, should be understood as a contest between those who, like Nietzsche and the Romantics push the logic of Protestantism until it becomes an extreme, subjective will to power and those who, like the liberals and empiricists, find a principle of balance and restraint. He argues further that those who, like Hume, promote radical scepticism, are the allies with the catalysts for all that is worst in romanticism. This narrative helps explain one of the great eccentricities in the book, namely the pivotal role that Russell confers upon Byron. Byron is never mentioned in any of the other histories of philosophy, either those prior to Russell's or those subsequent, but in Russell's volume he receives an extended discussion and declared one of the founders of the madness of Romanticism, nationalism and fascism. Another important item in this history is the bitterness that he directs against the scepticism of Hume. Many authors have reacted with outrage at Russell's characterization of Plato and Hegel but none seem to have noticed the scorn against Hume. This has a bitter edge. Plato and Hegel are, after all strangers; Hume is one of his own, a contributor to the empiricist tradition. Russell's attack on Hume is to my mind one of the centrepieces of the volume, one of a series of attacks on scepticism throughout the history of philosophy and the one subject that connects this book to our own intellectual climate.

Since Russell was fond of calling himself a sceptic, and approved of a volume that described him as a 'passionate Sceptic', the reader is unprepared for the severity of his criticism of scepticism in various sections of the book. In my opinion his criticisms of scepticism are among the shrewdest passages in the book and even among the shrewdest passages in his non-technical writing. Russell examines the scepticism of the Sophists, the Pyrrhonic scepticism of the Hellenic world and the scepticism of Hume. He accuses all of the same vice, a combination of subversion and conservatism. We are accustomed to the former accusation, but so far as I know Russell is one of the few commentators who calls attention to the latter. Sceptics cannot criticize the standards of society because they have no criteria with which to criticize. They conclude that since everything is false one may as well become a conformist and follow the rules of those in power. I say that this is shrewd on Russell's part but one must recognize that Russell is sceptical on moral issues and is therefore exposed to the same problem.

Scepticism, according to Russell, is the denial that anything can be known. While scepticism is healthy concerning some issues, such as the truth of religion, it is destructive with respect to others. Russell even accuses total sceptics of insincerity. Thus Russell writes of the Hellenic sceptic Pyrrho:

> He is said to have maintained that there could never be any rational grounds for preferring one ground of action to another. In practice this meant that one conformed to the customs of whatever country one inhabited. A modern sceptic would go to church on Sundays and perform the correct genuflexions, but without any of the religious beliefs that are meant to inspire these actions. (Russell, 1961, p. 241)

Concerning Hume he writes: 'Hume's philosophy, whether true or false, represents the bankruptcy of eighteenth-century reasonableness' (Russell, 1961, p. 645). His scepticism never holds its grounds. In the early sections of the treatise Hume announces that he is a sceptic but, Russell accuses, in the later portions 'Hume forgets all about his fundamental doubts' (Russell, 1961, p. 646).

If the absence of standards of criticism in scepticism leads to conformity, the critical part of scepticism, that is the part which undermines rational enquiry, opens the door to the subrational. Thus Hellenic scepticism 'had enough force to make educated men dissatisfied with the state religions, but had nothing positive ... (thus) the way was left clear for the invasion of the Oriental religions' (Russell, 1961, p. 248). The consequences of Hume's scepticism were equally nefarious but more dangerous. Hume's critique was ignored by empiricists in England but taken up by Romantics in Europe.

According to Russell, Hume demolished every philosophy that laid claim to any rational foundation but gave legitimacy to those philosophies, like that of Rousseau and Nietzsche that saw no need to seek any rational grounding. Thus the way was open to madness as there is 'no intellectual difference between sanity and insanity' (Russell, 1961, p. 646).

The importance of these passages can hardly be exaggerated. Russell dreads scepticism because it remains a great temptation but its consequences are horrific. The reader senses Russell's abhorrence of this philosophy. Scepticism is to Russell as Banquo's ghost to Macbeth. Russell concedes that Hume has shown genuine difficulties in eighteenth-century empiricism by raising his famous difficulties with the principle of induction. Russell also concedes that his own proposals for the solution to this problem raise difficulties of its own. But in this chapter his argument is more existential than logical. To concede to Hume is to open the floodgates. Empiricism, with its insistence on the discipline of observation is our only protection against the extreme consequences of the Protestant principle. Without empiricist criteria for truth Russell argues 'the lunatic who believes that he is a poached egg is to be condemned solely on the ground that he is in a minority' (Russell, 1961, p. 646). So, of course, is the lunatic who maintains that he is a member of the master race.

Here Russell is skirting dangerously close to a contradiction. He has maintained throughout that philosophies should not be argued on the basis of their moral or political consequences. But his criticism of Hume is based very largely on the consequences of Humean scepticism. In these passages Russell's defence of empiricism prefigures the defence of empiricism today against the ideas of the chanting students whom I have quoted above. I shall turn to this topic presently.

The drama of modern philosophy which is now evident centres on the role of the empiricist criterion of truth – in Russell's account the role of induction and the correspondence theory of truth. The most important challenge to the empiricism as a method and as philosophy comes from within modernity. Russell sees a more important threat to empiricism from modern scepticism and pragmatism than from the various traditions of metaphysics. His account of the metaphysical tradition is filled with interesting, sympathetic nuances. The danger to the scientific outlook come from philosophies that have emerged since the Protestant Reformation not those that came before it. Ironically one of the most dangerous of these challenges comes from scepticism, the other from the pragmatism of John Dewey – both philosophies that are usually thought of as belonging to the same family as that of Russell.

Russell's lengthy chapter in Dewey focuses on Dewey's principle (or Russell's interpretation of it) that ideas are to be judged by their consequences. Russell ridicules this idea, in some of the wittiest passages in the book. But he closes the chapter in an impassioned passage that can be quoted as the summary of the argument of this history and as well as a summary of Russell's argument for empiricism.

He accuses Dewey of 'cosmic impiety' and berates all forms of pragmatism and scepticism as follows:

> The concept of truth as something dependent on fact has been one of the ways in which philosophy has inculcated the necessary element of humility. When this check on pride is removed, a further step is taken on the road toward a certain kind of madness. (Russell, 1961, p. 782)

I indicated above that Russell's critique of scepticism, and now of pragmatism is connected to the current debates about philosophy, the 'hegemony' of western thought, and the validity of a kind of multi-cultural relativism. One of the flash points of these debates concerns the validity, or as we would say now, the privileged position of scientific knowledge. There are of course those who, citing Nietzsche, claim that scientific knowledge is one perspective among many. Ernest Gellner is one of the front line defenders of Russell in this dispute. In an article in the *Times Literary Supplement* of 16 June 1995, he directs his criticism against modern relativists who argue that we are faced with a choice between a relativism that accepts all cultural expression as equal or bigotry. He calls the former position 'the great carnival'. He writes: 'one simply cannot understand our shared social condition unless one starts from the indisputable fact that genuine knowledge is possible and has occurred' (E. Gellner, 1995, p. 8). This is Russellian.

In reply then to the second issue: does Russell raise important questions in the history of ideas? The answer is emphatically yes and Russell's text is one of those that has become even more important in the light of the new contests between empiricism on one side and the post-modernists and pragmatists on the other.

The History as Eurocentric
There is no doubt that Russell's history concentrates on philosophy as a product of European civilization and the West. On the other hand he consciously combats Western hubris by rejecting the narrative of progress that would make Europe a model for all the world to follow, and invites Western thought to join a worldwide community.

The History of Western Philosophy is divided into three sections, a division that suggests the philosophy of Compte, which is a narrative of progress. But if there is a narrative of progress it is a very hesitant one. The first section deals with the ancient world, a world of free worldly activity but which is unable to find an orderly structure so that it finally succumbs to the power of Rome. The second section, the Christian centuries, does have an ideal of world unity but is unable to realize it. It is plagued by dualism, cannot find a reason for creation of the world and can never close the gap between dream and reality. 'The mood of thoughtful men throughout the whole period, was one of deep unhappiness in regard to the affairs of the world' (Russell, 1961, p. 406).

So far then he seems to be following Hegel. He has presented the thesis and the antithesis. What is needed he writes is 'a durable and satisfactory social order' which combines 'the solidity of the Roman Empire with the idealism of Augustine's City of God' (Russell, 1961, p. 482) but he emphasizes that the modern world seems incapable of providing this synthesis. He proclaims that a new philosophy will be needed. This is far from the triumphalism that we associate with the story of Western thought.

In one passage Russell urges that we overcome Eurocentrism. 'To us it seems that Western European civilization is civilization but this is a narrow view ...' (Russell, 1961, p. 482). Often he sounds like contemporary followers of Foucault and Edward Said. 'There is an imperialism of culture that is harder to overcome than the imperialism of power.' '... if we are to feel at home in the world after the war, we shall have to admit Asia to equality in our thoughts, not only politically but culturally' (Russell, 1961, p. 395).

It is true that science is a product of Western Culture but Russell usually describes science as the product of individual genius rather than a particular culture. He would have said with Gellner 'The recognition of the inequality of cognitive claims in no way involves unequal treatment of people' (Gellner, 1995, p. 8). Science, he is saying, belongs to the world. Since Russell visited China in the twenties he seems to wonder whether it came to the right civilization. Here it usually grows in a hostile environment. He fears that at present it will be valued only for its technology. In brief then, *The History of Western Philosophy* does not speak of an ending or a new height. If anything it awaits a new chapter.

Let me then summarize a number of these points. When Russell's work was first published many philosophers assumed that he had set out and indeed accomplished a clean sweep of the past in order to make way for the methods of logical analysis. But the text does not sustain this reading. As a philosopher Russell addresses other philosophers. Russell does not present a sequence, he presents a forum where the centuries converse with one another, the twelfth addresses the nineteenth, the Hellenistic philosophers address us. In this sense Russell's history is a model for Rorty's concept of philosophy as a conversation.

As a history of ideas Russell's text presents another set of ideas. Here we have a drama of contending ideas in which the outcome is vital for the future of civilization. I am suggesting that we set the issue of totalitarianism aside and probe deeper. There we find that Russell has brought together much that he has thought and written since the 1920s. His principle theme is that there is a tension between science and philosophy in the modern world that has become more dangerous than any similar tensions in the previous eras. Thus, according to Russell, the tensions that beset analytic philosophy are not to be found in the conflicts between older pre-industrial philosophies and those of modern science, but rather between science and the philosophies that have arisen in the modern era. *The History of Western Philosophy* then gives us the portrait of a struggle within Russell, between the revolutionary who has overthrown the philosophy of the past and the traditional philosopher who seeks the foundation of analytic philosophy and induction, the sources of what the Greeks called Phronesis.

BIBLIOGRAPHY OF WORKS CITED

Boas, G., 1947. Review of *History of Western Philosophy*, *Journal of the History of Ideas*, vol. 8, no. 1.

Russell, B., 1961. *History of Western Philosophy* (London, George Allen and Unwin).

Times Literary Supplement, 1946. *Anonymous Review of History of Western Philosophy.*

Gellner, E., 1995. *Times Literary Supplement*, 16 Jan.